ANCIENT WEIGHTS AND MEASURES

SIR W. M. FLINDERS PETRIE

OXBOW | books
Oxford & Philadelphia

This edition published in the United Kingdom in 2023 by
OXBOW BOOKS
The Old Music Hall, 106–108 Cowley Road, Oxford, OX4 1JE

and in the United States by
OXBOW BOOKS
1950 Lawrence Road, Havertown, PA 19083

Paperback Edition: ISBN 979-8-88857-010-4
Digital Edition: ISBN 979-8-88857-011-1 (epub)

First published by the British School of Archaeology in Egypt, 1926
Facsimile edition published in 1974 by Aris & Phillips Ltd

Oxbow Books is grateful to the Petrie Museum for their collaboration in bringing out these new editions

Printed in the United Kingdom by CMP Digital Print Solutions

For a complete list of Oxbow titles, please contact:

UNITED KINGDOM
Oxbow Books
Telephone (0)1226 734350
Email: oxbow@oxbowbooks.com
www.oxbowbooks.com

UNITED STATES OF AMERICA
Oxbow Books
Telephone (610) 853-9131, Fax (610) 853-9146
Email: queries@casemateacademic.com
www.casemateacademic.com/oxbow

Oxbow Books is part of the Casemate Group

Front cover: Bronze weight in the form of a bull's head. From Amarna, Egypt, Dynasty 18 (*c.* 1550–1069BC).
Petrie Museum UC45602. Image © Mary Hinkley, UCL Educational Media.

CONTENTS

LIST OF PLATES

KEY TO STANDARDS OF WEIGHT

Grains	Original elements	Ancient name	Modern names	Original elements	Grammes
113·9					7·38
	116	P	Euboic?	7·52	
	121	PEYEM		7·86	
	124			8·06	
125·0					8·10
		D	Babylonian		
	127·5	DARIC	Assyrian	8·26	
	131·5		Euboic	8·55	
			Italic mina		
132·7					8·60
	134·0	S	Attic	8·68	
	135·8	STATER		8·80	
137·5					8·91
	144	Q QEDET	Egyptian	9·33	
152·4					9·87
	154·4	N	Milesian	10·00	
	162	NECEF	Alexandrian	10·50	
			Syrian talent		
168					10·89
	171	K	Persian	11·08	
	185	KHOIRĪNĒ		12·00	
188					12·18
	196	B	Nub	12·70	
	210	BEQA	Aeginetan	13·61	
210					13·61
			Phoenician		
		L	Maccabean		
	220	SELA	Ptolemaic	14·26	
			Alexandrian talent		
			Italic mina		
227·8					14·76

PREFACE TO THE 2023 EDITION

In the 1970s, a much-anticipated new series of publications illustrated objects and themes related to the excavations of the archaeologist William Matthew Flinders Petrie (1853–1942) in Egypt, and aspects of the collection of University College London's Petrie Museum of Egyptian and Sudanese Archaeology. A young couple setting up in business in the early 1970s, Aris and Phillips published these works, written by members of the UCL Egyptology Department, in their *Modern Egyptology* series. Building on Petrie's own observations, the authors of these volumes aimed to complete the great task of publishing the Petrie Museum of Egyptian and Sudanese Archaeology's vast collection, and to present some of the research that Petrie himself was not able to address in his own published works during his lifetime. As the current Curator of the Petrie Museum, it is a great privilege for me to support Oxbow Books in their mission to republish the series, which remains a key source of information for all those interested in object-based approaches to the study of the ancient world.

The Petrie Museum, part of University College London (UCL), is home to one of the largest and most significant collections of Egyptian and Sudanese archaeology in the world. Free to visit, this extraordinary collection tells stories about the lives of ordinary people who lived along the Nile Valley thousands of years ago. Originally set up as a teaching collection, the Petrie Museum comprises over 80,000 objects housed together with an internationally important archaeological archive. It is a collection of world firsts and 'oldests': the oldest woven garment; the oldest worked iron objects; the first known depiction of loom weaving; the oldest known written document about women's health; the earliest veterinary treatise; the oldest will on paper. The Museum has Designated Status from Arts Council England, meaning that it is considered to have outstanding resonance and national cultural significance. The collection has a substantial, visible international reputation for research, supporting hundreds of researchers every year, both remotely and in person.

The Petrie Museum is named after Flinders Petrie, who was appointed in 1892 as the first Professor of Egyptian Archaeology and Philology in the UK at UCL. Over three-quarters of the material in the Museum comes from excavations directed or funded by Petrie, or from purchases he made for university teaching. In 1880 at the age of 26, Petrie travelled to Egypt to survey the Great Pyramid. For the next five decades he was at the forefront of the development of archaeology in Egypt and later in Palestine, and his detailed methodological approach continues to shape the discipline today.

Petrie worked at more sites, with greater speed, than any modern archaeologist: seeing his life as a mission of rescue archaeology, Petrie aimed to retrieve as much information as possible from sites that were shrinking dramatically in size as Egypt modernised during the late 19th and early 20th centuries. He published a large part, but not all, of the finds from his excavations in his illustrated typological volumes, arranged according to object types and themes. Today, much of the Petrie Museum's collection is displayed and stored in a way which reflects these publications: for example, several storage cupboards are dedicated to the material illustrated in the 'Objects of Daily Use' volume, and objects in the drawers are arranged according to the order of the published plates. This offers a unique opportunity for researchers to engage with Petrie's typological and methodical approach to archaeology, as well as with the history of museum collections.

The first catalogue to be published in the *Modern Egyptology* series was *Amarna: City of Akhenaten and Nefertiti* in 1972 by Julia Samson, Petrie Museum Honorary Research Assistant. As official publishers to the UCL Egyptology Department the series went on to produce facsimile reprints of eight of Flinders Petrie's most important site reports and many of his object catalogues, originally published through the British School of Archaeology in Egypt. The substantial annual royalties from these reprints were paid into the 'Petrie Fund' at the time, which provided special grants to students in financial need.

In many ways, the new reprints of this classic series can be seen as the latest layer in a vast 'publication stratigraphy' of the thousands of finds from Flinders Petrie's excavations, which now live in museum collections around the world. On reading these volumes, I hope that readers will also be inspired to learn more about the Petrie Museum collection and its fascinating history.

Dr Anna Garnett
Petrie Museum of Egyptian and Sudanese Archaeology,
University College London
January 2023

PUBLISHER'S PREFACE

Oxbow Books is pleased to present this title in our *Classics in Egyptology* series. This series of facsimile re-issues is comprised of two sub-series. The first consists of 16 typological catalogues produced by W.M. Flinders Petrie based on his massive collection of Egyptian artefacts. Mostly excavated by Petrie during many seasons of campaign in the last years of the 19th and early decades of the 20th century, they now reside in the Petrie Museum at University College London. Published between 1898 and 1937 and long out of print, the catalogues were re-issued in facsimile by publishers Aris and Phillips in the 1970s. These were followed in the next 15 years or so by publication of a number of newly commissioned titles, based on more recent examination of elements of the Petrie Collection by contemporary experts, under the name *Modern Egyptology*. A selection of these additional titles forms the second component of our own series.

The archaeology of Egypt continues to fascinate. Multi-disciplinary investigation and research continues unabated, encompassing methodologies, scientific and data processing techniques, theoretical approaches, and even whole paradigms that were unheard of in the 1970s and undreamt of when Petrie was working in Egypt. Yet all the titles included in this series continue to be invaluable sources of basic data, providing an unparalleled resource that can easily be cross-referenced with the actual materials they describe and discuss. They remain within the Petrie Collection where they may be accessed and re-examined as new research flourishes. As historic documents, the Petrie catalogues stand as exemplars of the craft of typological classification, the backbone of modern archaeology – much of which, though refined by absolute dating and another 100 years of research, still stands the test of time.

A note on presentation

The facsimile titles of Petrie's catalogues re-issued in the 1970s were produced from scans of the original publications. Scanning technology at that time was not of the standard or resolution of today. The scans are no longer available, nor has it been possible to obtain, and in doing so destroy, original copies of the Petrie catalogues. These titles have therefore, of necessity, been rescanned from the 1970s re-issues. Where necessary the pages have been digitally enhanced for clarity of reading and to ensure the good quality of the plates, though inevitably a few are not of the standard we might wish, because of the quality of the previous scan, and occasional blocks of text are not precisely 'straight' or evenly situated on the page. However, some pages in the 1970s re-issues had been inserted in the wrong order and this has been corrected. The originals were produced at a folio size. The pages have been reduced slightly to standard A4 for ease of shelving and because this has the effect of slightly improving the scanned images. In some cases, illustrations were presented to scale and the original scale is given on the plate. There were also no digital files available for titles included in the *Modern Egyptology* series, so these too have been scanned from printed copies.

WEIGHTS AND MEASURES.

INTRODUCTION

1. THE subject of ancient weights and measures has been more neglected than other branches of archaeology. Only two or three dozen Egyptian weights had been published, when my excavations at Naukratis brought to light some five hundred. This former paucity was entirely due to neglect; it has been the same in most other excavations, whereas the work of the British School has added almost every year to the known material. Thus we have now at University College over four thousand weights, or about two thirds of all the Egyptian weights known; most of the remainder being those published in *Naukratis* and *Tanis II and Defenneh*, which were presented to American museums.

2. In view of the mass of material, it has seemed best to simplify future reference by incorporating in one series the scattered publications since those of Naukratis and Defenneh. Hence the numbering in those volumes is to be retained; while the shorter numbered lists published since, are here cancelled, and included in the single series of the present volume. The former series of type drawings of form are retained, as in *Naukratis*, except in two types which it was desirable to re-classify. The much larger variety of types now known has been incorporated (on the decimal system) by adding—for instance—types 331 to 339 between types 33 and 34. No additions have been made between the first ten types, in order to avoid confusion with subsequent numbers. Thus the present work forms a homogeneous whole with the earlier work of forty years ago. As much fresh information has accrued since that date, modifying the arrangement of the weights, there is here included a skeleton list of the latest attribution of all the earlier weights published in *Naukratis, Defenneh,* and the Cairo *Catalogue.* Thus nearly all the Egyptian material for study is at hand in this volume. The whole subject of Arabic glass weights is deferred for a second volume, to follow the present one.

3. A revision of earlier studies was necessary, owing to the great advance made in recent years in Palestinian metrology. Four standards of weight have been found named on weights from Palestine (pl. xxiii), the Necef, the Peyem, the Beqa, and another with the monogram of XO, which I here render as the Khoirinē, on evidence stated further on. Of these four standards, two had been already recognized in Egypt, but without original names, and two are quite new to us, and serve to clear up the Egyptian metrology, so that no limbo of unclassified material now remains.

Thus, by the material now known, we are forced to recognize eight standards in use in Egypt, which we shall specify and discuss. Each has so much variation between the different examples, that they form a continuous overlapping series, which can best be stated as starting from the peyem, beginning at 114 grains, to the sela, or Phoenician unit, ending at the double of that, 228 grains. Between these limits there is no unassigned place in the scale, and the variations are such that the ranges of the eight standards slightly overlap. Such a situation might seem to reduce the subject to a mere arbitrary assignment of any object to some standard, and even raise the question whether there were any definite standards. The subject is, however, cleared so soon as we reach the lower multiples. Some standards were multiplied by 3, others by 4, others by 5. Hence we find clear separations arising, such as, for instance, the result between 500 and 600 grains; there are only 14 weights altogether in this 100 grains of range, while, on the other hand, there are 15 weights of the single value of 287 grains, amid a multitude of others larger and smaller. Thus the different kinds of multiples serve to delimit the ranges of the standards, and so classify the weights.

The classification is also greatly helped by the different types of form which were favoured for different standards. Thus in the *beqa* (or Egyptian *nub*) series there are 50 square weights and 40 duck forms, whereas in the *stater* (or Attic standard) there are only 10 square stone weights and 23 duck weights. Hence by searching for varieties of form, which may be much more usual in one standard than in another contiguous to it, and mapping out the examples in a diagram, it is soon found what the limit is of one standard apart from the other. Of course it must be remembered that there was no fixed division between different standards; each had its variations, and they usually overlapped. If we had the same amount of irregularity now in our weights, there would be an overlap between the high pound weights and the low half kilogramme weights. All we can do is, by examination of all the material, to fix the points which divide best between the standards, and further to separate those which overlap, as far as possible, by evidence of forms and materials. All this only refers to a small percentage of the whole weights, for not more than two or three *per cent* are so divergent as to interfere, but it is needful to state exactly how they are here dealt with.

In such discussion of treatment, we must always remember that we are only taking a fore-shortened view of many thousands of years of changes, and that most of the variations which we observe might be simplified into quite separate lines of descent, if we knew the historical variation. The usual position is like that of looking along a crowded street, and seeing only a solid barrier of traffic, instead of looking down upon it, and so tracing the crossing lines of each separate unit of the whole confusion. We shall endeavour here to use every indication of the historic changes; for, though far from complete, they are invaluable as disentangling our view of the subject.

4. No attempt will be made here to deal with the whole of the immense subject of ancient metrology. This is only a publication of material, and in the necessary classification of it we may reach some solid foundations for the whole subject. The mass of fragmentary literary information, and results from other countries, will only be touched on where needful for the Egyptian material. Above all, nothing will be based on, or modified by, theories of connected standards; we only deal here with the material facts. The whole subject has been badly confused by the speculative metrologists, who have wasted much paper by theorizing. BOECKH, SOUTZO, AURES, HULTSCH, LEHMANN-HAUPT and others have started theories which the vagueness of the subject would shelter, but which are quite incompatible with the historical facts in detail. Looking at the conditions of the ancient world, of a large number of communities each developing a strongly individual civilisation, the presumption is that there would be as many standards as there were languages. The vision of our reducing all to one original standard is as hopeless as the old idea of one primitive universal language.

5. Some writers have preferred to pay attention only to the small minority of marked weights, as giving a greater certainty of meaning, and have ignored the general mass of material. That is, however, unsafe as marks often show what a weight was not, instead of what it was. The meaning of this is that the marks are often secondary, being added to a weight of one standard in order to show what was its equivalent on another standard. There is a parallel to this in modern times, when the coins of one country are countermarked with a fractional value of another currency in order to pass in a different system. In other cases only the secondary value is marked, and is shown to be secondary by its not being a likely number, and by the weight being a simple number of some other and commoner standard. Thus

10 darics	marked 9 =	9 qedets (2640)
20 "	S =	Roman Semis (2417)
30 " ½ mina	9 =	9 double beqa (4302)
½ qedet	nub =	⅓ beqa (Cairo 31601)
1 deben	6 =	6 double peyem (Br. Mus.)
1 "	8 =	8 khoirīnē (3746)
5 "	3 =	30 double peyem (2031)
10 "	70 =	70 beqa (4399)
10 "	60 =	60 double peyem (Br. Mus.)
10 khoirīnē	9 =	9 beqa (4254)
10 light beqa	9 =	9 heavy beqa (4302, 4542)
10 beqa	8 =	8 double daric (4416)
10 double beqa	19 =	19 heavy beqa (4417)
10 beqa	30 =	30 half qedets (3141)
10 "	8 =	8 double daric (Golenicheff)
100 "	15 =	15 deben (4491)
40 minas (sela)	270 =	270 deben (Cairo 31652).

In all these, the simplicity of the multiple on the commoner standards, and the irregularity of

the marked numbers on the rarer standards, shows clearly that the marking was secondary, as we might now mark 35 ounces on a kilogram weight.

In other instances, marks have been altered. There seems to have been a standard of $1\frac{1}{2}$ of the *nub* or beqa; on one weight (4552) a I has been altered to III, that is reducing from $1\frac{1}{2}$ to $\frac{1}{2}$ beqa as the unit; in another instance (4299), II has been altered to III, reducing from $1\frac{1}{2}$ beqa to 1 beqa unit. On another weight (4455, 4507) the value has been marked more correctly; 50 was originally on it, giving 208·66 grains for the beqa, and this has been altered to 51 by a fresh stroke, giving 204·56 grains unit. From all these it is evident that any number marked, beyond the simplest likely multiples, really shows that the weight was not made for that amount, but that its value on a fresh system has been added upon it.

The marks, when simple numbers, and undoubtedly referring to the original purpose of the weight, are often on a basis of a multiple of the standard. Thus a 5 qedet weight is marked I (Cairo 31289), and a 20 qedet (3673) marked IIII, and a 10 qedet marked II; also a 10 qedet (3260) is marked IIIII, and a 40 qedet (3343) marked ∩∩ (20); these show units of 5 qedet and of 2 qedet. The same is known from literary sources, where 5 deben has a name, *shed*.

6. Another point to notice, respecting marks, is that generic marks, or names for a weight, must not be confounded with specific marks which distinguish a standard. There were many different standards named mina or shekel; so finding "mina" or "shekel" on a weight does not show to which standard it belongs. Similarly in Egypt *deben*, though usually accepted as = 10 qedet, or between 1400–1500 grains, was also applied to other units. There is a weight (2046) of about 10 normal deben on which is clearly written "The 12 deben contained in the 2 weights of alabaster of Nefer-renpet." Here the named deben is obviously about 1156 grains, or a name for the 10 peyem weight. Similarly, there is, in Cairo, a weight of "300 deben" (no. 31651) the unit of which is 10 darics of 124·9 grains; the multiple of 300 proves this, as the daric was multiplied by 60, while the Egyptian deben was decimal. Again, a weight (of Ampy) at Berlin marked 10 deben, gives a unit of 218·8 grains, the sela, or Phoenician standard. The circle or ring marked along with a numeral, on weights, has sometimes been supposed to mean one specific

unit; but it is found on weights of six out of the eight known standards, only omitting the khoirinē and the stater (Attic); the meaning of it is therefore simply "unit."

7. It should be explained that the stone weights are treated here apart from the metal weights, as being the sole material for accurate discrimination. In most cases the stone weights have undergone no alteration; even when chipped, the original weight can be fairly closely inferred. But metal weights are nearly all so much attacked, that the alteration is serious; there has been gain by oxygen and carbonic acid, and loss by breaking away of the altered crust. A weight of metal which looks quite clear and smooth, may have had a large amount scaled off it, or have been cleaned in other ways. For the study of the units, only stone weights should be employed; the metal weights can then be attributed, after estimating the changes, and are of value for showing marks and types of form.

8. The choice of a modern standard to describe the ancient weights must be between the grain and the gramme. On the grain system there are thousands of weights already published, on the gramme system only a few hundreds at Cairo. The Continental scholars have devoted themselves to theorizing instead of collecting and publishing weights. It seemed best therefore not to break away from the great mass already in print, and split the subject by printing these fresh lists in grammes. To aid reference, I have here issued the Cairo weights reduced to grains, in the summary list, along with the weights of Naukratis and Defenneh. In the diagrams of weights here, the dividing lines by grammes are put above that by grains, so that the results can be read on either system.

The actual methods of weighing this collection were as follows. For all weights up to three pounds, a new commercial balance by Becker was used, which freely showed 0·1 or 0·2 grain with a moderate load. A new set of grain weights were used, the errors of which were not larger. For all fractions of 100 grains, a vertical slider was read; this held one end of a brass chain, and the other end hung from the balance pan. Thus any amount could be added or subtracted without the least agitation of the balance, the swing of the balance could be instantly checked by moving the slider, and a complete control quickly brought it to rest. By this means 70 weighings an hour could

be done to about 0·2 grain, and with 4000 weighings to be made, a speedy method was needful. The accuracy is amply sufficient for almost all the possible needs of the work.

For the heavier weights, up to about 30 lbs., a large mediaeval steelyard was rigged up, with the tip of the beam resting by a point in the balance pan; the leverage was about 1 : 10, and the amount of pressure was weighed in the pan like any other weight. The lever multiplier was ascertained frequently, by testing with a known weight. The knife edges rested on plate-glass planes bedded on plasticine to ensure a good contact bearing.

For a few very heavy weights up to 180 lbs., the weight was hung by a thin rope; a point at top and bottom of the rope was marked, and the distance measured; then the weight was pulled to one side by a horizontal spring balance, and the deflection and pull noted; several different readings were taken, and the weight calculated from them and averaged. This is sufficient to show what system the weight agreed with, and in no case could we depend on accuracy in such weights.

9. It need hardly be explained that the methods followed here, in classifying the weights, are those attained after many searches, and listing in many ways. A large amount of tentative tabulating had to be done, on various lines, before a conclusive method of handling each part of the material could be reached. The whole of the weights were first classified by form, and, under each form, according to the number of grains. The lists of these classes proved of great value for discriminating standards; but when once the useful differences are traced, the rest of such tabulation is needless to publish or keep. Similarly the actual weights, after classing by form, are all re-arranged according to the different standards, in the permanent order of the collection. In this volume all this scaffolding is removed, and might not be realised when looking only at the conclusions here stated. If any one wishes to revise the conclusions, they must go through the stages of classifying, and many trials of diagrams and curves, which have led to the present order; without such detailed study of the material, the situation cannot be grasped for any revision.

For the general state of our knowledge of ancient weights and measures, see the *Encyclopaedia Britannica*, 1890, art. WEIGHTS, and later materials in *Palestine Exploration Fund, Quarterly statement*, 1912, and *Transactions of the Victoria Institute*, 17 May, 1915.

CHAPTER I

THE FORMS OF WEIGHTS.
PLS. III–VIII.

10. BEFORE considering the history of the various standards of weight, it is necessary to observe the different forms which were in use at the principal periods, as such serve to give the approximate age of the weights.

Cylinder and Dome, pl. v, 456, 458; viii, 881, 883. The earliest weights are the small blocks of limestone found in early prehistoric graves of the Amratian age. There is no sign of wear on these blocks, nor of any use of them as tools. There does not seem to be any possible purpose for these pieces except as weights. When they are compared together, they are all found to be within the range of the "gold" unit or Beqa, with simple multiples such as 40, three of 20, 15 and 6. Though some of these are cylindrical, and others conical, they all have the curious feature of domed ends, so that they never can be set upright. The age of these is given by the grave groups in five instances; only one is without a history, for it was bought. The earliest fixed points are sequence dates 32 and 33, or within the age of the white-line red pottery of the Amratian civilisation. The latest fixed point is S.D. 46, or in the earlier part of the Gerzean civilisation. Hence this form characterizes the Amratian period and hardly extends into the next age.

Cone, pl. viii, 913–915. This type begins with rounded cones of limestone paste, covered with black line patterns, of Gerzean age. Later, the cone was flat-based and pointed, as found in alabaster in the Semainian age just before the Ist dynasty. All of these cones were found singly or in pairs, but never in larger numbers, so do not appear to be gaming pieces. They agree in the Gerzean age to the Daric standard, and in the Semainian to the Qedet standard which was official in historic times. The conical form, roughly made, lasted to the xiith dynasty at Kahun. Cones with wide domed tops are figured in the xviiith dynasty, as in *Qurneh*, xxxv, and L. *Denkm.*, III, 39: also in the xxvith dynasty tomb of Aba at Thebes (*M.A.F.*, V, 656, iv). There is no trace of cone weights from Naukratis or Defenneh.

11. *Square.* The next form to arise was the square block, somewhat oblong (vi, 65). This was found in a tomb of the beginning of the Ist dynasty (*R.T.*, II, xxxii, 61). Shortly after, there were many rudely squared weights, and ground slips of stone (*Tombs of Courtiers*, 9). This form was soon improved by rounding the edges to prevent chipping, until in the ivth dynasty—the age of mechanical perfection—the most suitable form was adopted (vi, 649, 653–654); this exhibits the greatest rounding of the edges compatible with leaving flat faces to prevent rolling. It is a form which is more perfect than that of any standards made since. It is dated by the weight of Khufu (Hilton Price catalogue), and the inscribed weight (vi, 656) of a nomarch Nefer-măot, no. 4740, a ivth dynasty name. Rather less rounding is seen in the vith dynasty (*Abydos*, II, xv, 14), and less still in the jasper weight of Khety of the ixth dynasty (no. 4466, pl. xi). In a representation of weighing, in an Old Kingdom scene, the weights are shown as sharp-edged cubes. In the xiith dynasty, the square weights mostly have sharp edges, as at Kahun, though some were rounded. After that, the rounding of the square weight ceases.

Oblong. The oblong weight appears in the figures of weights painted in the tomb of Hesy, of the early part of the iiird dynasty. Presumably these had the slight cylindrical curve of the top (as in the weight of Khufu), which is so usual in the xiith dynasty. Such was the typical form of the gold standard, but seen here in the splendid weight of prince Herfu (vii, 694). The same continued into the xviiith dynasty, shown by the weight belonging to Amenhetep I (Brit. Mus.), and the figures in the weighing scene at Deir el-Bahri. After this it disappears; but a weight of Taharqa, here (pl. x, 2398) of oblong form, has a slightly domed top, curving in all directions. Nothing of the kind occurred at Naukratis or Defenneh, and it therefore did not continue in the Saite or later civilisations.

Pillow forms. A variety of the oblong form is the pillow type, with all the edges and faces rounded. Such is dated by my finding granite blocks of this form in the workmen's quarters at the pyramid of Khafra. Two examples of this form shown here (pl. vi, 658; nos. 4103, 4081) are of diorite, which clearly points to the age of the ivth dynasty. Some of the Kahun weights are roughly made of this type, and some with rounded edges, but almost

flat above and below. After the xiith dynasty the type disappears.

12. *Black quartzose cube, cuboid, and rough forms.* These forms (iii, 4–19) merge so indistinctly into each other that they must be taken together, though the finest are exquisite cubes with flat polished faces, and the roughest have scarcely any regular shape. All of the more regular are of black or dark grey rock, apparently a black hornblende base penetrated by white quartz veins, or a magma with more or less quartz. At first sight, the rough forms seemed as if they must be merely hammer-stones, and several have been so used, but this is a common fate of even the best weights. The great amount of labour given to working down such a hard stone, usually with smooth, and often polished, faces, points to their being weights. The possible attributions of them confirm this; were they mere hammer-stones the irregular forms would be equally found of all varieties of handy size, but, after classifying them, they are found to group into particular standards. In the qedet, the necef and the stater they are rare, only 2 or 3 *per cent.* In the beqa, khoirīnē and daric they are 12–14 *per cent*; in the peyem 21, and in the sela (or Phoenician) they are the commonest type of all, amounting to 27 *per cent.* These hard black weights are not found in the Old Kingdom or in the xiith dynasty at Kahun. Two of the xviiith dynasty from Gurob may well be of the later occupation. I have found them in the late town at Gizeh, overlying ruins of the xxiith dynasty, and they are common at Naukratis and Defenneh. It seems, then, that they arose about the Bubastite age, and probably continued to near the Ptolemaic age.

13. *Domed top*, pl. iii, iv, 24–34. As early as the ivth dynasty, a circular weight with a domed top and fairly sharp edge is found, with the name Ra-ne-onkh deeply cut in the style of that age (no. 2152). It is a very imperfect example of the domed-top type, but it long precedes any others that are known. There is no dated example until we reach that of Onkh-nes-ra-nefer-ab (no. 2597) in the xxvith dynasty. The entire absence of the type, among the weights of the xiith and xviiith dynasties at Kahun and Gurob, and in all the paintings of the xviiith dynasty, makes it unlikely that it was used in those periods. The great multitude of weights of this form seem to belong, then, to the Saite age, and continued till Roman times (see *Illahun*, 33).

Domed, v, 37–40. Linked with the previous type, and passing into it, is the domed form, without the top being bounded by an edge. This seems to have arisen in forms contracting upward from the base, as early as the xiith dynasty (Kahun); but, in the more usual form, widening from the base upward, it appears rarely at Gurob, and perhaps only late there. It becomes extremely common, along with the dome topped type, in the Saite age; one example bears the name of Atha, son of Hor-uza (no. 2882), others in Cairo have inscriptions of Taharqa (31652) and Nekau (31604).

14. *Barrel*, vi, 485–53. The barrel or spindle form, flattened on one side, is probably Syrian in origin, along with the duck form. The earliest example is a small malachite weight found in the tomb of Zer, of the Ist dynasty (*R.T.*, II, xxxv, 78). None have been found of the xiith dynasty, and it is not till we reach the great age of intercourse with Syria, in the xviiith dynasty, that this form is common in Egypt. Seven weights were of this type out of 32 found at Gurob, a large proportion. In the ruins of the temple of Merenptah at Memphis, xxth–xxvth dynasties, there are 6 in 56, or 11 *per cent*. Yet when we reach the Saite age, at Naukratis and Defenneh, out of 1270 weights only 4 barrel forms of stone occur, though there are some small bronze barrel weights for goldsmith's use. In place of 22 *per cent* of barrel forms in the xviiith dynasty, or 11 *per cent* after that, there is only $\frac{1}{3}$ *per cent* in the xxvith dynasty—they are practically extinct. Hence all the stone barrel weights in Egypt should probably be assigned to the xviiith–xxiiird dynasties.

Duck, vii, 77–80. In Babylonia and Assyria, the duck form of weight is a well-known type, but it is not found in Egypt till the xviiith dynasty. It is seldom that the head of the duck is retained in Egyptian examples; one or two here show it slightly, and the only clearly marked neck, head, and eye, is on a fine specimen in haematite from Sparta. In general, the Egyptian form is more like an egg with a pointed end, flattened below to prevent rolling. In the best examples the small end is raised clear of the base, in the worst the flat base is the widest part of the mass. In the ruins of the Merenptah temple, xxth–xxvth dynasties, there are 4 duck weights in 56, or 7 *per cent*. On reaching the Saite age there is, of all varieties of the duck type together, less than 1 *per cent*. Many of these are of poor and degraded forms. On comparing this with the proportion in series where the duck was a regular type, there is 6 *per cent* in the stater (Attic) and 8 *per cent* in the khoirīnē. So it is clear that, in spite of Defenneh being on the Syrian road, the duck type was nearly extinct there in the xxvith dynasty.

15. *Animal types. Front.* Apart from the Babylonian duck type, there are many animal types apparently of Egyptian origin. Of these we mainly learn from the painted scenes of weighing. There is no trace of such forms in the earlier times, either actual specimens or in paintings. At the beginning of the xviiith dynasty, an ox weight is figured at El Kab (L. *Denkm.*, III, 10). Under Hatshepsut, there are the ox and ox-head forms at Deir el Bahri. Under Tehutmes III, the calf and ox-head (L. *Denkm.*, III, 39). A little later a lion weight, and an ox-head weight (*Mém. Miss. Franç.*, V, 210, 569 ii). At Qurneh, about this age, there occur a hippopotamus, an ox, and an ox-head (*Qurneh*, xxxv). From Tell Amarna, under Akhenaten, there is an ox-head of bronze weighted with lead (no. 4939 here); and about the same age one from Gurob (no. 5030). In Cairo is the large stone ox-head with the name of Sety I. Coming to the xxvith dynasty, the tomb of Aba at Thebes shows a gazelle weight (ROSEL., *Civile*, li; Cailliaud, 17). This last may be only taken from an earlier scene, as the whole tomb is an archaistic copy, mainly from the tomb of an earlier Aba at Sheykh Sayd. Hence we can only be certain of evidence for animal weights in the xviiith and xixth dynasties. Apart from those due to Greek influence, as some are here, we should assign all Egyptian animal weights to the period of the New Kingdom.

16. Setting aside, then, weights of vague and ill-defined types, we may now sum up the usual ages of the definite types. These periods are not entirely exclusive, as there may be a small proportion beyond the ages given, but they may be taken as serving to date weights in general, if no more precise evidence is at hand.

		Types in plates
Cylinders and cones, domed base	Amratian, prehist.	456, 88, 913–914
Pointed cones	Semainian, prehist.	915–917
Round-top cones	xviiith dynasty	921–927
Square, sharp edges	Ist „	62–64
Square, edges greatly rounded	ivth „	656

		Types in plates
Square, edges less rounded	ixth „	653–654
Square, edges slightly rounded	xiith „	646, 649
Oblong, cylindric top	iiird? xiith–early xviiith dyn.	691–694
Pillow	ivth–xiith dyn.	658
Black quartzose cube, &c.	xxiind?–xxxth d.	144–185, 55, 57
Domed top	(ivth) xxvith dyn.– Roman	24–36
Domed	xxvith–xxxth dyn.	37–45
Barrel	xviiith–xxiiird „	48–53
Duck	xviiith–xxiiird „	77–81
Animal	xviiith–xixth „	Front.

(The weights marked Merenp, from over the ruins of the Merenptah temple, Memphis, are placed to the xxiiird dynasty.)

CHAPTER II

MULTIPLES AND FRACTIONS.

17. THE general principles of the assignment of multiple and fractional weights to different standards should be noticed. Each standard had its regular system, as we have a system of 16 drams = 1 ounce, and 16 ounces = 1 pound. Occasionally a different fraction or multiple may occur for convenience of approximation to another system, as we had at one time postal weights of $\frac{1}{3}$ ounce as an equivalent for 10 grammes, and France now has a unit of 15 grammes as equivalent to our $\frac{1}{2}$ ounce. In general we should not accept any multiple which is unlikely, such as 11, 13, 23, 28, 33, 46, which all appear as supposed multiples in a recent paper on weights; nor any multiple which is out of the usual system of the standard, as 16 in the Assyrian sexagesimal system, or 6 in the peyem system which is decimal and binary. For purposes of classifying weights, the table on pl. xxv is the most ready way of seeing to what standard or standards any weight should be assigned. Some amounts are ambiguous, as for instance 600 grains may be either 5 peyems or 4 darics; or 800 grains may be either 5 necefs or 4 beqas. In such cases the only course is to place the uncertain weights together, compare the forms and materials with the certain ones of each standard in question, and then assign each weight its probable place. Thus the really uncertain material is seen to be only a minute amount of the whole. In order not to prejudice the question, any weight which might be supposed to belong to either of two systems, is entered here under each, the detail being given in the most likely position, and a bare mention of the weight in the less likely list, with the initial of the standard where it is fully stated.

18. The treatment of fractional weights is somewhat different. There is not the same range, as $\frac{1}{6}$ is the smallest fraction usually found, so that only five fractions need be considered, and the $\frac{1}{2}$ is usually obvious. The fractions of different standards are not well fixed, except the daric, the stater, and the sela. The method here followed, for separation of the small weights, was as follows. In order to separate at 23.5 to 26.5 grs. between $\frac{1}{8}$ B. and $\frac{1}{5}$ P., $\frac{1}{5}$ P. would not extend over 25.0; if it existed side by side with $\frac{1}{8}$ B. then there should be more weights from 23.5 to 25.0 where they overlap, than from 25.0 to 26.5 which can only be $\frac{1}{8}$ B. Yet the numbers are equal in those two ranges, therefore there are no $\frac{1}{5}$ P., but only $\frac{1}{8}$ B. B. is proved to divide in $\frac{1}{8}$th by the uniform series of haematite conic weights of 200, 50 and 25 grains. The sela we know to be divided into 4 drachms of 56 grains, and that in $\frac{1}{8}$th; hence 34–38 grains cannot be $\frac{1}{6}$ L. and must therefore be $\frac{1}{5}$ K.: and 26–28.5 grains is $\frac{1}{8}$ L. As K. divides by 5, then 28–31 grains cannot be $\frac{1}{6}$ K., but must be $\frac{1}{4}$ P. As P. divides by 4, then 38.5–40.5 cannot be $\frac{1}{3}$ P., but must be $\frac{1}{4}$ N. This covers all the scale, and the results are:—

peyem	114–125	÷ 4	28.5–31.2 grains
daric	125–132.5	÷ 6	20.8–22.1 „
stater	132.5–137.5	÷ 6	22.1–22.9 „
qedet	137.5–152.4	÷ 5	27.6–30.5 „
		÷ 3	45.8–50.8 „
necef	152.4–170	÷ 4	38.1–42.5 „
khoirinē	170–190	÷ 5	34.0–38.0 „
beqa	190–211	÷ 4	47.5–52.7 „
sela	211–228	÷ 4	52.7–57.0 „

Here it will be seen that there is an overlap of $\frac{1}{4}$ B. = 47.5–52.7, and $\frac{1}{3}$ Q. = 45.8–50.8. Now no $\frac{1}{3}$ Q. weight could exceed 51 which is = 204 on the beqa system; and the larger beqa weights, under 204 and over 204, are in the proportion of 4 : 3. As there are 14 small beqa weights *over* the limit, there should be by proportion 18 *under* the limit, within the Q. region (3 : 4 :: 14 : 18). Hence

we have to weed out 18 small weights as beqa from the mixture of qedet and beqa of 45·8—50·8 grains. On examination, it was found that there were just 18 of these of the conical dome form common for the beqa, having the rest of the domed-top form characteristic of the qedet. There is therefore little or no uncertainty in discriminating the two standards in the small weights.

CHAPTER III

System of the Catalogue.
PLS. XXVII—XLII.

19. BEFORE describing the Peyem and other standards, the arrangement of the tabular catalogue, at the end of the volume, should be noted.

The weights are classed according to the eight different standards. The order is according to the amount shown for the unit, from light to heavy. Where examples agree in the unit to a tenth of a grain, they are classed in the order of the multiple of the unit.

Column of number. As the long lists of weights of Naukratis and Defenneh are quite independent of the weights here, they continue to stand as a permanent record, numbered from 1 to 1292 (*Naukratis*, I, 75—79; *Nebesheh and Defenneh*, 82—88, in *Tanis*, II). The short lists subsequently published from other places are cancelled, as the examples all appear in this larger catalogue. The numbers here begin with 2001, to avoid clashing with the above lists. In the list of qedet weights, *d*, means a duplicate, which has been removed from the College collection and is not numbered. In all the columns, repetitions of current numbers and words are left blank, as the more open arrangement of figures is easier for reference.

Material. The obvious nature of the stone is named, rather than a purely geological definition, which would be less clear to archaeologists. Where more than one word is required, abbreviations are used. Bk., black; Br., brown; Gn., green; Gy., grey; Y., yellow. B. or Bas., brown basalt, the commonest material for weights; Bl. gl., blue glaze; Gls., glass; Glzd., glazed; Gy. volc. ash, grey volcanic ash; Gran., granite; Limest., limestone; Mem. glass, Memphite glaze factory; Porph., porphyry; Qtz., quartz; Qtzite., quartzite, silicified sandstone; Qtzose., quartzose, hard silicates with quartz veins; Steat., steatite.

Form. Numbers refer to the plates of types, pls. iii to viii.

Grains. This is the present weight, when undamaged; if damaged the amount of loss estimated is added, so as to restore the original weight. The amount of loss estimated is stated as —*n* in the last column.

×. This is the multiple of the unit in the weight. For heavy weights it is the multiple of the super-unit, such as D., deben; M., mina; T., talent.

Unit. This overlaps a little from one standard to another; the discrimination between the standards is detailed under *delimitation* in the following accounts.

Detail. This gives the name of the source when known; the date when known; the amount of loss, if any; the cross reference to another standard, when a weight probably belongs to a different system; the marks, if any, which are more exactly figured in pls. x to xv. "Merenpt." refers to the Merenptah palace site at Memphis; "Gebln." to Gebeleyn; "Karn." to Karnak.

The registers of metal weights (xliii—xlvi) are differently arranged, as the metals have both gained and lost; hence the total amount of change, by gain of oxygen and carbonic acid, and of loss by corrosion, scaling, cleaning and wear, must all be stated, in order to show how much uncertainty there is. After the number and form, as before, there is the present weight, NOW, the total amount of the changes, CH., the estimated ORIGINAL weight, and then the multiple, unit, and details.

The Peyem standard.
PLS. XXVII—XXVIII.

20. THIS standard is guaranteed, and named P-Y-M (pl. xxiii) by three weights found in Palestine, of 112·2, 117·4 and 119·6 grains, averaging 116·4 grains.

There appears to be a reference to this word in a passage I Sam. xiii, 19—22, which is amended by Signor Rafaelli and Rev. Mr. Segel, thus:— "And all Israel went down to the Philistines to forge every man his ploughshare and his *'eth* and his axe and his goad; and the inducement was a *peyem* for the ploughshares and for the *'ethim* and 3 *killeshōn* for the axes and to put a point on the goad." The *bakhshish* or bribe of a *peyem* seems to be this standard weight of silver; the *killeshōn* is supposed to be the *karasha* of the Aswan papyri,

about 860 grains, or 5 khoirīnē (*Pal. Exp. Fund, Quarterly statement*, 1916, 77).

The existence of the peyem in Egypt is proved by twelve marked weights:—

No.	Weight	Mark		Unit	Peyem	
2017	1834	÷	4	458·5	114·6 ×	4
2023	2296·4	÷	10	229·6	114·8 ×	2
2025	1379·3	÷	6	229·9	114·9 ×	2
2028	230·0	÷	1	230	115·0 ×	2
2031	6900	÷	3	2300	115 ×	20
2037	1382·2	÷	3	460·7	115·2 ×	4
2042	231·1	÷	1	231·1	115·5 ×	2
2066	1870·2	÷	4	467·5	116·9 ×	4
2086	117·8	÷	½	235·6	117·8 ×	2
2132	481·0	÷	2	240·5	120·2 ×	2
2214	495·4	÷	2	247·7	123·8 ×	2
2235	248·7	÷	1	248·7	124·3 ×	2

The median of these is 230·8 or 115·4 for the peyem, closely agreeing with the Palestine average of 116·4. In Egypt it seems that the double peyem was regarded as the unit. Further the importance and early date of this standard is shown by the large weight (2152) of 48476 (÷ 400 = 121·2) with the name of the "*nesut rekh* Ra-ne-onkh" (pl. x). The style of the signs and the name, alike fix this to about the vth dynasty. This person is probably the same as that of a tomb at Saqqarah (MAR., *Mast.* F. 1); or possibly Ra-ne-onkh without the title *nesut rekh*, of a tomb at Gizeh (L. *Denkm.*, II, 91 a). It is evident that the peyem was decimally multiplied.

Coming down to the xviiith dynasty, there is a limestone ball (2046) from Tell Amarna, stated to be 12 deben; allowing a maximum for loss, it may have been 14360, and could not therefore be 12 deben Egyptian; it was probably only 13870. The unit would be 1197, or 1156 if without loss. It is evidently the deben, or 10, of the peyem.

This standard is also known from documents of the xviiith dynasty. In papyri (*Z.A.S.*, 1906, 45) values are reckoned in rings of gold weighing 12 to the deben; that is to say, the same unit as recorded in the last paragraph. As the extreme range of the qedet deben is 1375 to 1524, the unit of the ring was between 114·6 and 127 grains; the range of the peyem is 114 to 125 grains. The ring appears to be called *shoti* in a papyrus, so that may be the Egyptian name of the peyem.

21. *Delimitation.* It might be thought that the list of marked multiples above was merely taken out of a list which might be continued far to either side. On the contrary, this standard has a very high proportion of marked weights, 12 in 219 or over 5 *per cent*. In the adjoining daric system, twice as numerous, in 434 weights there is only a single one with its number of shekels on it. In the sela system (Phoenician), on the other side, there are 5 marked weights in 162, or 3 *per cent*. The normal Phoenician standard of 224 is never above 230, and it would be impossible to assign to it weights up to 248 as above. The division between the peyem and the sela is best shown by the large weights. These are of 21277, 21900, 22130 grains on the sela; then a gap, and the peyem begins 22930, 23480, 23800, 24190, 24260, 24300, 24450, 24600, 24760. Thus the average interval between the sela weights is 430 and between the peyem 240 grains, while there is gap of 800 grains between the systems. In the double of these weights the same gap is seen; the sela between 42180 and 44574 averaging 160 apart, then a gap of 1500, and then an average of 600 apart in the peyem. Again in the duck and barrel weights the same interval is seen, between 112 and 114 grains unit.

The division between the peyem and the daric is indicated at once by the cessation of marked weights of the above list, ending with 124·3 grains. It is also shown very clearly by the heavy weights. The peyem weights from 22930 to 24760 average 240 grains apart, then comes a gap of 890 grains, and then the daric weights average 180 grains apart.

On the double scale this is still plainer, as there are 8 peyem weights between 46054 and 49700, and no daric or other weights larger, up to 55200 where the qedet system is reached. On looking at the total curve of weights of all kinds there is a very sharp drop at 125·0, down to less than a third of the number, and this clearly marks the limit of the peyem. Thus the extent of range of the peyem variation is well distinguished, and the named and marked weights leave no possible doubt as to the reality of the standard.

22. *History.* So far, we have been dealing with this standard on lines that have been familiar, without any historic discrimination of period. This is equivalent, in length of period, to lumping together all weights from the Hyksos down to our own time; obviously we must expect confusion in so long a period. We can now begin the new method of separating ages by the forms of weights,

as described in chapter I. This opens an entirely new prospect in metrology. In place of having a very few weights dated by inscription, and which may be exceptional in amount, we can, by forms, put into their probable historic order most of the weights that we have. Beside the criteria of form which we have noticed, there are some other guides; the source of the weights may indicate the age, for instance those from Kahun being of the xiith dynasty; the material, for instance the haematite weights being of the xviiith dynasty. Using all the guidance, the following peyem weights are dated to the earlier periods, as marked in the catalogue.

Old Kingdom unit	Mid Kingdom unit	Empire unit
114·9	114·6	115·0
115·0	114·8	115·1
115·5	115·0	116·0
116·1	115·2	116·5
116·5	116·4	117·0
116·9	117·2	117·7
117·0		118·0
	120·2	119·7
121·0	121·0	120·1
121·2		120·1
121·7	123·7	120·5
	123·8	121·3
124·2		121·5
124·2		121·6
124·3		122·7
124·3		122·8
		123·6
		123·8
		124·0

Later than these, the rough and cuboid forms belong to the xxiind–xxvith dynasties, and the dome-topped forms to the xxvith–xxxth dynasties.

To examine these results, it is best to form a diagram, placing all the units of one age at one level, as in pl. I. Here the five periods are separated, and at once the result appears that the early weights group on three different values, 115–117 grains, 121–122, and 124 grains. In passing from the vith to the xiith dynasties, the first group spreads wider, the second and third groups shift toward the first. In the Empire, the spread of each group is still wider, and the second and third groups are fused. By the xxiind dynasty the spreading has almost united all the groups, which are finally mixed into a general diffusion in the xxvith dynasty. In each group, the limiting examples of each

period are joined by dotted lines. This primitive isolation of three original units, and the gradual spread of their range until they are finally merged into a single widely inaccurate series, is most instructive; and, as we shall see, this is like the history of most standards of weight. It shows for the first time the real history of weights; and any theories of connection of standards must be based on the original values of certain components, and cannot be left merely in the vague uncertainty of the corrupt period. Whether there is any real derivation of standards one from another in the earlier times seems very doubtful.

In the diagram, the weights of the 1st age of Gezer are marked G in the xviiith dynasty line; those of the 2nd age (1300–800 B.C.) are in the xxiind line. These conform to the division between the high and low. The weights of the 3rd and 4th ages (800–100 B.C.) are placed in a line below, " Gezer late." They still show a gap at about 119 grains. The letter P shows the values of the weights inscribed " peyem " found in Palestine. One such is lighter than the limit of the diagram. The scale of grammes is above, that of grains below, so that the results can be read in either standard.

23. *Notes*. The marked weights have been listed above, and the marks will be found on pl. x. The transcription of the inscribed weight from Tell Amarna I owe to Dr. ALAN GARDINER. It may be rendered "The deben 12 borne by the stones (or weights) 2 of alabaster of Nefer-renpet." The present weight is 13860 grains; and an irregularity of the side is an early break, which may, or may not, have been before the inscription. From all the details it seems to be an original irregularity; the weight was not a finely finished example, but only a rough block, trimmed for copying the fine weights belonging to Nefer-renpet. Hence I should accept 13870 as the original, allowing for small bruises. This is expressly said to be 12 deben, showing a standard of 115·6 grains at Tell Amarna in the time of Akhenaten, very probably from some Syrian standard, agreeing with the central value of the low family of the peyem. A group of disc weights may be noted, as agreeing closely together, nos. 2133, 2157, 2175, weighing 481·2, 486·0, 489·4 grs. 2051 is a different estimate of 2031, accidentally entered in duplicate. Two fine weights from Gebeleyn (Brit. Mus.) give 6 and 60 × 245·2, the double peyem, marked B in diagram pl. I.

CHAPTER IV

THE DARIC STANDARD.

Pls. XXVIII—XXX.

24. OF the existence of this system from very early times there is no question; it appears in the standard weights of Dungi, and the copy of those by Nebuchadrezzar, and plenty of lion and duck weights of the later period. Among the metal weights at University College, there are lion weights of 1 daric and two of 20 darics. Owing to the many different systems in which the name shekel was used, and the single and double shekel in the Assyrian system, it is needful to use the later name daric, which has only one meaning. There is only one weight marked with number of darics (2379), and that is roughly done.

25. *Delimitation.* The lower limit has been already placed at 125·0 grains, by the evidence just stated for the peyem. The upper limit is the division between the daric and the stater (Attic system). This is not easy to define, as the fractions ($\frac{1}{6}$) are the same, and the daric is often decimally multiplied like the stater. Further, the mina of 60 darics and its half, overlap on 50 and 25 necef and on 40 and 20 beqa. The classes which are clear of these other standards are:—

Duck weights,		none between	131·6 to	134·5
„	„	255·0—270·1	127·5	135·0
„	„	658·0—672·2	131·6	134·4
„	„	1311·6—1337·0	131·2	133·7
Barrel weights,		none between	129·9	133·0
„	„	255·5—271·0	127;7	135·5
„	„	661·5—671·8	132·3	134·4
„	„	1319·5—1335·0	131·9	133·5
Fine edged dome top				
no daric, stater begins		1317	0	131·7
„	„	2661	0	133·0
Flat top, 1 daric, stater begins		1315·3	0	131·5
Rounded		3261·8—3331·6	130·5	133·3

From all these classes there is clearly a gap between 131·9 and 133·0, narrowed by one class rising to 132·3, while two others begin at 131·5 and 131·7 without any daric below them. Looking to the whole material, 132·7 seems to have an equal number of stragglers on each side, and may best be adopted as the dividing point, with 6 or 8 of each standard across the border, but distinguished by form, material, or multiples. The Gezer weights agree with this, the gap between

132·9 and 133·9 being much larger than any other interval lower or higher than this.

26. *History.* Rounded cones of limestone paste, which were moulded by hand, with a threading hole through the upper end, are found in the Gerzean age (*Prehist. Egypt*, xlix, 6—10). They are decorated with black line patterns, and no purpose can be assigned to these unless they are weights. There is also a double cone of clay, white washed and painted similarly, with a thread-hole. On comparing the weights of these, they agree in simple proportions. There are also two stone rings, too large for a thumb, too small for a wrist, and a finely wrought syenite slab, which agree with the weights of the cones.

Cone	485·5	÷ 4	121·4
Breccia ring	4435·0	÷ 36	123·2
Cone	313·5	÷ 2½	125·4
„	941·3	÷ 7½	125·5
Alabaster ring	3763·8	÷ 30	125·5
Syenite slab	3785·6	÷ 30	126·2
S.D. 40, cone	1267·0	÷ 10	126·7
Cone	261·7	÷ 2	130·8

These multiples agree on a system of decimal and sexagesimal, the $7\frac{1}{2}$ being $\frac{1}{4}$ of 30, the $2\frac{1}{2}$ $\frac{1}{12}$ of 30 or $\frac{1}{4}$ of 10. The range of the daric is 124·3—132·7, and that agrees fairly with the variations above. There seems, then, good evidence for granting that the Mesopotamian daric standard was brought into Egypt by the eastern invaders of the Gerzean prehistoric age. These are not incorporated in the catalogue of weights as there might be a hesitation as to their purpose, and the importance of them lies in their date.

The weights that can be approximately dated by the forms, in historic times, are marked with the dynasty number in the catalogue. In the diagram, pl. I, it will be seen how they are distributed. There appear to be two groups in the early period, five agreeing on 127·5, and seven between 130·4 and 132·8. Those of the first dynasty, marked I, are in the higher group. In the xiith dynasty, the 127·5 group spreads to 126·0—128·7, and the higher group extends to 129·6 toward the lower. By the xviiith dynasty, the groups have become almost fused in Egypt, only showing a little gap at 128·6—129·0, wider than any other gap, except at the extremities. The Gezer weights are marked G. Probably 127·5 and 131·5 should be accepted as the earliest forms. The lower of these is the stand-

ard of the Assyrian weights, and Nebuchadrezzar's copy of the early standard of Dungi gives only 126·0 for the unit. The late coin of the daric was intermediate, 129·2; most likely it was a mean example of the fused standards in late times. The higher value appears in some coinage, as the Lampsacene staters of the satrap Orontes, averaging 130·4.

27. *Notes.* The multiples of the daric standard were on two systems, the sexagesimal or old Babylonian system, and the decimal. Multiples on both systems are found from the Old Kingdom to the end, altogether 16 clearly sexagesimal, to 31 decimal. Looking at the higher and lower standard, they are almost alike in both; in the lower 15 sexagesimal and 29 decimal, in the higher 26 and 41 respectively. It appears, then, that both systems of multiples were used throughout. On comparing curves of the distribution under the two systems, there is scarcely any change in common. The only point that might be significant is that the sexagesimal curve has maxima A and B, at 127 and 131; these may well show the original units which group on 127·5 and 131, as stated above.

There is more uncertainty in the mina weights of this system than in any other, owing to the coincidence of three standards, the mina of 60 darics 7500–7960, 50 Necef 7640–8500, 40 Beqa or *nub* 7520–8400 grains. Thus all the daric minas except the lowest might be claimed on other standards. On comparing all the ambiguous weights with those of B which are above the mina limit, the probable division seemed to be that all the irregularly rounded, cuboid, and flat-top domed weights belonged to the daric, and the square, cylindroid and banded alabaster weights to the beqa. On comparing the daric and necef series, the higher multiples up to 31900 and 78600 stop with the D range and do not extend to N alone; hence doubtful cases should be given to D. Accidentally, no. 2355 is also entered as 2348 without addition for loss.

The notable weights in this series (pl. x) are those of Taharqa (2398) and of Onkh-nes-ra-nefer-ab (2597); they do not agree, giving 128·2 and 131·6 for the daric. The former is inscribed "son of Ra, Taharqa, by Osiris in the midst of Sais, beloved." This is probably the Osiris Unnefer of Nesaft, in or near Sais, see BRUGSCH, *Dict. Geog.*, p. 358. Another peculiar weight (2638) is a large duck with well-formed head, weighing 250 darics of 126·8, or

240 (4 minas) of 132·1 grains. Unfortunately the marks on it (pl. x) are bruised and worn; they might read 12 or 16 or 4. As they cannot agree with 250 shekels, or any derivative of that, it is probable that this was 4 minas. There is a fine haematite weight of duck form, with the head and eyes carved, from Sparta, 20 darics of 128·6. A weight from Malta is of a pointed dome form, pierced with a hole for a cord; it is a half mina, yielding a daric of 128·2. Both these latter I owe to my old friend Greville Chester, as likewise all the weights from Syria and Gebeleyn, beside others. One obvious 10 daric weight (2640) of 1321·9, has been re-marked with 9 cuts to show its value as 9 qedets of 146·9.

This standard was of great importance early in the Mediterranean. The Knossos octopus weight is 29 kilos = 447,500 grs.; and 20 bronze ingots with marks (*Bull. Paletnol.*, 1904, 101) vary from 27·0 to 33·3 kilos, median 29·4 = 453,000 grs., giving a shekel of 125·8 grs. No very exact result can be stated until these are all accurately weighed and changes estimated.

CHAPTER V

THE STATER STANDARD.

PLS. XXXI–XXXII.

28. THIS standard, otherwise called Attic, is here named from its most celebrated example, the immense coinage of gold staters of Philip of Macedon. We do not know any early name for it, and to call it Attic or Solonic is only to put back the name a couple of centuries in some thousands of years of history.

Coming in between two well-known standards, the Babylonian daric and the Egyptian qedet, the stater has been often confounded with one or the other, and its separate existence as a standard has been denied. There are but two early marked examples here, 2803, of the Old Kingdom form, giving a unit of 134·4, and 2911 of the Middle Kingdom, giving 135·7; one weight in Cairo (31613) with a scarab on the top and number "60," is 600 staters of 134·1. These are far removed from any qedet weight, the lightest of which with numerals gives 140 grains, and they are too high for any known example of the daric standard.

29. *Delimitation.* The gap between this and the daric has been described above. The most con-

clusive point is that some varieties of form are unknown in the daric standard, and only begin with the stater. The separation between this and the qedet is marked by the far greater proportion of duck weights of the stater; in proportion to the numbers of other forms, the duck weights are 5 *per cent* of the staters, and less than a thousandth of the qedet, fifty times more numerous in one than in the other. In the class of good domed weights there is a clear gap between 2698·9 and 2768·8 or 134·9 to 138·4 grs. unit; again, in rounded weights there is a gap between 3471·7 and 3522·9, or 138·87 to 141·32. On looking at the whole of the series in curves, it appears that 137·5 is the point where the two standards are equally usual; each must have a few examples extending across this point, which can only be distinguished when peculiar in form, material, or multiple. The heavy weights bear this out, though they are not very numerous. There are eight of 400 qedet, ranging from 151·7 to 138·0 for the qedet, and nothing whatever below that, till reaching 400 × 124·2 on the peyem standard; thus there are no weights of 400 staters or darics, and the qedet begins at 138·0. In the next grade, there are sixteen weights of 500 qedet from 151·4 down to 138·5, and then only one below that, of 135·4. Of the 1000 qedet series, there is a gap between 1000 staters of 134·5 and 1000 qedet of 138·5. Thus the heavy weights prove that the qedet series ends at about 138·0. From this, and the previous difference of 50 to 1 in the proportion of duck weights, between the two standards, it seems impossible to doubt the distinction between the stater and the qedet, however much they are naturally confounded by their nearness, and by examples crossing the border lines, especially in the later confusion of standards.

30. *History*. In the diagram, pl. I, it appears that there were two forms of the standard in the Old Kingdom, about 134 and 136; a unit of the latter value is supported by a weight in Cairo (31281). The same separation appears in the few weights of the xiith dynasty. After that there is no clear break, and only a confused mass of weights in the Greek period, hence the lack of discrimination in writers on metrology. The Gezer weights of the xviiith dynasty onward do not show any such grouping.

The lower standard is what is best known from the Attic weights of 134 grains in trade, though never exceeding 133 for coinage. The higher standard of 136 appears in the early haematite weights from Troy, pl. xlix, between 136·4 and 137·4. Thus the varieties we see in early Egypt continued to be reflected in other countries to a later time.

Notes. Outside of the barrel and duck weights there is little that is distinctive between this and the qedet; as a whole, the stater is of rounded forms, seldom fine or clean-cut, and often bad and ill-defined, whereas the qedet is the best cut of any group, and generally of clean forms and sharp edges.

Of peculiar weights, beside the two marked ones noted already, there is no. 3042 of 274·8 with a large Δ cut on it, showing it to be 4 drachmae of 68·7. As a whole, the stater series is not distinctive or interesting in detail. A fine weight of basalt of the ivth dynasty in Turin is inscribed for the *kher heb*, Hep-ata ("Law of the prince"). It is marked 10, giving a unit of 267·9, or 2 × 133·95, marked T on the diagram, pl. I.

CHAPTER VI

THE QEDET STANDARD.

Pls. XXXIII–XXXVII.

31. THIS is by far the most numerous standard in Egypt, and has generally been regarded as especially Egyptian. It is the basis of nearly all statements of weight from the xviiith dynasty onward. The multiple of 10 qedets was termed the deben, and 10 debens were termed the sep, in the xxvith dynasty (*P.S.P.A.*, 1893, 309). Deben is however a name applied also to other standards.

The marked weights are not more than a hundredth of all, in this standard. Their evidence is varied; two give the qedet, and two the deben, on the basis of 140–150 grains (3102, 3218, 3453, 4491); five give the double of this as the qedet (3178, 3260, 3343, 3484, 3547); one gives a quadruple qedet (3234). There was, then, the confusion of single and double values, as known in the daric and other standards.

The marks are more usual on the light varieties, mostly on a standard of 138 to 141, special emphasis being on values of 140·0 "of the treasury of Heliopolis" (Brit. Mus.), and 140·4 "of Heliopolis" (Louvre), and about 139 "of the treasury" (4985); others are nos. 3102, 3178, 3218, 3234, 3260, 4491. The heavier examples that are marked are much more scattered, 142 (3343), 144·0 (3453), 144·3

(3484), 145·6 (3547), 149·5 (3746), and the most important 150·0 with the name of Aohmes II (Brit. Mus.). There is also a deben of the Old Kingdom (3746) of 1494·7 grs., roughly marked 8, probably to correspond to 8 khoirīnes of 186·8. It is evident that the high value of 150 had strong support, though in Saitic times there was a ruling Heliopolitan value of 140 grains.

In late times, there was a fractional standard called the *khenp*, a word that has too many meanings; the khenp-deben was $\frac{1}{5}$th of a deben, the khenp-qedet was $\frac{1}{2}$ of a qedet, thus making a binary system of $\frac{1}{2}$, 1 and 2 qedets (*P.S.B.A.*, 1893, 310–312). The $\frac{1}{2}$ qedet and 2 qedets were the Egyptian drachm and tetradrachm.

Delimitation has already been noted between the stater and qedet, and that between the qedet and necef will be noted under the latter.

32. *History.* The history of this standard is not well defined, owing to its not being so common as some others in the early periods. The earliest stage appears to be at the rise of the Ist dynasty, when half a dozen alabaster cones (viii, 915) were placed in graves, sometimes singly, or else two together (*Tarkhan*, II, p. 11, pl. ix). As the cone with a curved base occurs in prehistoric weights and with a flat base it is common in xiith dynasty weights, there is fair ground for accepting the Tarkhan cones as weights. As they occur singly, or two together, they cannot be pieces for a game. The details of these are:—

No.	Grave	s.D.	Grains	÷	Unit
3272	1568	78	845·3	18	47·0
4050	717	79	478·2	10	47·8
3499	717	79	144·8	3	48·3
3541	728	78	872·6	18	48·5
4352	1892	77	980·0	20	49·0
4363	728	78	985·0	20	49·2

The standard thus appears to be the qedet, but divided by three, and this is the case in 45 instances in the list of historic times. The multiples 18 and 3 might as well be 6 and 1 qedets; but the multiples 10 and 20 strongly show that the third of a qedet was the unit. These were misunderstood at first and are entered in error to 3 and 7 qedets in the list. The qedet here would be from 141 to 147 grains.

Referring to the diagram, pl. I, it is seen that the Old Kingdom weights extend over the whole space between the values 141 and 148 as given in the Ist dynasty. There seems to be probably a gap between 145·6 and 147·7. If so, we may look on the early weights as indicating two families, centering on 144 and 149. On reaching the xiith dynasty such a division disappears, and no clear families can be traced. In the xviiith and xxiiird dynasties the mixture is so continuous that it is useless to figure it, and all that can be said is that there was a low group of 138·4; but from 140 to 148 there is no separation, and a grouping at 151 in the xviiith dynasty is lost in the xxiiird.

If it were possible to get sufficient examples from single localities of an early period, perhaps the origin and growth of the variations might be traced. For instance, 9 out of 12 from Kahun of the xiith dynasty are between 140·6 and 144·0, pointing to a standard of about 142·5, with rare examples of 147·2 and 149·3. In late times there was a definite standard of 140 at Heliopolis. In the Delta, in Greek times, there is so close a relation between the curves of distribution at Naukratis and Defenneh (*Tanis*, II, pl. L) as to point to five standards between 138 and 149, equally diffused.

The best that can be said seems to be that there was during the Old and Middle Kingdom a principal standard of about 145 grains, with local variations up to 150; and that in the xviiith dynasty two extreme groups of 138·5 and 151 became attached to the qedet, more probably by assimilating some foreign standard, rather than by variation of the earlier qedet. The gold shell of Taoa (Theban xviith dynasty) points to 151 being a southern unit. The Heliopolitan standard of 140 points to 138·5 being of northern or eastern origin. The great mass of hundreds of small weights of late period are so generally diffused that they are of no value for determining the standard.

33. *Notes.* There are not many peculiar weights in the qedet series; they are mostly plain conventional forms of the Saite age, and so much commoner than other standards that they did not require marks.

3102 has the names and titles of Apries with the numeral 40 (pl. viii); this serves to vouch for multiples by 4 and 40, but, owing to a large piece being broken away, the original weight of the deben is not precisely fixed.

3162 has the seal hieroglyph of the chancellor, lightly engraved on the top.

3218 is a splendid hippopotamus head in haematite, marked |||||∩|||||, ten qedet in two methods of numbering. It is from the Set temple of Nubt, a temple standard.

3336 is of brown serpentine, oblong, with rounded top edges, obviously Roman.

3392 of alabaster, thin, with rather bulgy outline, is from Nubt.

3594 has the mark Λ, probably 10; and, if so, 10 thirds of the qedet; the form seems influenced by the cheese-shaped Roman weights.

3687 is a finely polished block with slightly curved faces, of black quartzose stone.

3722 is a mace head form of black and white porphyry; that it is a weight is suggested by a similar form of grey syenite from Meroe, 3795, which also agrees with the qedet standard.

3876 is a simplified duck form of yellow limestone, with a large plug of lead up the axis, for adjustment.

4982, 5003 are hollow cases, filled with lead.

4985 has the mark of the *per hez* or treasury, and agrees in the light standard.

5015 is of black steatite of Roman age, and therefore placed with late weights.

5028, 5046, 5049, 5095 are a set of four weights found together, and then completely cleaned, with full allowance for the scale removed. They serve to show exactly how much variation existed in a single set.

5034, 5044, 5080, 5086 all have loop handles on the top.

5068 is an octagonal barrel weight, with an eye at the end; through this is a ring of four-sided rod, thinned to the ends, which are coiled round each other in Egyptian fashion. It has been adjusted by adding three turns of strip copper, around the ring.

5094 is a very large bronze weight, which had a handle let in to the top of it, now lost.

CHAPTER VII

THE NECEF STANDARD.
Pls. XXXVII–XXXVIII.

34. This standard was first found named in 1890, and by 1912 no less than six examples were known from Palestine bearing the name in early Hebrew (xxiii); five of these are single necef, and one is a quarter necef. The name is written with the letters *nun-tzaddi-pe*, and in English usage it may best be called necef, the vowels being unknown to us. The name may perhaps appear in Egypt as the *nusa*, see *P.S.B.A.*, 1892, 440. The Palestine weights yield 153·5, 154·3, 156·8 and 157·6 grains for the unit (excluding two damaged examples), the mean being 155·5.

On the Egyptian side, there is the literary evidence of $\frac{1}{9}$ of a qedet of gold being a unit of value at Karnak (*P.S.B.A.*, 1892, 440). The range of the qedet implies that this gold unit was between 153 and 169 grains. Thus it agrees with the *necef*. There is also the evidence in the inscriptions of Tehutmes III, that the irregular multiples of tribute stated in qedets, agree to regular multiples of a basis of about 160 grains. There are many other Asiatic examples of weights also on this basis (*Encyc. Brit.*, 80 grain standard).

The marked weights here catalogued vary in the multiple adopted for the unit.

No. 4045	398·1	marked 5	gives	$\frac{1}{2}$ of 159·2
„ 3939	38·5	„ $\frac{1}{4}$	„	1 154·0
„ 3962	154·9	„ $\frac{1}{2}$	„	2 × 154·9
„ 3927	307·5	„ $\frac{1}{2}$	„	4 × 153·7
„ 4071	40100	„ 5	„	50 × 160·4

Thus the unit was taken as the Palestine unit of 154, or the half, or double or quadruple of it; the mina was of 50 necef.

35. *Delimitation.* The square weights are less than 1 *per cent* of the qedet, while they are 5 *per cent* of the necef. On looking at the distribution of these, there are but 4 in a range of four grains, from 148 to 152, followed by a close group of 5 in the space of 153·6 to 154·3; hence it seems that the division is between 152 and 153·6. The heavy weights also show a break, eight 40-deben weights ranging from 55,200 to 59,750 (= 138·0 to 151·7), and then ceasing; after which, the 500 daric weights run from 64,830 to 66,000 (= 129·65 to 132·0); in these, therefore, there is no example of 400 necef. On searching the curve of distribution between 152 and 153·6 it appears that the point of crossing of the qedet and the necef is at 152·4; and probably some qedet extend over 153, while some necef may begin at 151·5. Thus between 151·5 and 153·5 the separation of the weights must depend upon the forms. The necef was very commonly dome-topped, with the sharp edge of the xxvith dynasty style, like most of the qedet; but it was very rarely domed from the base upward, like

many of the qedet weights. As noted above, the square weights are five times more common in the necef than they are in the qedet. The limits of the necef and the khoirīnē will be noted under the latter.

36. *History*. On looking at the diagram (pl. I) of the distribution of these weights, arranged according to period, it appears that there were two standards somewhat separated at first. The lower is from 153·2 to 154·3, or 155·6 in a Cairo example; the upper is from 160 to 164·5. These two, which were quite separate in the square weights of the Old Kingdom, became spread nearer to each other at 157·0 and 159·7 in the xiith dynasty, and became almost unified in the xviiith dynasty. A separation still existed in the xxiiird dynasty between 156·9 and 160·8; and the Gezer weights show the same separation, being all of the lower standard in the xviiith dynasty. The late weights of the Saite age are indicated by the number of each grain, and show a maximum at 154, and then a fairly steady dwindling down to 168. The history, therefore, seems to be that the unit of 154 grains was the early form, preserved in Palestine as 155 grains; that another unit of 163 grains existed in the Old Kingdom, which became confused with the 155 grain necef in the xviiith dynasty, but was never unified with it, and while separate in the xxiiird dynasty, was spread out by variation as a long and diffused extension of the 155 grain necef in the Saite age.

37. *Notes*. Regarding the various ambiguous examples which might be attributed to either the necef or the daric mina standard, we have already noted (under the daric) that in the higher multiples, up to 10 minas, the series ends with the range of the daric, and does not extend into the range where the necef is alone. This gives ground for attributing all such weights to the daric, and they are accordingly marked in the necef series with D prefixed, and given in full in the daric series.

Peculiar weights of this series which should be noted are no. 3914, 765·8 grains, with the *khent* sign on the top; no. 4045, 398·1 grains, a rough cone of alabaster with five holes marked on the base; and a red marble disc, no. 4101, 164·0 grains, with the Christian monogram on the top, probably the latest example of the necef. On the whole, there is not much of interest or peculiarity in the series, which is largely of the Saite age, as shown by the quantity of dome-topped weights like the qedets.

CHAPTER VIII

THE KHOIRINE STANDARD.

PL. XXXIX.

38. DURING recent years many weights have been found in Palestine bearing a sign, of which one example occurs in Egypt, see no. 5152, pl. xiii. This sign appears to be a monogram of *kh* and *o*, presumably the beginning of a name *kho*——. With this sign are various multiple numbers I, II, L, ⊥, which, by the weights, have obviously the values 1, 2, 4 and 8; there is also a $\frac{1}{3}$ unit marked LL. The name will be considered further on.

Unfortunately there has not been any critical examination of the Palestine weights to determine their gain or loss. It is not possible therefore to come to any exact conclusion as to their mean value, or range of variation. It may be said that the stated range of the *kho* series (omitting one extreme instance) is from 173·6 to 179·4, with a mean value of about 177·5 grains.

The number of weights which appear to belong to this standard in Egypt is less than that of any other standard; there are barely 150 in this collection. Of these, only three of stone are marked with numerals; (4230) of 362·7 grains is 2 × 181·3; (4149) of 1710·0 is 5 × 342, the double of 171; and (4253) of 36976 is 10 of 3698, or 200 of 184·9. One of bronze 5152 has the monogram XO, and is 2 of 189 grains.

39. There is an interesting group of five cowry shells carved in grey syenite, evidently all from one source, though bought singly. The largest weighs 4 of the next one, and that double of the next, and these are respectively 2, $\frac{1}{2}$ and $\frac{1}{4}$ khoirīnē; the others agree to $\frac{3}{10}$ khoirīnē. See pl. xvi.

No.	4248 (ix)	368·0 grs.	2 × 184·0
„	4214	89·8 „	$\frac{1}{2}$ × 179·6
„	4217 A	45·0 „	$\frac{1}{4}$ × 180·0
„	4205 A	53·6 „	$\frac{3}{10}$ × 178·7
„	4196	53·3 „	$\frac{3}{10}$ × 177·7

No other weights cut in the form of a cowry shell occur in the whole collection. These are marked on the diagram, pl. I, by Φ along the top of the khoirīnē series. See pl. xvi.

Turning next to the name, the cowry was named by the Greeks *khoirīnē*, as Prof. D'Arcy Thompson has kindly informed me; his notes on the subject are added here as an appendix. This name seems at once to give the source of the monogram *kho*

found upon the weights. The *khoīrīnē* shell was very familiar to the Greeks, as it was that used in ballotting. May it not be then that these shells were used for rough weights? To any one familiar with the broken brickbats, chunks of stone, scraps of China plates, and many other casual masses which are common as weights in Oriental markets, a lot of apparently uniform shells will seem respectable as weights. Through the kindness of Dr. Bather, my enquiry about Aegean cowries has been answered by Mr. Cosmo Melvill, who states that a specimen of *Cypraea lurida* weighs 214 grains, and *C. spurca* and *physis* about 120 or 130 grains. Dr. Harmer further states that *C. lurida* from Cape de Verde Islands is 200 grains, and from St. Helena is 142 grains. There is, then, no improbability in a growth averaging about 180 grains having been found in the Mediterranean; or the standard may be older than the use of the shell, and examples chosen which agreed with it. We may thus fairly link together the khoīrīnē shell, the artificial cowries of syenite, and the weights marked *kho*.

Delimitation. The break between the necef and the khoīrīnē is shown in the simplest way by the single unit stone weights. Of these there are 35 of the necef between 152·4 and 167·9; after that an entire break, and then 14 of the khoīrīnē between 172·4 and 185·2. Looking at the whole series, 168 grains is the point which best divides the standards.

40. *History.* On mapping the distribution of these weights according to age (pl. ii), there appear two groups. An example at 171·0 in the Old Kingdom (with marked numerals) appears to be the parent form of two in the xviiith dynasty, of the same value, and 172·7. On the other hand, the great mass of examples begins with 185·0 to 187·4 grains, and spreads out in the xiith dynasty to 176·5 to 188·5, and to 176·1 to 190·0 in the xviiith dynasty. By the xxiiird dynasty, examples appear, fusing together the two groups; and in the xxvith dynasty there is an almost continuous variation centring mainly about 176, but tailing off to 190. This is the foundation of the Palestine group with marks, centering on 177·5. The Gezer weights of the xviiith dynasty show the division as in Egypt at that date, between 172 and 177·6; but the later weights agree with the fusion of varieties seen in Egypt. This history of the standard, thus traced by the forms of the weights, is a warning against accepting any late group, such as the Palestine

marked weights, as a basis for discussing the origin of weights.

41. *Notes.* The value shown by the cowries is marked along the top of the diagram. One remarkable weight should be noted, no. 4254. This jasper weight of king Khety of the ixth dynasty (xi, 4466) bears on the end of it, apart from the inscription, the numeral 9. It is very unlikely that this was the original intention for the weight, but, like many other numerals, it has been added to show the value by a fresh standard. Unfortunately, fractures have destroyed the accuracy of this weight, but it was originally about 1850 grains, or 10 khoīrīnai, and it thus shows that we are justified in tracing the khoīrīnē back to the Old Kingdom. The weight has been converted into 9 of the gold standard or beqa. The first weight on the list, no. 4141, is very low, and would not be placed to this standard, were not its form like that of no. 4220, and its material, amazonite, like that of no. 4231. The cowroid forms, nos. 4142, 4231, agree with the syenite cowries, and the khoīrīnē connection of this standard.

CHAPTER IX
THE BEQA STANDARD.
PLS. XL—XLI.

42. THIS standard has been recognised in Egypt during the last twenty years, and commonly called the gold standard, as the weights often have the hieroglyph of gold upon them. As there are here as many as 24 examples bearing numerals, it is scarcely requisite to extract them from the catalogue, in which they are all marked. The range of variation of these marked weights is from 189·7 to 215·2 grains for the unit.

In other collections several examples occur of weights of this standard with royal names and numerals, which are entered in the diagram. The weight of Khufu of 2060 grains, gives 206·0 for the unit. That of Senusert I is 4 units of 213·0. Of Amenemhet III there is a weight of 4 units of 196·1. In the xviiith dynasty is a weight of Amenhetep I giving 5 units of 207·6, and one of Tehutmes III giving 6 units of 197·1. A weight which is probably of the Old Kingdom, by the name, Ampy Ptah-ne-kau, gives 10 units of 218·8; but this is higher than any other marked weight, and probably belongs to the sela, the so-called Phoenician standard. Thus weights which by the royal

3

names were probably more accurate than usual, vary from 196·1 to 213·0, without any regular order of changes.

The name of this standard is given by three marked weights found in Palestine (xxiii), each with the word *beth-qof-ʿayn*, spelling beqʿa. These weights are of 90·6, 94·3, and 102·6 grains, the half of a 181 to 205 grain unit. This standard was used in the earliest Hebrew literature, as it is named as the weight of the gold ring given to Rebekah, and the poll tax stated in Exodus xxxviii, 26. This is evidently half of the Egyptian gold standard, and there is no reason for forcing it into any supposed relation to the Hebrew shekel of any period. The double unit, like the Egyptian, is indicated in Palestine by a small weight in the form of a tortoise, marked 5 or $\frac{1}{5}$; as it weighs only 38·6 grains, it must be $\frac{1}{5}$ of 193 grains.

43. *Delimitation.* The lowest value shown by a weight (4299) marked *nub* "gold," is 189·7 grains. The barrel form which is often seen in all other standards (especially in the daric) is entirely absent from the beqa, there being no barrel weights of a unit between 191·7 and 218·4 grains. Other forms of the beqa exist, but are not found in its lighter variations, so that there is a wide gap between the higher khoirīnē and the lower beqa weights. Thus, there are no examples between the following values of the unit :—

Duck weights	to 188,	none to 199·1
Domed „	up to 190,	„ to 199·9
Rounded „	up to 191·7,	„ to 199·6

Looking at all the examples about the critical range, it seems that 188·0 may be accepted as the best dividing point, with a few of each family crossing this division.

44. *History.* The history of this standard (pl. ii) begins earlier than that of any other. Six of the prehistoric graves at Naqada each contained one block of limestone, of some form which had no parallel among working tools (vi, 456, 458; viii, 881, 883). The list of these, and three similar blocks of unknown source, is as follows :—

No.	Grave	Sequence date	Weight			Unit	Form
3175	461	40–61	2785	÷ 15 =	185·7		913
				or ÷ 20 =	139·2		
4296	B. 107	33	5676	÷ 30 =	189·2		881
4321	1773	31–41	7694	÷ 40 =	192·3		881
4332	?	?	1163·6	÷ 6 =	194·0		456

No.	Grave	Sequence date	Weight			Unit	Form
4358	1873	46	589·7	÷ 3 =	196·6		646
			790·0	÷ 5 =	197·5		A
4392	1866	43	3996·6	÷ 20 =	199·8		456
			418·4	÷ 2 =	209·2		B
4543	1563	32	4224·5	÷ 20 =	211·2		883
4553	?	?	2180·2	÷ 10 =	218·0		458
4555	?	?	118·0	÷ $\frac{1}{2}$ =	236·0		456

Three of these (4296, 4321, 4543) are cylinders with rounded ends (forms 881, 883); three (4332, 4392, 4555) are domes with rounded bases (form 456); only one weight (4358) is of the bulgy square form (646) usual in the Old Kingdom. Two are of unusual forms, A a porphyry turtle, B a porphyry cylinder; as the forms are not characteristic of weights, they are left here unnumbered. The cylinders with rounded ends are the earliest, being of s.d. 32, 33, and between 31 and 41, all therefore of the Amratian prehistoric civilisation. To the Gerzean civilisation belongs the dome with rounded base (4392) s.d. 43, and the bulgy square (4358) s.d. 46. As regards the standard, all but two of these are simple multiples of a unit between 188·7 and 211·2 grains, agreeing closely with the limits of the beqa in dynastic times. The multiples 3, 6, 15, and 30 show strongly a triple form. This triple multiple would bring it into relation with the later qedet, 3 of the lower family of the beqa being equal to 4 qedet: this relation may account for the frequency of 40 qedet weights (= 30 beqa) and $\frac{1}{3}$ qedet (= $\frac{1}{4}$ beqa) in later times. But though the first may be the qedet, one could not ascribe all the above examples to the qedet, for multiples of $13\frac{1}{3}$ and $26\frac{2}{3}$ would be quite unlikely. It might be supposed that the prehistoric Egyptians had not reached the art of weighing; but their high mechanical ability, and the presence here of a small balance beam, of a red limestone which is peculiar to prehistoric times, give ground for crediting the above blocks as being weights.

At the beginning of the Ist dynasty, conical weights were used; two of these were found at Tarkhan (4352, 4363; viii, 9, 156), as noted under the qedet; they are of 980·0 and 985·0 and appear to be 5 beqa of 196·0 and 197·0 grains. Of about the same age is the gold bar of Aha, weighing 216 grains, which can scarcely be unconnected with the gold standard (*Royal Tombs*, II, 21).

In the Old Kingdom, the lower standard is the more compact, 196 to 202. The higher standard

spreads out from 206 to 213·5; and the extreme amounts are the important examples, above mentioned, which are likely to be standards, one the gold bar with the name of Aha, the other the fine weight with the cartouche of Khufu. Intermediate examples show that these are not isolated values, nor due to casual error. It will be seen on pl. ii that the heavier group continued to extend toward the lighter, the ixth dynasty weight of Khety, and the second marking (4445) of weight (4507) 208·7, coming below the Khufu standard. The weight of Khety, however, must not be taken as exact, for the marking of 9 upon it, as before said, is probably only a secondary assignment of the 10 khoirine weight.

In the xiith dynasty, the range is wider in the low standard, 188 to 202·1, and the high standard is also widely spread from 204·4 to 215·2, but not quite reaching the Aha weight. In the xviiith dynasty, the gap between the upper and lower standards is even wider than before (201 to 205·5), and there are royal weights in both, as before. It is not till the debasement of the xxiiird dynasty that the two standards are finally confused. The Gezer weights of this period and earlier, are eight of the low standard, and only one of the high; this points to the low standard being Syrian.

Amid this wide inaccuracy and duplication of standard it should be observed how several important weights agree on 196—197, the Ist dynasty cones, the splendid weight of Herfu, that of Amenemhet III and later of Tehutmes III. These seem to mark a definite standard amid the wide range of 188 to 202 grains.

45. *Notes.* This standard is one of the most interesting on account of the many marked and dated examples, and the fine forms often occurring. The most beautiful weight in the collection is the large one, pl. vii, type 694, of light green veined marble (4355), in perfect condition and polish, made for the "Hereditary prince, royal seal bearer, sole companion, keeper of the seal, Herfu, living again." Unfortunately the locality of this is unknown, as I bought it from Aly Araby; see a scarab of Herfu in the Louvre, Salle des Dieux (*P.H.S.*, 444). Other weights of the same form bear the sign of gold, and numerals (4416, 4547). Two weights of the Old Kingdom (4455, 4507), much rounded, with finely cut numerals, are of a beautiful red-veined limestone, which I have not seen elsewhere; these are from Quft (pl. xi). Another Old Kingdom weight

(4399), now much broken, must have been splendid when originally made, as it is of fawn-coloured chert, well rounded and polished (pl. xi). A pleasing series of weights are those of haematite from Tyre, of truncated cone form (viii, 893), nos. 4360, 4382, 4388. They agree closely in a mean standard of 199·2, varying less than 0·2 grain from it. Two curious weights of white marble from the temple of Byblos (4325, 4385), bear a pair of breasts on the top, in one instance united by a cross handle. They vary somewhat in unit, and the lighter might equally well be 5 minas of the daric; but the heavier one is beyond the range of the daric, and so both probably belong to the beqa in its later character as the Aeginetan standard, of which these weights equal 4 minas. Similar weights in the collections are from Syria and Knidos, and belong to different standards.

A rather irregular series of unusual form are the sharp-edged discs nos. 4365, 4439, 4488 A, 4517, 4544, 4554. They have, all but one, been worked out of thin veins of quartz, varying in colour from white to yellow, pink, and brown. Two of the six are known to come from Quft, and from the similarity of material and form they were doubtless all made there. The average unit of these is 208·4 (mean diff. 5·6), and hence they belong to the higher standard. Four other weights from Quft average 206·4, and it seems therefore that the high standard is south Egyptian.

The Golenicheff weight of 2025 is probably 10 beqa, though marked 8 for the double daric system (*Rev. Eg.*, 1881, 177).

CHAPTER X

THE SELA STANDARD.

Pl. XLII.

46. This is a very well known standard of weight, usually called the Phoenician or Alexandrian. As we have used the original or specific names of the other standards, instead of local names, it is desirable to use one of the ancient names here. The shekel is only a general term, and the sole distinctive name is sela, which was the later Jewish name of this shekel. As S is already appropriated to stater, the second letter L will be used for *sela*.

The marked weights here are:—

No.	Grains	Mark	Unit	Period
4590	8570	÷ 20 =	428·5	XII
4593	429·4	÷ 2 =	214·7	VI
4612	432·4	÷ 2 =	216·2	VI
4626	1303·6	÷ 3 =	434·8	XXVI
4665	882·4	÷ 4 =	220·6	Ro.
4669	3534·4	÷ 8 =	441·8	Ro.
4688	8900	÷ 20 =	445·0	XII

It appears therefore that the double unit of over 400 grains, as well as the single unit, belong to both early and late times.

47. *Delimitation.* The *nub*-marked weights of the beqa extend up to 215 grains. The good domed weights are entirely absent between 1592·8 (the necef) and 2192·4 (the sela), so the khoirīnē and the beqa were omitted. In the larger weights, of rather over 4000 grains, there occur clear gaps in the series. Thus in the cuboid weights there are 5 between 207·8 and 209·8 of beqa unit, and then a gap to 11 between 213·8 and 226·3 of sela unit. Similarly in the roughly rounded weights there are 6 between 199·7 and 209·6 of beqa unit, a gap, and then 7 between 215·1 and 227·5 of sela unit. These various limits indicate that the beqa usually ceases at 210 (though four marked ones are known above that, up to 215); and the sela begins about 214. Looking at the whole series, probably 210 grains may be accepted as the best division, as there are special reasons of form and material for any exceptions on either side which cross that limit. The boundary between the peyem and the sela was dealt with under the former standard.

48. *History* (pl. ii). This standard begins in the Ist dynasty, with a block of porous basalt, weighing 438·9 grains; from the tomb with the name of a queen Sma-nebui, apparently about the time of Mena. This falls in the middle of the range of Old Kingdom weights, which show a unit from 214·7 to 227·0. In the xiith dynasty, the examples were rather more scattered. In the xviiith dynasty, the middle values became commoner, about 218; and these increased still more in the xxiiird dynasty. The Maccabean shekel was 220 grains. The Gezer weights of late periods show much the same variability.

49. *Notes.* As a whole, this standard is marked by the large proportion of irregularly formed weights, more than a quarter of the whole; while fewer dome-topped weights of the regular Egyptian form appear than in any other standard. Barrel weights are scarce, and there is but a single duck

weight. A peculiar form is the half of a thick disc; one of these (no. 4714) has an inscription on the edge (pl. vii, 701), of the "Hereditary prince, purifier in the temple of Ptah, *sam* priest, high priest of Memphis, Hora." Several unusual forms occur in this standard, such as no. 4579, a roughly cut ram in limestone; no. 4626, a wolf's head in basalt; no. 4719, a duck's head; no. 4697, a large rectangular marble weight with the figure of a man on the top, from the Lebanon; no. 4716, a triangular prism (viii, 874), apparently of jade, with the name of Ptah finely cut on the end; no. 4557, a curious lump of haematite; and, above all, the finely inscribed weight (pl. vi, 656) of Nefer-maot, no. 4740, certainly of the early ivth dynasty.

A weight at Berlin has upon it "copper 15"; as it weighs 6343 grains, it shows a unit of 423 grains, or twice 211·5, which is evidently this standard. There is here the wolf's head (4626) weight marked *gamma*, 3, showing a unit of 434 grains, which accords with a triple multiple of this standard. But it seems possible that both of these are re-marked, and were originally 50 darics of 126·9 and 10 darics of 130·4. The weight of Ampy Ptah-ne-kau at Berlin, inscribed "deben 10" is 2188 grains, and the unit of 218·8 agrees much better with the sela than with the beqa.

50. The values which we have found for the original units, (before their fusion formed the standards known historically), are the material necessary in any search for an original connection between them. Many theories exist of one unit being formed by multiples or fractions of another; the original bases of any unit are the quantities involved, and it is useless to compare the vague values made in times long after a unit originated.

The following are, then, the amounts which have to be considered in any theories of derivation of standards, and the equivalent cubic inches of water.

	Grains	Mina	Cub. ins.	Grammes
peyem	116	5800	23·0	7·5
	121	6050	24·0	7·8
	124	6200	24·6	8·0
daric	127·5	7650	30·3	8·25
	131·5	7900	31·3	8·5
stater	134·5	6725	26·7	8·7
qedet	145	7250	28·8	9·4
necet	154·5	7725	30·7	10·0
	162	8100	32·1	10·5

	Grains	Mina	Cub. ins.	Grammes
khoirīnē	{ 171	8550	34·0	11·05
	{ 185	9250	36·7	11·95
beqa	{ 196	9800	38·9	12·7
	{ 210	10500	41·7	13·6
sela	220	5500	21·8	14·25

One of the widest uncertainties in the later state of the standards is in the similarity of 6 darics, 5 necef, and 4 beqa. On referring to the original components, and multiplying them as above, the results are:—

daric	necef	beqa
765	772	784
790	810	840

Thus none of the original components are alike, and the resemblances of later forms are merely casual.

Another possible connection is that 5 peyem are 4 qedets. This is by the qedet 580, and by the lowest component of the peyem also 580. Both of these are at least as old as the ivth dynasty, and probably the qedet is of the Ist dynasty or earlier. The scantiness of early material leaves the direction of derivation uncertain.

The lower khoirīnē seems to be the source of the late Persian 86-grain unit, which has hitherto been taken as derived through a silver weight equal in value to a gold standard. This implies that the khoirīnē is $1\frac{1}{3}$ darics. By the daric, this would give 170 and 175·3; the khoirīnē is 171 and 185. Looking at the diagrams, pl. i, ii, it is unlikely that the primitive daric should be 128·25, or the khoirīnē 170. Thus the question remaining is whether the Persian unit is derived from $1\frac{1}{3}$ daric or from the khoirīnē; the data are too scanty and diverse for the settlement of this. Other supposed relations of weights may require to be tested, and the original standards are the only source for proving any derivations.

In the table above, the mina of each unit is stated, and the equivalent volume of water in cubic inches. This is required for testing possible connection of weight and water volume, which seems probable in several cases.

CHAPTER XI
WEIGHTS FOUND AT GEZER.

51. THESE weights are all published in Prof. MACALISTER's report, and are here reduced to grains (in pl. xlix) in order to compare with the Egyptian weights. After the classifying of the previous weights, there is little question about the attribution of these, except that a few of the smallest, of which the fraction is doubtful, are omitted here. There are five periods distinguished in the publication; but as there is no clear line between the first and second they are both marked here as 1, including all down to the end of the xviiith dynasty, 1330 B.C. Class 2 comes down to 800 B.C.; class 3 from 800 to 550; class 4 550 to 100 B.C. The few names that occur on these are not always satisfactory. The beqa 94·3 is very low, but is vouched as such, by the name on it. The peyem 112·2 is also very low, but likewise is named. The khoirīnē weights marked as such, with the multiple in italics in the list, are all well in their group. A weight with the name necef on it, however, is only of 143·2, obviously a qedet, 10 grains too light for the lightest necef; probably it was a necef ground down, or made as a qedet, and then marked necef by accident or fraud. The whole question of loss and alteration is unstated, and may easily increase many of these.

The relative numbers in each standard, and each period, are here given, reduced to percentages of the total (230).

Period	1	2	3	4	all
peyem	1	1	3	4	9
daric	3	—	3	2	8
stater	1	2	1	2	6
qedet	5	7	5	13	30
necef	3	2	3	2	10
khoirīnē	3	3	4	8	18
beqa	1	3	2	5	11
sela	1	2	2	3	8
Each period	18	20	23	39	100

The qedet greatly preponderate in every period. Next to that the khoirīnē; and it is strange how the three least usual units are what might be expected to prove the commonest, the well-known daric, stater or Attic, and sela or Phoenician. Looking at the different periods, the peyem increases in later time, the daric loses ground, the stater is not at all increased by the Greek influence, the qedet gains largely as well as the khoirīnē. These changes are instructive as they are not at all what might have been expected. It is as clear here, as it is in Egypt, that all of these units were in use as early as the xviiith dynasty.

The comparison of these with the Egyptian weights has already been stated in the account of each standard.

CHAPTER XII

THE METAL WEIGHTS.

52. As the purpose of studying the stone weights was the recovery of the original standards, and tracing their changes, it was needful to exclude the metal weights which have almost always undergone alteration. The metal weights, also, are mainly of later period than those of stone. Metal was rarely used for weights before the Greek period; and after it came into use, stone weights are only a minority, except for large sizes where metal would be expensive. The difference of period is so marked that a few stone weights of late age are included here in the metal group. Metal has usually both lost and gained in weight. The loss is by wear, by solution of compounds, and, especially on bronze weights, by scaling of compounds; the gain is by the oxygen and carbonic acid locked up in the compounds, for nearly half the weight of green carbonate of copper is gain from the air. The uncertainty in estimating the changes, obliterates the value of a weight for precise enquiries; but it generally leaves the weight of some value in coarser grouping, and only in few cases does it render uncertain the attribution of a weight to a standard. In comparing several estimates, made thirty years apart, there was found an average difference of 1 grain on a total change of $2\frac{1}{2}$ grains.

53. The considerations in the treatment of metal weights are different from those regarding stone weights. Owing to the late date, there is no question as to original values of standards, all those were long past; nor is there any historical difference to be taken into account, so far as we know. The use of metals in coinage has led to a depreciation of the standard in most cases, quite different from the casual variations before the influence of coinage; different types of one standard came into use, for trade and for coinage, as in the Attic and Roman systems,—stater and uncia. The use of coinage also led to fresh divisions, such as the drachma rather than the stater (Attic) or the shekel (sela); also to fresh subdivisions, as the twelfth of the stater (Attic). The ranges of variation became wider than before; the marked nomisma, or sixth of the uncia, is found from 59·6 to 73 grains, im-

plying a libra from 4300 to 5260 grains. In view of this vagueness and of the balance errors affecting very small weights, we must not hesitate at granting a much wider range to these little weights of the Attic system than is due to the early stater system; the uniform style of little square leaden weights from 57 to 74 for the drachma belong rather to the common Attic system widely in error, than to the daric, peyem, and qedet which occupied those limits in earlier times. Hence all the practical considerations of study in the great trading, coining, cosmopolitan age of the Roman Empire, must be widely different from those which have led us back to the isolated conditions of the origins of local standards.

In this late section there are many weights from Syria and Asia Minor; but as trade was so general in the Graeco-Roman age, it is not unsuitable to take together all the eastern weights. I owe all these Greek weights, and some of the Egyptian examples, to the zeal of my old friend the Rev. Greville Chester, whose collecting tours, down to his death in 1892, were a means of saving a great quantity of antiquities from ignorant destruction and loss.

A class of very small bronze weights here has been kept apart from the other metal weights, for two reasons. First, they are so small that the uncertainties of original balance error, and of corrosion, make it only just possible to class them aright, without any hope of their giving help in defining the standards. Second, they are nearly all from Defenneh, from the early Greek goldsmiths' workshops, and thus dated between 660 and 560 B.C. Their only value, therefore, is in showing what standards were used in the jewellery trade at one place and in one century.

54. In studying metal weights it is necessary to make allowance for the changes which they have undergone. The principles of this, and a table of the allowances needed for various corrosion, I published in *Naukratis*, I, pp. 70–71, in 1886. All the weights reported here have had changes estimated; and, as most have both gained and lost, the sum of the changes is entered in the list, to show how far the result is uncertain. The estimation of change must always be vague, in fact the only satisfactory material would be entirely uncleaned weights, reduced to a metallic state by chemical means. The main use of examination is to reject from the series such weights as have undergone

large changes. In the diagram of results, none are included which have more than two *per cent* of total change, and these results may there be fairly trusted to about one *per cent*.

In the diagram of metal weights, pl. ii, there are short curved lines below the row of marks showing the unit of weight. These lines show the *maxima* ⌢, and the *minima* ⌣ of the distribution of the stone weights. The details of references to other sources will be described below, under each standard. In the following notes, numbers with star * are shown on pl. ix frontispiece.

55. PEYEM, xliii. A notable group here is of three square weights (pl. xii, 4747, 4751, 4764) with an anchor in relief, the Seleucidan emblem. These must be presumed to belong to one standard. That of 3503 grains, if halved (1751), is near 1816·; and the ratio to 4570 is as 3 : 4; the proportion between these is then 3 : 6 : 8, on a basis of about 570 to 605 grains. As this is Syrian, we cannot refer the base to 4 qedets, and as the multiples are by 3, the base cannot be 3 Aeginetan or beqa, as 9 and 18 are very unlikely in that system. This limits these to being 15, 30 and 40 peyem, and as that unit is well known in Syria, this is the more probable. The bronze weight bears the name of Papios in relief (pl. xii). The disc of bronze (4773) from Tartus, of 495 grains, with *tzo* in Phoenician, may refer to *tzor* small, as being the small division of a unit. The usual heavy weight is 400 peyem, and this weight would be a hundredth of that. There are only two animal weights, calf and frog, of this standard, 4749,* 4775.*

56. DARIC, xliii. The best known form for this standard is the Assyrian lion weight. There are here two fine examples of 2610 and 2635 grains, quite uninjured; one lion (4848)* is of the raging Assyrian style, the other (4841)* of the bourgeois Babylonian type (pl. ix). They agree with the high group of the standard (marked L in diagram), while the great lion weights centre on 127·2 (marked here AL) which is the low standard, and none of them reach 130 grains, unfortunately the amount of cleaning is not stated (see *Rev. Eg.*, ii, 174–176). No. 4782 is from Magnesia ad Sipylum; it is credited here to the daric, as there is no evidence of the peyem as far west as Lydia. The same may be said of no. 4783* from Ephesos, with heads of Severus and Caracalla. The small couchant lion, no. 4788,* has a ring on the back, a miniature of the Assyrian lions. The thick disc of lead with a handle, no. 4789,* has in raised letters cast on it LPMαTOYP. This probably refers to its issue by a Roman governor at Tyre, like no. 5158 issued by a governor at Berytus. The only known family name to agree with these initials is Lucius Pomponius Molo, who was in the mint at Rome in 94 B.C. The weight from Lachish, no. 4799, is a square of sheet lead, stamped at each corner with a die (pl. xii) from the gold stater of Philip II, which gives its period. The large weight no. 4800, from Ephesos, with a tripod in relief, is of the same group as the other triangular lead weight from Ephesos, no. 4840.

A square bronze weight, xiii, no. 4806, has deeply incised letters on it, EM⊥; ⊥ is known by the khoirine series to be = 8, and an eighth of this agrees with the daric. On the other side it bears K, which may mean 20 drachms of the sela. On a brown serpentine weight no. 4821, Π is evidently for πεντε, five shekels. Another marked weight in the same material has B, referring to the double shekel, no. 4856. A rectangular bronze weight, no. 4849, bears a thunderbolt in relief on the top, and, incused below, a bull of curious disjointed style. By these types it is probably Seleucidan.

The distribution in the diagram, pl. ii, shows a clear gap at the same point as in the stone series, 129 grains. As this is the value of the daric coinage, it seems that the coinage had no influence on a standard value, but the weights continued to be copied from the trade standards. This unit had a wide range in the Greek world, being the regular standard of the earliest coinage of Asia Minor,— Cyzicus, Lampsacus, &c.—as well as of Corinth and early Magna Graecia, before it became modified to suit the Attic system.

57. STATER (Attic) xliii. In this system, the reduction to a unit is here continued on the stater basis, for convenience of comparison with the stone weights. But the actual numeration marked on the weights is nearly always on the drachma, or half-stater basis, and the divisors would be simpler on this drachma·value. This was not so originally, as the two marked weights of early times show the stater basis.

The most usual class of this Attic standard are the small square leaden weights, the commonest of all in Greek times. The weights with two and three dots (4860, 4868) prove the usual division of the drachma into six obols. Among the animal weights, the "flat bull head" (4925)* of Greek work,

is in front view, and is flat on the back. The
" bull head, Amarna " (4939)* is an all-round figure
of purely Egyptian work of the xviiith dynasty.
The haematite wolf head, or fox head (4938)*, is
probably prehistoric Greek. The Asklepios weight
(4946)* is a square of sheet lead, bearing an oval
stamp in which is a figure of Asklepios. The weight
no. 4964 apparently represents a flat seed; it is the
only trace of the principle of the seed-weight, so
essential in India and China. The distribution
diagram, pl. ii, shows that the majority conform to
the trade value of the Attic standard, and that
the coinage value has had very little effect on the
weights; the number agreeing with the coins is
only what might be expected as a lower extension,
like the upper extension, of the trade value.

58. QEDET, xliv. This is an almost entirely
Egyptian standard; at Gezer, about a quarter of
the weights agree with it, but it is rare in Syria,
and unknown in the Greek series. The metal weights,
by their forms, are nearly all distinctly Egyptian.
There is only the figure of a dove, no. 5050*, which
could be accounted as Greek work. The bull's
head from Gurob, no. 5030, is in the round; the
flat bull's head, no. 5073*, is of the form usual in
foundation deposits. No. 5044, though stated as
found in the tomb of Den, is apparently of late
date; it has had a handle broken off, and is much
battered, so, if really found there, it was probably
dropped recently by a native. In the distribution
diagram, pl. ii, it appears that the most usual values
are 142–144 and 149–151. There is no prominence
of the low 140 grain value. For other notes on
these, see the qedet stone series, sect. 33.

59. NECEF, xlv. The first example (5096) is placed
here, instead of with the qedet, as it resembles
no. 5113 which is clearly the necef. In the higher
values there are many animal weights; altogether,
23 *per cent* are animal weights, while there are only
4 *per cent* of these in the qedets. The distribution
is much scattered, and shows no relation to the
ranges of stone weights. This was the Greek system
in eastern Asia Minor, and probably native to
North Syria and the Hittites. It was also one of
the systems later called " Alexandrian." The iron
weight (5116) is the only one of that metal here.

60. KHOIRINE, xlv. There is sufficient gap between the last group and this to distinguish the
beginning; and at the end is a marked weight
(5152) certainly of this standard. Possibly some of
the lighter beqa (or Aeginetan) weights which

follow, really belong here. The proportion of animal
weights is as in the necef. The distribution of these
has no relation to the grouping of the stone weights.
This system was well-known in Asia Minor, used
for the silver coinage of Phocaea, and passed on
to Massilia.

61. BEQA (Aeginetan), xlv. One of the lowest
examples of this (5154)* is so assigned because of
the form of a tortoise, the type of Aegina. Another tortoise weight is no. 5186*. In Greek times
the drachma, or half-stater, was the unit, and hence
all these numbers of multiples should be doubled,
which renders them much smoother, 3 and 5 and
150, in place of $1\frac{1}{2}$ and $2\frac{1}{2}$ and 75, also $\frac{1}{4}$ and $\frac{3}{8}$ in
place of $\frac{1}{8}$ and $\frac{3}{16}$. The double drachma is kept
here in order to compare it with the beqa or *nub*
weights of earlier ages. No. 5158 records the name
of Licinius Cnaeus, perhaps born in the joint censor-
ship of L. Licinius and Cnaeus Domitius, 92 B.C. He
appears to have been governor of Berytus. A group
of weights with a head of a ram or lamb, probably
belong together; they are nos. 5163*, 5169*, 5195*, of
3, 5 and $1\frac{1}{2}$ drachms, all cast in open moulds.
These are probably of Phokis, as the ram's head
is on the coins of Delphi with the Aeginetan standard. The heart shape, no. 5178*, is of Egyptian style.
The little discs of calcite from Ephesos (5180, 5188,
5193) are of $\frac{1}{4}$ and $\frac{3}{8}$ of a drachma. An unusual
type here is the square with concave sides, type 614;
three here, nos. 5162, 5177, 5185, are of 10 obols,
5 and 150 drachms, which seem peculiar to this
system.

The distribution of these weights shows no relation to that of the earlier beqa standard; but they
closely conform to the usual range of the coinage,
and the variation of the Aeginetan trade standard
of Greek times.

62. SELA (Phoenician), xlvi. The most distinct
series of this unit is that of the thin weights of
cast lead, with a raised border and a letter-numeral,
belonging to Berytus and Marathus, type 612. The
similarity of the eight listed here (xiii, 5205–5208,
5228, 5237, 5273, 5275) is the ground for placing
so low a unit as 197 grains (no. 5205) to this system.
There is however as low a variant in a series of
disc weights from Carthage (197 to 234 grains)
which must belong to this standard. A large
example is the pan-shaped weight with ribbed inside, no. 5214, which gives a mina of 60 sela; such
a multiple is supported by xiii, nos. 5218, which is
marked Llll, *librae tria*, showing a libra in Roman

times of 20 sela, and the use of a weight of 60 sela. Two Egyptian examples from Memphis are curious, roughly carved as a lion and ram, xvi 5215, 5230. No. 5235, xiii, bears *sigma* upon it, probably for *siglos*. The numeral 5 on no. 5243 is doubtless placed for a fifth of the sela. Among the animal weights that of the calf, no. 5253*, is unusual for the size and good work; it is a *cire perdue* casting, filled up with lead. The two weights from Cyprus are alike, nos. 5256, 5257, but clearly not double one of the other: the only relation is 25 to 12, and this would be 25 and 12 drachmae of the sela. In these, and many other instances, the multiples show that the drachm of $\frac{1}{4}$ sela was the unit regarded rather than the whole sela. A fine series was found at Tell Amarna (xiii, 5276–5281), dated to Roman times by a variegated glass whorl found with it. These six weights of lead are in good condition, not deeply corroded, and without any loss, each plainly marked. The details of them are given at the end of the list of the sela (xlvi), and the mean value entered in the list (5267). The mean variation and balance error is under five grains. In the diagram, the mean is a thick stroke, with a bracket over it showing the extent of variation. It is an unusually high value of the sela, suggesting that it may have been modified to agree with the weight of the denarius some time in the second century. In the diagram, the distribution centres on the group of earlier weights, and the rather lower value of the Ptolemaic coinage does not seem to have lowered the average.

63. UNGIA, xlvi. This Roman system does not appear in the earlier stone weights; and only a few stone ones are here, all of the regular Roman form. The standard of the libra was probably derived from the Aeginetan system, the descendant of the beqa; but being divided in Italy into 12 unciae, and these into six sextulae or nomismata (= solidus coin), and these again into 24 siliquae, this duodecimal series entirely broke the resemblance to the Aeginetan system.

The first three and last of the list stand so far apart from any other examples, that they are clearly fraudulent. The rest form so connected a series, that they must be granted to vary to the outrageous amount of a tenth of the whole; being marked weights there is no denying this irregularity. The usual marks on them are Λ for libra; Γο for oungia, uncia; N for nomisma or solidus; with the usual letter-numerals. The marks are often placed in a wreath with a cross between them, sometimes in an archway supported by twisted pillars (xiv, xv, 5323, 5378). The peculiar types are noticed, in order. The reason for the abundance of these weights was the fixing of the solidus under Diocletian at 72 to the libra, or 6 to the uncia, at which it was long maintained; also the custom of weighing all gold in payments, which kept up its weight for coinage, but required weights on all occasions of purchase. No. 5293, xiv, has the *khirho* monogram inlaid with silver, which is very rare on weights; there are no others here, or in the British Museum. The weights which have been cleaned are inserted here at their present amount, and they have probably lost but little; + *x* is placed in the column of original weight to show that they are not complete. There are six official weights in the list, which should be noted together. No. 5296, xiv, xvi has on one side three busts with the letters **KHT**, evidently intended for Konstantinos IV (Pogonatos) with his brothers Heraklios and Tiberios, and therefore between 668 and 674 A.D. On the reverse is a female figure holding a balance. No. 5297 is a square weight with the head of Honorius inscribed D.N. HONORIUS and on the reverse a female figure holding a balance and EXAGIVM SOLIDI. This is too much worn to prove the original amount, so it is entered at the weight stated by Cohen. No. 5320 is inscribed ΔIKEON, as being an exact standard. No. 5341 has two busts in relief, stamped in thin sheet copper, and then soldered on to a square weight with flat faces. 5332 A is of the same type, but solid. No. 5386 has three busts incised upon it, and is probably of the period 668–674 A.D. like no. 5296; the weight shows it to be for the double triens, or $\frac{2}{3}$ of the solidus.

Nos. 5300, 5369, 5371, were all together in a box for scales, but have no other connection. No. 5301 is a pan weight intended to hold a nest of fractions, such as was usual a couple of centuries ago. 5303 is marked *sigma* for the *semi uncia*. 5326, 5346, 5393 are marked IB for 12 *scripulae*. 5312 is marked H for 8 *siliquae*. 5304, 5349 are marked IB for 12 *siliquae*. 5391 marked IB is probably an error for NB, two *nomismata*. Unusual multiples are 5315, 4 *nomismata*; 5290, 5 *nomismata*; and 5384 marked 4, showing a division of an eighth of the uncia, probably the silver coin of Diocletian. No. 5317 is of alabaster, with IB on one side and on the other T, with small letters around it, apparently ΠΛΛΥΛΟ, or ΑΓΟΡΑ; the form is clearly of Roman age. What

the letters can mean on a half libra, six unciae, is not apparent. The **IB** might refer to 12 sela of light value; we note below an approximation of the sela and uncia, which might support this reading. No. 5329, the bronze head, is a steelyard weight, so exactly four unciae that it may be accepted as that, though steelyard weights are usually of irregular amounts. No. 5345* has, incised on it, figures of two saints galloping on horseback, with a dog running; the faces and other parts are inlaid with silver, and the limbs with red copper; below is incised **ΓΑ**, one uncia. These two saints are probably the same as appear armed on foot, on a libra weight, British Museum, 483. No. 5358 is a bearded head roughly cast in lead, probably of the 1st or 2nd century.

64. The most important part of this series is the set of weights and scales in a box with tray (pl. xvi). The scales and box will be described with the balances, the weights are described here, the list being given at the end of the table of the ungia. In the lower box are five brass weights (5399–5403) in their original holes, quite unworn and untarnished, with the maker's polish still on them. Each bears the numbers of the ungiae in an ornamental wreath. Their condition is perfect, and they do not seem to have lost a tenth of a grain since they were made. Their accuracy is also good, an average error of 2·4 grains; thus they give one of the best determinations of the uncia standard. There is one smaller weight in the lower box, and six smaller weights in the tray. These latter have also been accurately adjusted, having an average error of only 2 grains, the smaller ones only vary 1 grain. Among these are two coins, ground down to weight; they are of Constans I and Constantinus II as Caesars. The coinage of this family had entirely disappeared in deposits of 480 A.D., and there were only a few *per cent* in a deposit of 420 A.D. So this set of weights is very probably before 400 A.D., and may best be put at 350 A.D., as the coins were not in the original set, but only supplementary. The mean value of the uncia from this set is 427·2 grains, marked by a thick line in the diagram, with a bracket extending over the variations. This is a very high value, beyond all the ordinary range; it seems likely that it was a variant of the uncia, used in Egypt to fit the old Ptolemaic coinage system of the sela.

Another, smaller, set of weights was found with scales in a box: one bronze nomisma and three glass weights of the half, third, and siliqua. These agree well together, with an average variation of only 0·3 of a grain. The standard is also very high, 435·5 for the uncia; marked on the diagram like the previous series. No. 5367 is now placed in the sela series, according to the mark **B** upon it.

Referring to the general distribution in the diagram, apart from these two high series, it falls into sections; 415 to 422 grains agreeing with the gold coinage of aurei and solidi; 411–415 grains agreeing with the Roman trade standard of 4950 for the libra, 412·5 uncia, before the solidus arose; a lower group 404–408 grains with the **ΔIKEON** weight, agreeing with 6 drachmae (3 staters) of the trade stater (135–136); and a lowest group, 390–395, agreeing with 6 drachmae of the coinage stater (130–132 grains).

Thus the Roman uncia passing into Oriental use was accommodated to older standards of the sela-Ptolemaic tetradrachm, and the heavy and light Attic tetradrachm, beside keeping its own two values of the coinage and trade uncia.

Reference should be made to the weights in the British Museum catalogue of *Early Christian Antiquities*, by Mr. O. M. Dalton, pp. 91–98. That collection is about half the number of these here; it has four weights dated by official names, and one of the imperial exagia with busts.

65. *Small metal weights.* The series of small bronze weights, nearly all below 50 grains, is not sufficiently accurate or well preserved to be of any value for fixing standards; but it serves to show what standards were in use at Defenneh about 600 B.C., by the goldsmiths who worked there. A few similar weights from other sites—mostly near there—are included. The multiple marks are in pl. xv, 5427–5651. The units found are:—

111	stater, Attic	46 %
13	qedet, Egyptian	5 „
50	necef, Syrian	21 „
1?	khoirīnē, Persian	
9	beqa, Aeginetan	4 „
58	sela, Phoenician	24 „
242		100 %

Thus the Attic examples are nearly a half, the Phoenician and Syrian make up most of the rest, while the Egyptian, Persian and Aeginetan are negligible. This agrees very well with the historic conditions of a Greek settlement on the Syrian road, except that the Egyptian is scarcely represented.

It shows how little the Egyptian demanded his old standard then. Probably the actual workmen were Greeks and Syrians. The day of the Persian had not yet come.

CHAPTER XIII

THE INDO-CHINESE-ETRUSCAN SYSTEM.

66. THE three sources to be considered here are:—
The Indian seed system in MARSDEN, *Numismata Orientalia*, edit. Edw. Thomas, 1874; indicated here as T.

The Chinese system in DECOURDEMANCHE, *Traité des Monnaies, Mesures et Poids de l'Inde et de la Chine*, Paris 1913; here D.

The Etruscan weights in *Monumenti Antichi*, I, 321, pl. x; here E.

The Indian system is based upon the weights of seeds, especially the wild Licorice, or *rati*, as the nominal standard. A higher weight was the cultivated bean, or *masha*, which appears to be the *Phaseolus vulgaris* of southern India, but as a cultivated plant its uniformity in different ages is unlikely. Other seeds whose weights are recorded as standards are rice, barley, common beans, and black beans. All of these are stated not only in simple relation to the *rati*, but in such numbers that they are all in simple relation to the larger unit of about 580 grains, called *Çatamana* in the silver standard, and *Pala* or *Nishka* in the gold standard. It is therefore the simplest course to regard each weight-seed as a source for fixing the original value of the *Pala* (T, 14, 65). The following are averages of large quantities:—

	Grains	×	Pala
Small beans	3·582	160	573·1
Rice	0·3585	1600	573·6
Barley, husked	0·5978	960	573·9
Common beans	9·10	64	582·4
Black beans	14·60	40	584·0
Rati	1·871	320	598·7

For the *Rati*, this is the average of the results of six observers, omitting the earliest as obviously wrong. The six agree, with an average difference of 0·05 on 1·87, or $\frac{1}{40}$; the mean having a probable error of 0·02, *i.e.*, it is as likely to be between 1·85 and 1·89 as beyond those limits. This gives 599 ± 6 as the value of the *pala*. The *Rati* is therefore the outlying member of the group; yet, as the best

known, we must give it at least equal weight with the others. The average will be 581 grains, mean difference 7, probable error 3 grains. The Bactrian coinage unfortunately does not help the enquiry, as the Attic was the standard during the fine period; when the native standard came into use the regulation was imperfect, and degradation set in. Hence the silver coin results vary far more than the above values from different kinds of grain: The early examples would give a unit between 577 and 612 grains, and they quickly diminish to a unit of 500 grains and less.

The safest conclusion therefore seems to place the Indian standard pala at

$$581 \pm 3 \text{ grains}$$

or as likely to be between 578 and 584 as beyond those limits.

67. On the Chinese weights M. DECOURDEMANCHE quotes (D, 159) values of the tael from a work *Notions techniques* by P. Hoang (Shanghai), which are as follows:—

	Su-chow	565·0
	Amoy	572·0
	Wen-chow	573·3
	By *che*, cubic measure	575·6
	Official	575·9
add {	Fine set, University College	579·78
	Burgess's value	579·84
	Customs	586·5

The official tael is probably the most recognized, 576 grains; the customs office would take the highest value possible, as silver only is received there; the lower values are probably due to the usual loss of standards used for payment. The set of weights at University College are so concordant (see sect. 97) that they are accurate copies of some standard, and they agree with Burgess, who had good official sources.

This tael is × 16 for the *kin* or catty of 9216 grains, which is decimally multiplied as the *teu* of 92,160, and *hu* of 921,600 grains. This last is the heavy talent of the Babylonian standard; the connection seems likely enough, and we may accept it without at all subscribing to the maze of theoretical connections of various standards with coins, which form the substance of the above work. The result of this connection would be that the tael was = $4\frac{1}{2}$ shekels. The values of the shekel, and the equivalent tael, are traced in Egypt as follows:—

4*

	Shekel	∴ tael
Early dynasties, two standards	127·5, 131·5	574, 592
Fused in xviiith dynasty, mean	129·0	580·5
Nebuchadrezzar's copy of Dungi's standard	126·0	567·0
Daric, Persian standard	129·2	581·4
Spartan duck weight	128·2	577·0

The history of the shekel (and with resulting values for the tael) seems then to be,—two early standards 127·5 (574) and 131·5 (592); their fusion by about 1500 B.C. as 129 (**580**); and the continuance at about this value into Persian and Greek times.

68. On the Etruscan side, there is published a series of 15 marked and 2 unmarked weights of one standard, and 8 other weights of different standards. As these have not been discussed, they are given here in detail. They are all from Marzobotto near Bologna, and therefore thoroughly in the Etruscan region. The weights are stated in grammes, and are quoted thus here to show how far rough the weighing has been; it should be repeated in a scientific manner. Of the main system, 11 weights have marks showing a unit of about 570 grains or 5700 (37 or 370 grammes), and 4 are of other multiples of that unit. Here they are all reduced to show a standard of about 37 grammes. The multiple signs are I = 1, + = 10, ++ = 20, \V/ = 50, >|< = 100.

Weight grammes	Mark	Multiple	Unit grammes
3500	100	100	35·0
3600	10	100	36·0
3650	10	100	36·5
1835	5	50	36·7
3700	10	100	37·0
3700	—	100	37·0
745	2	20	37·2
560	—	15	37·3
1880	5	50	37·6
26300	70	700	37·6
37800	500	1000	37·8
114	1	3	38·0
3800	100	100	38·0
305	10	8	38·1
3810	100?	100	38·1
115	1	3	38·3
38300	100	1000	38·3

The first is so different to the others that there is probably some special disturbance of wear, damage, or fraud about it. With it the average is 37·3 ± 0·15, without it 37·5 ± 0·1; the latter we accept here. It gives for the unit

578·7 ± 1·7 grains.

69. We now compare these results together. The unit from the

Babylonian talent, yielding 574 and 587, uniting in	grains	580
Indian seedweights	„	581 ± 3
Chinese modern weights (565–586)	„	576 ± 2
„ by Burgess, and a fine set	„	579·8
Etruscan	„	579 ± 2

These agree together within the half *per cent* of known probable error in each country. The comparison of modern Chinese weights with earlier weights is allowable, considering the close continuity of Chinese civilisation.

If, then, we allow of a presumable connection of these amounts, what historical view must be taken of their descent? First, we know that there was a widely spread system (which we need not detail here) covering Babylonia, Assyria, Persia, Syria, and extending to Egypt as far back as the period of the Old Kingdom. The talent of this system was uniformly divided by 60 × 60; and this covers every region south of the Caspian and Caucasus.

Next, we find this talent differently divided, by 10 × 10 × 16; and this extends over early India and China.

Then we find the suggestion that the latter system was carried into Etruria. This could not be by way of Asia Minor or the Mediterranean, because, if so, the Assyro-Persian division of the talent would prevail. The only road for it must have been north of the Caspian and the Euxine, through Turkestan. Such then is the route which this fact indicates for the Etruscan migration,—Turkestan, the Kirghiz, south Russia, Hungary, Carinthia, the Tyrol, and so to Etruria. This would accord well with the style of the bronze buckets of Carinthia, and with Isaac Taylor's Mongolian affinities of the Etruscan numerals; coming from the Indian border, there would be no difficulty in a large proportion of Aryan influence in the language. If the Etruscans entered Italy about 900 B.C. their movement from Russia upon the Balkan people was the precipitating cause of the Dorian invasion of Greece 1100 B.C. The Dorians in Greece are an earlier stage of the same pressure from the east which brought the Etruscans to Italy. There now enters into possible consideration the strange similarity of types and ideas in the Etruscan and the early Japanese pottery. If the Etruscans started in contact with Indo-Chinese civilisation, the movement of pottery types eastward would not be further than that of the weight

standard westward. It is now an open question of study how far a similarity can be traced between early Chinese and Etruscan ideas.

CHAPTER XIV

STEELYARDS. PL. XVI.

70. THE steelyard was unknown in Egypt or Greece until the Roman age. Its source is Italic, by the evidence of examples; this accords with the statement of Isidore of Seville that it originated in Campania. It certainly was not primitive, as the balance was the legal emblem of sale. To the present time, it is the characteristic machine of Italy, except at Venice where the balance comes in from Oriental trade. In Egypt now the balance is universal in native hands, and the steelyard is only found in use under Italian influence. In the Middle Ages, however, the steelyard was used by Arabs, and then are two very large examples in the present collection (sect. 76).

The steelyards found in Egypt are always incomplete, the counterpoise being lost. In most cases the chains and hooks, or pan, are also lost or damaged. Hence no direct observation can be made on their ancient standard. This can nevertheless be recovered indirectly.

The regular form in Roman times was a steelyard with a groove at the end, in which a saddle rested, and from this hung the hooks or pan. Thus the steelyard could be revolved with any face of the beam upward, while the groove turned beneath the saddle. A suspensor was provided on each of two or three faces of the beam, at different distances from the pan; thus varying leverages were obtained, and one face would weigh from, say, o to 8 lbs., the next from 7 to 25 lbs., the next from 25 to 70 lbs. At the present time usually only two edges are used, and the pan hangs from a stirrup hingeing on the beam, and turning to either edge.

There seems to have been very little attention given to the right form of the parts. On the smaller steelyards there is a fixed ring for the suspensor, and this is placed parallel to the beam, so that a large error would occur by slightly different positions of the hook; especially in heavy amounts, where the length between suspension and pan is only a quarter of an inch. Sometimes the fixed rings are diagonal, in no case are they across the beam as they should be. The divisions of the beam are

often irregular. This may probably be due to errors in the weights by which the beam was graduated. No doubt they were all made empirically; a convenient pattern was found by trial and error, to give suitable scales, and this was copied again and again; the graduation was put on by placing weights in the pan, and these were probably irregular by four or five *per cent,* like the Roman weights already described. In no case can we expect to find results of value as to the exact amount of the standard; but assigning the steelyards to their respective standards is of use, as showing what standards prevailed at that age.

71. The divisions of the beam are of two classes; lines, with more or less indication of their meaning, and letter-numerals, which vaguely indicate the place without lines. The lines are often marked with only a dot on each side for the tens, and three dots on one side for the fives, abbreviated from the letter-numeral E. Where Roman influence was strong, the fives and tens are marked V and X without much more, though usually XX is marked and N is put for 50, borrowed from the letter-numeral. On some small beams the third side starts a higher multiple, 50 or 60 times that of the other sides. The first step is carefully to examine the scales, usually with a magnifier, and list all the marks. Observe how the second scale joins the first; sometimes a gap, sometimes an overlap, of a pound or two, the marks on the second scale proving the relation. Often the second scale will run up to 100 and then go on with tens, without repeating the 100 mark. If the third scale is lettered in multiples of the others, as 50 or 60 times as much, then it begins early in the alphabet, as Δ, Є, C, Z, &c.; what its relation to the other scales may be, is proved as shown further on. The next step is to measure each scale, and find the mean scale in inches, avoiding the discrepancies. There are three ways of reaching the mean scale; the most practical for this case is as follows. Supposing there are 8 divisions visible,—measure from 1 to 8, from 2 to 7, from 3 to 6, from 4 to 5, add these four together, and divide by the number of units 7 + 5 + 3 + 1. It is obvious that any one of these pairs might be shifted among the others without in the least affecting the mean. Hence this set of measurements gives all that is attainable. This mean scale is useful in reducing measures in inches to mean-scale values in the following processes. As the suspensor was always intended to be held up

by the right hand, the beam projects to the left, the direction of reading is retrograde, and often the letter-forms are retrograde.

72. To follow the method of examining a steelyard we will take the actual case of the Psykharido steelyard here, no. 2; the critical points of this on the three scales of different sides are here drawn full size (top pl. xvii), in three lines one below another. This is not a facsimile but a reasoned drawing, giving full numbering, and continuing the scales backward into *minus* quantities for the sake of study. All readings must be stated in terms of the scale on which they are read; for accuracy, it is usually better to measure actually in inches, and then reduce to scale values by the mean value of the scale, found as described in sect. 71. Of course the slide rule is necessary for all the proportioning in the subject. On this drawing, the centre of gravity of the beam is at the left; this is found by balancing on a knife edge, and should be pencilled on all sides of the beam. It may be thought that the position of C.G. cannot be used as it depends on the losses of chains, hooks, suspensors, and portions of the beam; but all these will also affect the weight, and thus the theoretical independence of all accessories is preserved. As the C.G. is a long way from the other critical points, slight errors are not magnified, and it is sufficient to read its amount on each actual scale, without referring to a mean scale. Of course any suspensors must hang free, or be placed exactly square with the beam, when balancing it. The suspensory points are here marked with a thick line, S, T, U on different sides. The saddle, for the hooks to carry the object, is at the right hand. For reference below, the lengths from C.G. to S, T, U are lettered b, c, d; and those from S, T, U to the saddle are lettered h, j, k. These lengths, as stated above, must be in terms of the scale in question. Let the weight of the beam be called G, grains or grammes. Regard that as a load on the beam at C.G. and the beam as without weight elsewhere; suppose the counterpoise at point of suspension, and inactive. Then

$$h : b :: G : \text{(saddle, hooks) and S units}$$
also $j : c :: G : \text{(saddle, hooks) and T units}$

$$\therefore \frac{b}{h} G = \text{(saddle, hooks) and S units}$$

$$\frac{c}{j} G = \text{(saddle, hooks) and T units}$$

$$\therefore \left(\frac{b}{h} - \frac{c}{j} \right) G = S - T \text{ units.}$$

(Saddle, hooks) may be any constant, modified by mutilations at either end. If beam is level when counterpoise is at S, then moving the poise the distance h away from the saddle will balance a weight equal to it on the saddle; that is, the counterpoise is always h units in weight. Therefore h, j, k are all an equal number of units; or the distance from suspensor to saddle reads the same on its own scale, whichever side is measured. If this is accurately so, then the formula can be simplified $\dfrac{b - c}{h\,(S - T)} G = \text{unit of weight.}$ It will be seen that the insoluble cases are where the readings $b = c$ within the amount of errors of work; any near equivalence of b and c, therefore, cannot be dealt with. Further, if the saddle end of the beam is lost, the position can be recovered, by continuing the scales to the right, and finding the place where two scales show equal readings from their suspensors.

Thus a fragment of a beam, which has two scales and two suspensors remaining, suffices for the recovery of the unit.

73. The theory being settled, the actual example will be worked. The first step, after weighing (5892 grains here), and marking C.G., is to measure the mean value of each scale, as described in sect. 71. Then take the distances h, j, k in inches, and reduce them to mean scale values. These last should be all the same numbers, and any differences between them show errors in making. Where one scale is marked with multiples of another scale, as ounces on one and pounds on another, then the same proportion will exist in the numbers of h, j, k. All this should be checked by taking the distances with dividers and reading direct on the beam scale. The actual distances in this case (see no. 2, pl. xv) are in scale values h 3·63, j 3·50, k 3·41. The scale readings are S = +·12, T = +2·08, U = +8·7; the C.G. is at 3·92, 11·16, and 35·3 on respective scales. Hence $b = 3·80$, $c = 9·08$, $d = 26·6$. Therefore

$$\frac{\dfrac{b}{h} \quad \dfrac{c}{j}}{S - T} G = \frac{\dfrac{3·80}{3·63} \quad \dfrac{9·08}{3·50}}{-1·96} \; 5892 = \frac{\text{unit}}{4940}$$

Thus the unit
shown by the 1st and 2nd scales is 4940 grains

similarly by the 1st and 3rd scales 4710 grains
similarly by the 2nd and 3rd scales 4530 „

To show on what actual quantities such differences as these depend, suppose that k is 3·25 in place of 3·41, a change of 0·036 inch due to uncertainties in the exact place of the suspensor, owing to long extension of the mean scale used. Then the values of the unit would be 4940, 4920, 4920. It is clear that even in a favourable example a greater accuracy than 5 *per cent* in the result is not to be expected. Only a thirtieth of an inch uncertainty in taking the scale value of U, modifying d and k, makes 5 and 8 *per cent* of difference in the unit deduced.

74. By similar reckoning on each of the steelyards, the values for the unit in grains are as follow:—

		S—T	S—U	T—U
1	Paulos	4440	4580	4440
2	Psykharido	4940	4710	4530
3		5240	4340	5520
4	Broken saddle	5200		
5	Smallest	5050		
6		464	435	454

These are evidently on the basis of the Roman libra and uncia. Also no. 7 (which cannot be reckoned owing to zeros being near the suspensors) shows 12ths of the unit, pointing to the libra and uncia, and works concordantly on this basis.

Another unit is found on other beams, as follows:—

		S—T	S—U	T—U	
8		2370	2710	2200	? 2 deben
9	Talit	7340			5 deben
10	F	2925	3400	3030	2 deben
11	Harpo	142·0	140·4	140·0	qedet & 5 deben
12		1340	3720?		× 60
13		111	300	106	2 qedet?

Some of these seem to belong to the Egyptian qedet and deben system. No. 11 is best given as 142, the other values depend on assuming an error in graduation on the U scale. No. 12 might rather be on the daric system, by the multiple being 60. No. 13 is very uncertain, but suggests the double qedet, by 300 grains. It should be noted that, in varying results, if only two agree they are in error, because an error in one scale will vitiate two results; the one result which differs from a similar pair is more likely to be correct.

There are, beside these, three others (14, 15, 16) whose scale zeros are so close to the suspensors that no result can be safely reached.

75. The work and condition of the steelyards are as follows:—

1. Name of Paulos. Heavy, fine work. Saddle, 2 chains and hooks, and 3 suspensor hooks, all quite perfect; with clean green patina. Pl. xvi.

2. Name of Psykharido, and other letters. Rather rough work, but solid and fairly accurate. Good state. No attachments.

3. Carelessly divided. Worn. No suspensors. Saddle; chains broken.

4. Beam broken through middle suspension. Erratic divisions. The lost dimensions are restored by continuance of the scales, to find the point of equal values on S and T scales; such restorations are in ellipses in the table, pl. xv.

5. The smallest beam. Moderately good work. No suspensors; 1 eye left, and two broken. Beam broken.

6. Roughly divided; signs vague. Suspensors lost. Saddle; chains broken.

7. Rough work, poor divisions. One suspensor, half eye of another, third eye lost. S loop for saddle. The zeros are too close to the suspensors to give a result; but units being divided in 12ths are probably librae with unciae. By trial, this unit works truly. All the above are for the Roman standard; the following are probably of Egyptian standard.

8. Tip of beam lost. Coarsely, but fairly well divided. One suspensor, and one detached. Green has been cleaned to bare yellow metal. Well preserved.

9. From Talit in the Fayum. Of rhombic section, with only two scales. Purely Roman in style. Suspensors and bearing-pins lost. No attachments.

10. Rough, careless work. Black patina. Good condition. One suspensor. No saddle.

11. Name of Harpo(-krates?). Round beam. Dot divisions, with letter-numerals between. Parts of two suspensors and counterpoise loop. Ring of U scale half gone.

12. Fairly good work. One suspensor, eyes of two others broken.

13. Average work. Only letters marked, and no real divisions. Two suspensors, one eye lost, beam broken. Knob beyond the saddle lost.

The following from bad division, and having zeros near suspensors, are so erratic that the standard cannot be fixed.

14. Well made. Black patina. Saddle; chains and hooks broken.

15. Fair work. Only letters, and no real divisions. No suspensors. Two eyes and one broken. Saddle. Unit in 10's and 60's, so probably daric.

16. Name of Herōdou. Stoutest work, lettering late Ptolemaic? three eyes broken, one whole; saddle. Unit divided in 8ths; perhaps sela.

The system of the marks (pl. xvii, lower part) is usually the Syro-Greek system, which is common on coins and monuments. The fives between tens are marked E alone. Numbers over 100 (P) are only marked in tens, as N for 50 or 150. The Roman V and X system is also used, but with only one X for tens above twenty (nos. 5, 7, 10, 12).

76. Two large steelyards of Arabic times were bought in Cairo, from the sale of *waqf* property. These are both of steel, inlaid with silver numerals, and the lesser one with inscriptions. In the drawings, pls. xviii, xix, the slings and hooks for suspension, and the saddles for hanging the scale pan, are omitted for clearness.

The length of the larger steelyard is $93\frac{1}{2}$ inches in all, of which 16 inches is occupied by the butt end with the suspensors. The support for the scale pan so far above the axis is very badly designed, as the whole accuracy therefore depends on the beam being exactly level, and from that position it tends to fall either way, as it is very unstable. Each of the four sides of the beam is divided; the sides one above the other belong to one way of suspension, *i.e.* the beam was read from the side, and not looking down from above. The counterpoise being complete with its hook, the values can be directly ascertained. Reading on face A, the distance of the support A from the fulcrum, 6.30 inches : the counterpoise of 140,320 grains in weight :: the unit of division, 3.186 inches : the unit of weight 71,000 grains, or 10.14 lbs. Face B will be noticed later. On reversing the beam, face C belongs to the support C. Here 2.58 inches : 140,320 grs. :: unit of division 1.275 inches : 69,300 grs. unit. On face D 1.30 inches : 140,320 grs. :: unit of division 0.643 inches : 69,400 grs. Thus the different faces give a unit of

A 71,000 grs. 8.5 to 32.0 units = 320 lbs.
C 69,300   31.5 to 90.0   =   900
D 69,400   80.0 to 182.0   = 1820

$\frac{1}{2}$ counterpoise 70,160.

It is obvious that the counterpoise is a double unit, which simplifies the divisions, as they are then based on half the distance of fulcrum to support.

The poise itself is of course the best defined, and is clearly a tenth of the Arab *kantar*, being 10.02 lbs., and the kantar at present is 101.31 lbs. The irregularity shown by different faces is merely due to the difficulty of division on so unstable a leverage. The numeration is on two systems, one for tens, the other for hundreds; the tens are proved by lying between the hundreds; the hundreds are proved by the thousand being marked *alf* "thousand," in the series on face D. The numerals are set out on pl. xix.

We turn now to face B, which is on a different unit. Dealing with this as before, 6.30 inches : 140,320 grs. :: 0.715 ins. : 15,927 grs. This unit of 15,927 grains is explained by the lesser steelyard.

The lesser steelyard is 53 inches long, of which 11 inches is occupied by the butt. Face A is complicated by having two sets of divisions, belonging to supports J and K. The lower set, J, belongs to the support J, and the upper K series to support K. Face B is entirely blank. Reversing the steelyard, face C is complicated by having the two series of divisions for supports L and M; for the sake of clearness here, there is copied off above the beam the L series separate from the M series. There are also a few marks of a third series which appear to be only mistakes for the two series. Face D has the series belonging to support N. The rule which serves to prove which support and scale belong together, is that the distance from the fulcrum to any support is always the same number of units of its own scale, whatever the position may be. This is the simplest way to state the matter, when there are several scales to compare. Here we find the fulcrum to the support at

J	K	L	M	N
0.693	0.675	0.655	0.660	0.631 unit.

N is so uncertain, (by its being so near the fulcrum and so high above it,) that it is best to take the mean of the others, which is 0.670. The unit of weight multiplied by this 0.670 is equal to the counterpoise. We know the counterpoise (less its hook) to be 104,800 grs. The theoretical value, deduced from the beam and divisions only, is 107,550 grs. The hook might be assumed as an iron rod $\frac{3}{8}$ inch thick and 9 inches long, about 2000 grs., so that the whole counterpoise would be about 107,000, or possibly rather more. Hence the unit of weight of all the series of divisions is 107,000 $\div$ 0.67 = 159,700 grs.; as both the factors

are liable to be greater, the result of differences would not much affect this, but it might possibly be 2000 or 3000 grs. different. Practical trials of the balance gave 159,800 and 160,700 grains as the unit.

The inscriptions, though partly worn away, afford some help. On face C, line L begins with the name çīr, usually rendered *seer* in commerce. Forty seers make one maund; both these terms are vague general names, as shekel is. The weight of this seer is 2·28 lbs., so the maund would be 91·2 lbs. Among the various examples, the maund of Basra is 90·25 lbs., and we may assume that this steelyard was used for trade from the Persian gulf. On the face D is the guarantee *rotl waf khazany*, "exact rotl of the Treasury." This identification of the unit explains the meaning of face B on the larger steelyard; the unit there we found to be 15,927 grs., and the seer *khazany* is 15·970 grs. The close similarity does not mean much, as either might be one or two *per cent* different, but certainly they are intended for the same unit.

The source of the numerals here used is the alphabetic system of classical times, in a corrupt form of Greek minuscule. Such was used by the Copts, as Mr. Knobel has pointed out (see L. STERN, *Koptische Grammatik*). The 40–60 are also closely like the Gobar figures in the xth century in a Persian M.S., coming from India of the viiith century. The Greek E for five was continued as a subdivision mark from the steelyards of Roman times. The units of weight here are, however, the Egyptian kantar and the Basra seer. Besides the inlayed silver figures there is a punched series of lines for numbers, which have been marked since the silver inlay, as they are accommodated to it. These are obscure; the 40, 70, 90 and some hundreds, have a pair of curved lines; a C form is at half of each ten and half of each hundred, and might be degraded from *nusf* "half." The other lines are so corrupt and variable that it is difficult to trace the system.

CHAPTER XV
MEASURES OF CAPACITY.

77. COMPARATIVELY few measures of capacity have been recognized in Egypt hitherto. Eight vases of stone with the capacity marked in *hen*

measures are about all that have been acknowledged by Egyptologists. As these capacities are mostly odd numbers, and heavy alabaster vases are not suited for making measurements, it is probable that these markings are only records of contents, and do not imply that the Egyptians used them for guages. Where then are the numerous measures which must have been commonly used among a people so fond of accounts and registers?

A considerable number of pots and vases are found which are obviously likely to be intended for measuring, such as plain cylinders (xxi, 77–80) and conical cups with broad flat brims (xxiii, 201–206). The difficulty really lies in recognising what is or is not a measure. There can be no possible doubt about xx, 102, which is a regular cylinder divided on the inside by bands marking quarters; each quarter is half a *hen*, and the whole is two *hens*. From this there is every grade of form, down to purely ornamental alabaster vases (xxii, 832); how far are we to credit them with being measures? When we look at modern usage it seems probable that there are three classes to be distinguished; (A) measures made for the purpose of guaging, (B) jars made for general use, approximately according to measure, like the usual pint and quart jugs which are the commonest vessels now, (C) jars which have been accurately guaged, and marked with contents, to show the amount placed in them, often an irregular quantity. The value of these for fixing standards is very different; class C serves to prove the approximate amount and name; A serves best to fix the exact amount; B is of little use, but should be included in lists, though not used for fixing the standard. Another consideration is that class A must have been filled to the brim, if there is no definite mark below that; whereas B would only be filled as much as was convenient to carry, and there is no certainty what that limit might be. In the present guaging of such vessels we can only fill them all to the brim, and therefore the contents of class B will be recorded in excess.

78. The safest way to begin to handle the subject is to start with forms of class A, which are most probably measures, and if they agree with a definite system, accept that as a framework. Then other vases, the purpose of which is uncertain, or of class B, may be accepted if they fall within the variation already known from class A. Considering that a range of variation of an eighth of

5

the whole amount exists in one standard of marked weights—the beqa, and a range of a tenth to a thirtieth in other standards, it is probable that a large range will be found in capacity measures. Another point to observe is that pottery measures —rough or glazed—cannot be made exact, owing to variability of shrinkage, and must not be relied on for accuracy. Only measures of metal, not seriously corroded, or of stone, can be accepted as good definitions. All of the vases here named were guaged by the weight of water contained up to the brim.

Several different standards may be expected among capacity measures. From the figures of such measures in the iiird dynasty, there appears to have been generally used then the Egyptian *hen* and the Syrian *saton* (*Ancient Egypt*, 1915, 40). Other measures that may be expected are the Syrian-Hebrew *log*, and in late times the Persian and Greek standards. As there were eight standards of weight in use, there would probably be also several standards of capacity, due to the many mixtures of surrounding civilisations.

79. The plain cylinder is a form most likely to be made for a measure. It was so made in the iiird dynasty (tomb of Hesy), in Roman times, and down to the present day. A cylinder without a brim, a spout, or a handle, is inconvenient for any purpose beyond merely filling and emptying it in bulk for guaging. There are seven such cylinders here, nos. 5, 10, 18, 30 (vases 77 to 80), and nos. 1, 14, 17 (vases 212, 213, 211); these are all simple multiples of the Syrian standard, 5, 4, 3, 2, 2, 2, and $\frac{1}{20}$. They form, then, a strong basis for this standard. Four of these are of bronze, giving values of 19·9, 20·6, 21·5 and 23·6 cubic inches. One of wood is as low as 19·2 inches; but a contraction of 3 *per cent* across the grain would be quite likely, which would allow this to be $20\frac{1}{2}$ c.i. Two of glazed pottery give middle values of 20·9 and 21·3. The stone cup measure from Edfu, apparently of the age of Khufu, is 20·8, see *Ancient Egypt*, 1923, p. 2. This has the triangle *q* on the brim, suggesting some original form of *kotyle*. The figures of measures of Hesy, give by the outside sizes 21·2 to 23·6 c.i., and, as the thickness might be about 1 *per cent* of the diameter, this would give 20·4 to 22·8 for the contents. From literary sources, the old Syrian system was on 21 c.i., and the Seleucidan 22 c.i. All of these agree as nearly as their uncertainty permits:—

		Mid
Khufu measure		20·8
Bronze cylinders	19·9–23·6	21·4
Glazed „	20·9, 21·3	21·1
Hesy „	20·4–22·8	$21\frac{1}{2}$
Early Syrian standard		21
Late Syrian „		22
25 beqa of water cube of 20·4–21·4		
25 sela (mina) „ „ 21·3–22·5		

It appears, then, that the earliest measure 20·8 agrees with the larger form of the early beqa; the later measures 21·4 might connect with either beqa or sela. The connection is passably likely, but yet the variations leave some latitude for making a connection.

Having then a variation of 19·9 to 23·6 cubic inches for the unit, it is reasonable to include various other vessels which give multiples of quantities between those, as in the Catalogue, nos. 1–35. Another class of vessels, which seem obviously measures, are the conical cups with flat brims, pl. xxiii. Most of these are only fragments, and the capacity can only be found by linear guaging. All of them are of glazed pottery. On both accounts, therefore, no exactitude should be expected. They are all multiples of the same Syrian standard as before, 4, 2, 2, 2, 1, and $\frac{4}{10}$. The values they give are from 19·5 to 24·6, with 22·0 as the mid value. This agrees with the more accurate bronze measures more closely than could be expected.

The large situlae with handles are of nearly the same capacity, xxi, nos. 69, 70, and contain 4 of the Syrian standard, giving a unit of 21·6 and 22·4. In these different classes, in which all examples conform to one standard, there is good evidence that they are certainly measures, and that hence any vessels giving simple multiples of this unit, between 19·9 and 23·6, or 19·5 and 24·6 glazed, probably belong to the same system. Beside these, two border cases, just beyond those limits, are included in the catalogue, sect. 83.

Of all these, taking the bronze vessels alone, the median is 21·0 ± 0·25 c.i. The Khufu standard cup is 20·8. The two Old Kingdom vessels give 20·6 and 24·0, mean 22·3, but probably the larger one was intended to be not quite filled. The extreme values that could be allowed to the sela would be 216 to 224 grains, corresponding to 21·4 to 22·2 c.i. On the whole 21·0, or perhaps later 21·5, seems most likely to be the true value; and 21·5

is the median of the whole list. The multiples by 6, 18 and 24 are correct in this system, as the unit was ×36 to form the saton measure.

80. Another class of vessels that belong to one standard are the tall drinking pots, xx, 27, 28, 29, which are copies of the usual pottery of the first half of the xviiith dynasty. These are simply related as $\frac{1}{2}$, $\frac{1}{2}$, and $1\frac{1}{2}$, of the Egyptian *hen,* giving values of 27·1, 29·3 and 30·1 c.i. This same standard is that of all the pots with handles, of Roman age, xx, 103, 104, 105, 106. The multiples are 2, $\frac{1}{3}$, $\frac{1}{8}$, $\frac{1}{16}$, $\frac{1}{24}$. These are regular fractions, $\frac{1}{8}$ *hen* is known as the *khǎy,* and it was also binarily divided into $\frac{1}{8}$ and down to $\frac{1}{52}$. Though these little bronze jugs do not promise much accuracy, they agree almost as well as the larger measures, giving 27·8, 27·8, 28·6, 29·3, and 31·1 c.i. for the unit. The hen was ultimately divided by 120 at Edfu (BRUGSCH, *Recueil,* IV, xciv).

The class of open cups also belongs to the *hen.* The only one that appears to be accurate is the finely made spouted cup, xx, 76, which is half a *hen* of 30·4. The little cast cups, xx, 139, 128, are $\frac{1}{10}$ *hen,* giving 29·4 and 30·3. The pottery cups, xxiii, 208–210, of $\frac{4}{10}$, $\frac{1}{4}$, and $\frac{1}{10}$ cannot be accurate; they show 29·9, 31·0, and 31·7 for the *hen,* but they may not have been intended to be brimful. A blue glazed cup or bowl, 41, fig. 207, xxiii, was of 2 *hen,* of 28·5; only a fragment remains.

Between the limits of size of the bronze vessels which appear to be measures, 27·1 to 31·1, there are various others, as in the catalogue, nos. 36 to 63, which should probably be included in the series. Of these, there are four good bronze vessels, making 10 bronze, in all, of fair size. The median of these is:—

10 bronze vessels	29·0 ± 0·3 cubic inches
8 marked vases	29·2 ± 0·6 ,, ,,
Hesy figures of measures	28·8 ± 0·6, allowing thickness
5 debens of water	28·8, limits 27·5–30·0

Looking at these, it does not seem that we can do better than keep to the most accurate of this material, the bronze measures, and take the *hen* at 29·0 cubic inches.

81. Having now grouped the two commonest standards, the residue remains to be examined. There are several capacities which are obviously connected, 16·11, 16·86, 32·01 to 33·8, 49·6, and, putting all of such together, there is a group of 12 vessels giving from 32·0 to 34·1 for a unit. This is evidently the Syrian log, which is stated at 31 in Phoenicia, 32 Judaea, and 33 Babylonia. All are of bronze or alabaster, and therefore may be accurate. The most probably correct is that with the cartouches of Amenhetep III, which is just at the mean value. The median of

11 vessels is	33·1 ± 0·15 c.i.
log is	31 to 33
necef mina of water	30·3 to 33·3
,, early values	30·7 and 32·1

As the necef was the standard of the north Syrian tribute, used later in Antioch and Cilician coinage, it is in the position to be connected with a Syrian and Babylonian measure. The amount of 33·1 c.i. is however too large for the early necef; and, if the connection be true, the log cannot have been started before the xviiith dynasty, when the standard varied up to, and over 166 grains. Yet the log was used at an early period, as the two spouted copper pots (xxii, 3, 5) of the Old Kingdom are 1 and $1\frac{1}{2}$ logs; so this throws some doubt on the connection of weight and measure.

82. Another group of measures clearly connected (xxii, 52, 57, 58, 59, 61, 64) are 8·87, 17·41, 25·26, 33·4, 35·3. These are all of bronze, all but one are similar to bowls of early Greek period. They give multiples $\frac{1}{2}$, 1, $1\frac{1}{2}$ and 2 of a capacity varying between 16·7 and 17·7. This is the Attic kotyle, as nearly as that is fixed. The sources for that, in standards cut in stone slabs, give 14·6–19·6, 16·2–18·2, 17–18, and probably $17\frac{1}{2}$ in the best value. The Egyptian median is 17·2 ± 0·15

Attic   about 17·5
if chous = 8 minae, therefore   17·6 to 18·2, limits
                                    of mina.

There is no proof that the chous measure was 8 minae, but that is the only practicable connection of Attic weight and capacity. The sextarius measures of Pompeii (see Appendix) would show a kotyle of 17·73, if the Roman and Attic were connected.

83. Beside the above there are two bronze bowls of about the Persian age (xxii, 60, 66) containing 37·25 and 37·63 c.i. These might be $1\frac{1}{4}$ *hen,* but the multiple is unlikely; on the other hand they are half of

74·5 and 75·26 c.i.
and the Persian kapetis is 74·4 c.i.

They are probably therefore Persian measures.

This comprises all the vessels that are likely to be measures, or to have been made to correspond to such.

The resulting values for the standards are:—

	Cubic inches	Cub. centim.
Syrian 20·8,	or 21·4 ± 0·3	341 or 350 ± 5
Hen	29·0 ± 0·3	475 ± 5
Log	33·1 ± 0·2	542 ± 3
Attic kotyle	17·2 ± 0·2	282 ± 3
Persian kapetis	74·9 ± 0·3	1227 ± 5

These values appear to be more accurate than the various information that we already have about these measures, mostly of late date. This is however the Egyptian version of the standards, which might differ slightly from the native values.

84. *Catalogue of Capacity measures*, pls. xx–xxiii.

The second number of each is that in the Catalogue of Stone and Metal Vases, except those marked 201–215 which are of pottery published here.

Syrian standard.

No.	Vase	Material	Cub.ins.	×	Unit
1	212	Wood, shrunk	38·4	2	19·2
2	53	Bronze	76·8	4	19·2
3	98	,,	39·0	2	19·5
4	203	Blue glaze	19·52	1	19·5
5	77	Bronze	99·66	5	19·9
6	91	,,	159·7	8	19·9
7	859	Alabaster xviii	20·2	1	20·2
8	99	Bronze	366·2	18	20·3
9	65	,,	81·4	4	20·3
10	78	,,	61·79	3	20·6
11	11	Copper	123·8	6	20·6
12	835	Alabaster xviii	41·4	2	20·7
12 A		Durite, Khufu	20·8	1	20·8
13	201	Lt. bl. glaze	41·6	2	20·8
14	213	Blue glaze	1·046	$\frac{1}{20}$	20·9
15	68	Bronze xxi	63·0	3	21·0
16	217	Blue glaze xii	0·53	$\frac{1}{40}$	21·2
17	211	Hard br. pottery	85·2	4	21·3
18	79	Bronze	42·96	2	21·5
19	15	,,	21·62	1	21·6
20	69	,,	86·55	4	21·6
21	922	Alabaster xxv	21·72	1	21·7
22	206	Lt. bl. glaze	8·71	0·4	21·8
23	832	Alabaster xviii	43·9	2	21·9
24	204	Gy. bl. glaze	44·25	2	22·1
25	70	Bronze	89·6	4	22·4
26	834	Alabaster xviii	11·3	$\frac{1}{2}$	22·6

No.	Vase	Material	Cub.ins.	×	Unit
27	92	Bronze	546·5	24	22·8
28	822	Alabaster xviii	11·5	$\frac{1}{2}$	23·0
29	202	Gy. bl. glaze, frags.	92·0	4	23·0
30	80	Bronze, Gr.	47·2	2	23·6
31	216	Gy. bl. glaze, frag.	72·1	3	24·0
32	10	Copper	144·2	6	24·0
33	821	Alabaster xviii	24·5	1	24·5
34	205	Gy. bl. glaze	49·3	2	24·6
35	906	Alabaster xviii	24·7	1	24·7

Egyptian Hen.

No.	Vase	Material	Cub.ins.	×	Unit
36	27	Bronze xviii	13·55	$\frac{1}{2}$	27·1
37	105	,, Ro.	1·74	$\frac{1}{16}$	27·8
38	55	,, xix	6·95	$\frac{1}{6}$	27·8
39	102	,, Ro.	55·90	2	27·9
40	905	Alabaster xix	14·07	$\frac{1}{2}$	28·14
41	207	Lt. bl. glaze, frags.	57·0	2	28·5
42	106	Bronze, Ro.	9·55	$\frac{1}{3}$	28·6
43	214	Wood	0·80	$\frac{1}{36}$	28·8
44	97	Bronze, Ro.	14·40	$\frac{1}{2}$	28·8
45	23	Bronze & glaze xix	3·61	$\frac{1}{8}$	28·9
46	104	Bronze, Ro.	1·22	$\frac{1}{24}$	29·3
47	29	,,	44·0	$1\frac{1}{2}$	29·3
48	139	,, Ro.	2·94	$\frac{1}{10}$	29·4
49	67	,, Gr.-Ro.	58·8	2	29·4
50A		Horn, Kahun xii	1·18	$\frac{1}{25}$	29·4
50	62	Bronze, Gr.	59·2	2	29·6
51	858	Alabaster xviii	59·4	2	29·7
52	923	,, xxv	9·92	$\frac{1}{3}$	29·8
53	209	Pottery	7·48	$\frac{1}{4}$	29·9
54	28	Bronze xviii	15·05	$\frac{1}{2}$	30·1
55	63	,, Gr.	30·1	1	30·1
56	128	,, Ro.	3·03	$\frac{1}{10}$	30·3
57	76	,,	15·22	$\frac{1}{2}$	30·4
58	904	Alabaster xix	3·84	$\frac{1}{8}$	30·7
59	210	Pottery	3·1	$\frac{1}{10}$	31·0
60	103	Bronze	3·88	$\frac{1}{8}$	31·1
61	96	,,	1·58	$\frac{1}{20}$	31·6
62	208	Pottery	12·68	$\frac{4}{10}$	31·7
63	127	Bronze, Gurob	1·60	$\frac{1}{20}$	32·0

Syrian Log.

No.	Vase	Material	Cub.ins.	×	Unit
64	90	Bronze	32·01	1	32·0
65	939	Alabaster	16·11	$\frac{1}{2}$	32·2
66	16	Bronze xviii	32·4	1	32·4
67	840	Alabaster xviii	32·9	1	32·9
68	3	Copper iv ?	32·9	1	32·9
69	841	Alabaster xviii	33·07	1	33·1
70	5	Copper iv?	49·62	$1\frac{1}{2}$	33·1
70 A		Copper xviii	33·26	1	33·2

No.	Vase	Material	Cub. ins.	×	Unit
71	935	Alabaster	8·35	$\frac{1}{4}$	33·4
72	18	Bronze xviii	16·86	$\frac{1}{2}$	33·7
73	109	Bronze, Ro.	33·8	1	33·8
74	75	Bronze	8·53	$\frac{1}{4}$	34·1

Attic Kotyle.

75	64	Bronze	33·4	2	16·7
76	61	,,	8·36	$\frac{1}{2}$	16·7
77	58	,,	25·26	$1\frac{1}{2}$	16·8
78	59	,,	17·41	1	17·4
79	52	,,	35·3	2	17·6
80	57	,,	8·87	$\frac{1}{2}$	17·7

Persian Kapetis.

81	60	Bronze	37·25	$\frac{1}{2}$	74·5
82	66	,,	37·63	$\frac{1}{2}$	75·3

85. *Notes on condition of measures.*

SYRIAN.

1. Wood cylinder, split in two, warped, bottom shrunk. Guaged lineally.
2. Bronze, green patina; cracked.
3. Bronze, side broken out. Guaged by proportion.
4. Blue glaze, burnt, blackened: perfect.
5. Bronze cylinder, thin coat of black oxide: perfect.
6. Bronze bowl, edge partly broken.
7. Alabaster; perfect.
8. Bronze, very thin, brown patina, perfect, except loss of handles.
9. Bronze, black patina, perfect.
10. ,, ,, ,, small break in edge.
11. Copper, green patina; perfect.
12. Alabaster, cracked and joined.
12 A. Durite, broken and rejoined. Of Khufu? (Pls. xvi, xxvi.)
13. Lt. blue glaze faded; perfect. Inscription impressed slightly, *Nefer user neb taui. User* probably blunder for *neter*.
14. Lt. blue glaze, broken and joined.
15. Bronze, thin brown patina; perfect. Funeral vase of Nesitanebasheru.
16. Blue-green glaze, apparently xiith dynasty.
17. Hard brown pottery; perfect.
18. Bronze, black patina; crack in edge.
19. ,, part bright, part red and green; perfect. Inscribed for the "washer of the sandals of Amen."
20. Bronze, figure of Isis standing, incised; green patina, perfect.
21. Alabaster; perfect.
22. Lt. blue glaze, chip off edge.
23. Alabaster; perfect.
24. Gy. blue glaze; perfect.
25. Bronze, green and red patina; holes in side for handle; perfect.
26. Alabaster; perfect.
27. Bronze, grey face, stout metal; perfect.
28. Alabaster, cracked and joined.
29. Gy. blue glaze, half of side and base. Guaged lineally.
30. Bronze, green patina, crack round half bottom, hole in side.
31. Gy. indigo-blue glaze, only quarter of side, slight indication of base. Chip in edge, patched with pitch anciently. Saqqarah.
32. Copper, green patina; perfect.
33. Alabaster; perfect.
34. Gy. blue glaze, complete.
35. Alabaster; perfect.

EGYPTIAN HEN.

36. Bronze, red rough patina; perfect.
37. ,, green patina, neck cracked round; complete.
38. Bronze, green patina; perfect.
39. Bronze, green patina; perfect. *Cire perdue* casting. Contents to lower ring 14·5, to middle 28·9, to upper ring 42·7, top 55·9 c.i. Mean unit 28·0 c.i.
40. Alabaster; chip from edge.
41. Lt. blue glaze, a third of the side and base. Guaged lineally.
42. Bronze, green patina; perfect.
43. Wood; perfect.
44. Bronze; lumpy green patina; perfect.
45. ,, green patina, marked "$\frac{1}{8}$"; upper part, blue glaze.
46. Bronze, green; part of brim broken.
47. ,, bright, partly green; perfect.
48. ,, cast; little break in brim.
49. ,, green patina; long cut in neck.
50. ,, black patina; perfect.
51. Alabaster; chip from edge.
52. ,, perfect.
53. Pottery, drab, xxviith dyn.? perfect; found with 59 and 62.
54. Bronze, green patina; perfect.
55. ,, black patina; perfect.
56. ,, casting; clean brown, perfect.
57. ,, black patina; crack in edge.

58. Alabaster; perfect.
59. Pottery, light brown, buff facing, chipped.
60. Bronze, green and brown; perfect.
61.   ,,   clean, and green patina; edge broken.
62. Pottery, light red; perfect.
63. Bronze, thick green patina, Gurob; perfect.

SYRIAN LOG.

64. Bronze, thick green patina; part of brim lost.
65. Alabaster; perfect.
66. Bronze, thin delicate work; bruised by pick on neck and shoulder.
67. Alabaster; perfect.
68. Copper, green patina; perfect. iind dynasty.
69. Alabaster; perfect.
70. Copper, green patina; end of spout lost. iind dynasty.
70 A. Copper, with cartouches of Amenhetep III.
71. Alabaster; perfect.
72. Bronze, green patina; perfect, and elastic cup.
73.   ,,   casting, Roman; part of foot lost.
74.   ,,   thin, green patina; perfect.

ATTIC KOTYLE.

75. Bronze, green patina.
76.   ,,   brown and green patina; perfect.
77.   ,,   thick, sharp, casting; perfect.
78.   ,,   thin as 76, 80; black patina; edge slightly broken.
79. Bronze, green patina; perfect. Tell Yehudiyeh, tumulus IV, 20.
80. Bronze, inside clean, out brown and green; perfect.

PERSIAN KAPETIS.

81. Bronze, green, thick, sharp, casting; perfect.
82.   ,,   black patina; perfect.

86. *Gold dust measures.*

A unique set of seven measures (pl. xxiii) was found in the South Town at Nubt (*Naqada* 67): as there were some traces of the xviiith dynasty there, such is probably the date of these measures. They are a series of binary divisions, the largest holding piled gold dust of 742·5 grains or $\frac{1}{2}$ deben, the others down to $\frac{1}{128}$ deben, which was the Ethiopian gold unit of the *pek*. The mean scale is to a deben of 1488 grains. As these are too small for liquid measure, and agree with the deben of gold dust, there can be no doubt of the meaning of them. The mean error is 6·5 grains.

CHAPTER XVI
LINEAL MEASURES.

87. THE cubits are all of wood, excepting a standard slab of limestone, and four fragments of stone cubits. The latter were made as ceremonial objects, of importance for the inscriptions which cover them, but varying so much in the amount of the digit that no precise result can be obtained from the short lengths of the pieces. The cubits are here arranged in the order of length.

For measuring these, a standard brass scale by Dollond was used, divided into tenths of an inch, supplemented by an ivory scale of fiftieths, read to thousandths by estimation. The brass scale is of true length at 62° F.; it was one of Capt. Kater's original standards in 1824, since verified at the Standards Office in 1876.

(1.) Square wooden rod, 0·75 × 0·75 inch, with caps of cast bronze on the ends, rather loose, Roman? The mean scale of the divisions is fairly regular but shows a much shorter unit than the butts; it appears as if the cast caps were put on entirely in excess of the scale length. As they were rather lumpy with rust, the ends were ground down on slate until the metal just showed on parts of the surface. The scale values were read along both ends of the cuts.

The divisions are in six palms of 3·4 inches in a cubit of 20·4, the end palm divided in one, one, and two digits. The palm spaces are, on opposite edges,

cap 3·611	3·407	3·396	3·412	3·424	3·623 cap
3·606	3·406	3·408	3·407	3·417	3·623

Thus the most skew line is not more than 0·012 askew. The mean palm value is 3·409 inches mean difference 0·003 inch; and the end caps are 0·20 and 0·21 in excess. The cubit of six palms would be 20·45 mid 0·02; and the total length is 20·868. The digit divisions agree to the palm scale, leaving all the excess on the end cap. The division in six is influenced by the Assyrian and Jewish cubit.

(2.) Very rough irregular slip from Gurob, Roman? (0·9 to 1·4 × 0·35 inch), cut from a scrap of furniture; marking lines are wide and faint. Divided into six palms in a cubit of 20·6, end palm is of four digits, second palm halved, sixth in four digits. The palm spaces, along the axis, are

butt 3·38	3·29	3·85	3·04	3·51	3·46

Beyond the end is another digit space. The mean, excluding the very rough butt, is 3·43 m. d. 0·24;

six such palms give a cubit of 20·58 m. d. 1·4. The total length from butt to a cut is 20·58; but no exact value can be taken from a measure so obviously rough.

(3.) A flat slip of wood from Kahun, 0·5 × 0·3 inch (xiith dyn.?), with wide cuts roughly made across it. The spaces are

butt 0·85 1·23 1·07 1·10 0·86 1·08 1·00

Excluding the butt, this gives a mean value of 1·03 m. d. 0·09. This is a twentieth of a cubit of 20·6 inches, m. d. 1·8. The result is very rough, but a decimal division of the cubit is known elsewhere (*Pyramids and Temples of Gizeh,* p. 180).

(4.) A round rod, 0·7 diameter, with two holes near one end. Rough cuts are made about a third around it, giving eleven digits. The lengths of the spaces are

butt 0·71 0·58 0·74 0·60 0·93 0·81 0·70 0·81
0·58 0·65 0·71

The mean digit, omitting the butt, is 0·737, mean difference 0·09; showing a cubit of 20·6 m. d. 0·3. This is just a normal value, though the divisions are so irregular.

(5.) A flat slip broken from the end of a bevelled measure, 0·75 × 0·17 inch, from Kahun, xiith dynasty. It only has two spaces, butt 2·89, 5·85, and traces of rough ink division in digits. This gives a space between lines of 2·96 palm, seven making a cubit of 20·72.

(6.) A thick bar of wood, 3·10 × 1·56, with bevel edge 0·9 wide. From Gurob, xviiith dynasty. It is divided on the bevel into six palms, forming the short cubit of 17·7 inches. At one end is a cut a tenth of an inch short of the butt. The cuts are very fine and sharp; but the surface is a good deal decomposed and powdery, and the ends decayed. The worst skew of the cuts is 0·012, average skew 0·005:

butt 0·114 2·946 2·976 3034 2·916 2·972 2·76 butt

The mean palm is 2·97, m. d. 0·03, six making 17·83, or seven = 20·8 m. d. 0·2. This is rather long for the palm of the normal cubit, 2·95, and still more in excess of the palm of the digit 2·92. Hence it seems impossible to take the cut near the end as belonging to the digit standard, and the excess of the butt as agreeing with the cubit standard, though this might naturally be expected where a measure seems to show a small variation of standard. The end cut was perhaps a correction, marking 17·72, corresponding to a cubit of 20·67.

(7.) A long rod, 0·75 × 0·50 inch, with a middle mark, and one near one end. From Gurob, xixth dynasty? It has been broken, but can be replaced within probably 0·01 or 0·02. The lengths are, butt 20·61 break (10·3–10·25 cut added) 20·32 0·73 butt.

How these are to be understood is not clear. 20·61 is obviously the cubit; but what can 20·32 and an additional digit mean? Both together, 21·05, is too much for a cubit. It seems like a true cubit of 20·61, and a cubit of 28 digits of 0·726 inches, with another digit added on.

88. (8.) A rectangular rod, 0·90 × 0·63 inch, with one edge bevelled. The whole of the narrow side is occupied with the titles and names of Tutonkhamen and his queen Onkhesamen. Found at Gurob, xviiith dynasty (*Illahun* 20, xxiv). One end has been broken off at a knot. The remaining end has a round hole sunk in it, 0·32 wide, 0·36 deep, as if to hold a terminal stud; therefore the butt length is only a minimum, and the real end is unknown. The divisions, from the butt end, are a palm, two halves, a palm, half and two quarters, a palm, a palm, and one lost. The palm series of spaces is

butt 2·811 2·973 2·885 3·062 3·000 3·035
2·846 2·962 2·865 3·051 3·010 3·060 broken

The worst skew of the marks is 0·018 and the average 0·012. The lines measured along were the back of the top, and the front of the bevel.

The mean palm, excluding the butt, is 2·99, m. d. 0·06; seven such would make a cubit of 20·9 m. d. 0·4. If the butt was of full length, the plug in the end must have projected 0·15 or more.

This concludes the class of the normal royal cubit of Egypt, divided into seven palms.

89. Next are four examples of the Assyrian and Jewish cubit of 21·4 inches, divided into six palms.

(9.) Rectangular wooden rod, 0·60 × 0·75 inch, with six palm divisions on the narrow side, the end one divided into four digits. The palms are

butt 3·518 3·502 3·507 3·555 3·498 3·466 butt

The mean palm, excluding the butts, is 3·518, m. d. 0·02; and six such are 21·11, m. d. 0·13. The butts are, one exact, the other 0·05 short.

(10.) Rectangular wooden rod; 0·50 × 1·05, with six palm divisions on the narrow side. At one end the name ANOYTI incised. The end palm is divided into digits, the fourth digit halved; the third and the fifth palm are divided into digits. The palms are

butt 3·614 3·566 3·592 3·572 3·464 3·674 butt
The mean palm is 3·555 m. d. 0·04; and six such are 21·33, m. d. 0·2. The ends are 0·06 and 0·12 in excess.

(11.) Rectangular wooden rod, 0·60 × 0·85 inch, with six palm divisions on the narrow side, alternate palms divided in digits. The palms are

butt 3·44 3·51 3·65 3·56 3·50 3·41 butt

The ends are evidently worn, 0·11 and 0·14 short; the mean palm is 3·555 m. d. 0·05, as previous.

(12.) Rectangular wooden rod, one edge bevelled, 1·25 × 0·6 inch; divided in palms, and a half at 4½ palms, broken away beyond.

butt 3·02 3·10 3·06 2·91 1·65 broken

The mean palm is 3·02, m. d. 0·07; of which seven would be 21·16 m. d. 0·10.

90. (13.) Roughly rectangular wooden rod, 1·1 × 0·65 in middle, tapering to pointed ends: divided in 7 palms, and a middle cut. Divisions at

butt 3·41 4·49 3·68 3·52 3·11 4·08 4·21 butt

The mean palm from the divisions is 3·64 m. d. 0·16, or for 7 palms 25·48 m. d. 1·1. The divisions are so wildly irregular and rough that the present total length 26·50 seems more likely to be true, especially as the mean of the two end palms is rather over the mean palm of divisions. This means, then, two feet of 13·25 inches.

(14.) Roughly rectangular wooden rod, with a bevelled edge. Divisions across the top and the bevel, marking 7 palms, and a middle cut.

butt 3·53 3·90 4·00 3·67 3·89 3·68 3·00 burnt butt

The mean palm is 3·82 m. d. 0·03, of which seven would be 26·74 m. d. 0·21. The cuts are well formed, and square with the edge. The butts are obviously shorter than the average palm, and one is burnt. This shows then two feet of 13·37 inches.

(15.) A piece of palm rib, 1·1 × 0·7, with ten very rough cuts upon it, 0·10 to 0·15 wide and askew. The fifth mark is larger, and there is a wide space after the tenth.

butt 0·93 0·85 0·67 0·80 0·93 0·93 0·74
      0·73 0·80 0·69 0·98

Mean value 0·816 m. d. 0·025, multiplied by 10 = 8·16 m. d. 0·25. The only likely origin for such a unit would be $\frac{1}{25}$ of the cubit of 28 digits, 20·40. This would require exactly the normal digit 0·729 inch. But the weathered condition of this, and the roughness of the divisions, suggests a late Arabic source. This completes the wooden measures.

91. The stone scales are, one of the 26·8 inch cubit in seven palms, and three fragments of the 20·7 cubit.

The 26·8 measure is remarkable, as the only known standard measure for comparisons in Egypt. It is a slab of limestone 26·9 × 12·75 to 12·9 wide × 2·3 to 3·0 thick. It is smoothed on the upper face, and across the whole breadth of it are six drawn lines. The average error of straightness and parallelism of these is 0·007 inch; the mean of the palms between the lines is 3·829, mean difference 0·006, or for seven palms 26·80, m. d. 0·04, ± 0·015. This is obviously the same unit as the two Kahun wooden measures of 26·5 and 26·74 which take back the history of the standard probably to the xiith dynasty.

The date of the stone standard is probably Ptolemaic or Roman; it was found in surface digging in material of that age at Memphis. The links of this to the northern countries will be noted below.

92. The fragments of other stone measures were ceremonial, without any accuracy of division. The first, pls. xxiv, xxvi, is of hard white limestone of smooth grain, very finely engraved with hieroglyphs; these are certainly not later than the xiith dynasty, while from the style, and the presence of Horus and Set as the double rule, the vith dynasty seems to be the age. It comprises parts of the 7th, 8th and 9th digits, marked by those nomes of Upper Egypt.

The second piece is of hard, almost crystalline, limestone, like that used at Amarna. It is clearly of late age, Saite or Ptolemaic. It comprises the 7th to 10th digits.

The third piece is of black basalt, the end of a cubit marked "royal cubit," and comprising the 1st, 2nd and 3rd digits, with a prayer to Tehuti-ap-rehui below. The mention of Baken-nefu recalls the prince Baken-nefi on the stele of Pionkhy, who is likewise linked there with the city of Te-huti-ap-rehhu.

The fourth piece is of a different character, being entirely private, and without any divisions. The form with a bevel shows that it has been a measure; it was dedicated for a lady Aset-reshu, who "beheld Isis," or died, in the age of 89 years 4 months and 20 days.

93. The various cubit rods that are already known elsewhere show several lesser units marked upon them, which are copied on pl. xxv from

LEPSIUS, *Die Elle*. A length of six digits is marked, or 4·35 to 4·4 inches: Eight digits or 5·8 to 5·9 inches: 10 digits called the "small span"; the only value which can agree to the name on all the rods = 7·3 to 7·4 inches. The "great span" of 12 or 13 digits, 8·7 to 9·6 inches. The "glorious measure" *zeser* of 15 digits, 10·9 to 11·1 inches. The *remen* cubit of 18 digits, or 13·1 to 13·3 inches. Another unit of 19 digits, or 13·8 to 14·0 inches. The lesser cubit of 22 or 23 digits, or 15·2 to 16·2 inches. Finally the royal cubit of 28 digits or 20·6 inches. It should be noted that though the lesser cubit is usually stated to be 24 digits, it is distinctly limited as not over 23 digits on the two most detailed cubits.

These various lengths are evidently other standards, approximately marked on the royal cubit; there could be no sense in specially marking such numbers as 15, 18 or 19 digits merely as such fractions of the great cubit. We must look to other sources to see what standards were known which could thus be notified. Apart from the decimal digit, which is a well recognized measure, a quarter of the diagonal of the cubit, there are

Digits	Inches		Pyramid courses
6	4·35—4·4	×3 13·1—·2, Northern foot	
8	5·8 —5·9	×2 11·6—·8, Roman foot 11·61	23·2
12, 13	8·9 —9·6	×2 17·8—19·2, Persian cubit 19·2	38·2
15	10·9 —11·1	Punic foot 11·1	22·2
18	13·1 —13·3	Northern foot 13·2	26·3
19	13·8 —14·0	Philetairean foot 13·8	28·0
22, 23	15·2 —16·2		

Thus all but one of these lengths are measures known in other countries. The Roman foot is old Italic or Etruscan, and early Greek; also the diameter of Stonehenge is 100 feet. The Persian cubit remains yet in its double, the modern *arish* of 38·27 inches. The Punic foot is best found from the sarcophagus at Byblos, 11·10, and varies from 11·08 to 11·17 over the Punic colonies (*Ancient Egypt*, 1923, p. 34). The northern cubit is the most interesting standard known, for its long history and wide spread. It was a third of a fathom of about 79 inches, and the double of the 13-inch foot. The varieties are

	Foot	Cubit	Fathom
On cubit rods	13·2	26·4	79·2
Standard block		26·8	80·4

	Foot	Cubit	Fathom
Kahun rods	{ 13·2	26·5	79·5
	{ 13·3	26·7	80·2
Asia Minor	13·3	26·7	80·1
Greece	13·3	26·7	80·1
Roman Africa	13·4	26·9	80·7
Stambuli cubit	13·3	26·6	79·8
Silbury hill	13·0	26·0	78·0
Belgic foot	13·1	26·2	78·6
English land measure	13·2	26·4	79·2
„ mediaeval foot	13·2	26·4	79·3
French architects	13·0	26·1	78·24

At Silbury hill the stones around it were a fathom apart, and the radius 40 fathoms. The Belgic foot was too firmly established to be ousted, and the Romans had to adopt it on the German frontier. The English land measure of 10 fathoms 1 chain, 10 chains 1 furlong, 10 furlongs one old mile, is much older than the foot and yard, which were inserted on the awkward basis of 5½ yards one pole. The mediaeval 13·2-inch foot is much commoner than the 12-inch in buildings. French architects used the *canne* of 78·24 inches.

The pyramid courses above stated, are thicknesses frequently repeated in the Great Pyramid, which suggest that standards of these values were known and used,—perhaps by foreigners,—side by side with the Egyptian standards, see *Ancient Egypt*, 1925, p. 39.

94. There remains the difficult question of possible relations of the lineal standards to those of capacity, which we have already seen to be probably linked with weight standards. An immense amount of theorizing has been spun upon this subject, and it is very hazardous owing to the uncertain values, the abundance of multiples that may be tried of both capacity and lineal units, and the effect of the complication of cubing the units. It seems highly unlikely that a primitive connection should exist between lineal measure and weight, as capacity measures are not likely to arise till both are fixed. Also it is unlikely that the attention should first be given to great amounts of cubic feet and talents, and not rather to pints and pounds. The most probable field for examination is in lesser amounts, as follow.

The Syrian standard of 21 cubic inches is the cube of a palm of 2·76 inches, giving a foot of 11·04, rather short for the Punic foot. Yet this is so near, and so probable in its local connection, that it seems likely. If the early measure is really

as low as 20·8 c. i. the palm would be 2·75, or foot 11·00, which would be too short.

The Egyptian hen of 29·0 cubic inches, defies any likely origin in Egyptian measures; 10 hen, 290·0 inches, is the cube of half the northern foot of 13·26, as found in Egypt. This is as close as our knowledge goes, but seems very unlikely. It would point to weight and capacity measures coming in by way of Syria from the north.

The Syrian log of 33·1 cubic inches is the cube of $\frac{1}{3}$ of the Persian foot of 9·62 inches; but there is no ground for taking that as divided into 3 palms of 3·211. The locality, however, is possible.

There is no satisfactory explanation of the Attic kotyle of 17·2 cubic inches. It is possible that the half a Northern foot of 13·01, cubed, might have been repeatedly halved down to $\frac{1}{16}$th. The fair Achaeans being probably northern in origin would be a likely source; and though the foot is a shorter variety than that which belongs to Egypt, yet it is in accord with Silbury Hill and the Belgic foot, as well as the later French *canne*. Another possibility is that as the *chous* was 8 minae, the mina was $1\frac{1}{2}$ kotyle or 26·0 cubic inches of water, the side of which was 2·96 inches; this might be a palm $\frac{1}{7}$ of the 20·75 cubit, formed from the Greek foot of 12·44 inches.

The Persian kapetis of 74·9 cubic inches multiplied by 16, or $\frac{1}{3}$ of the artaba, is the cube of 10·62 inches, half a cubit of 21·24. The four Egyptian cubits of this unit, described here, average 21·23. The length then agrees, and this unit, rather longer as 10·7, is that of Persia.

So far as those relations go, it may be fairly said that the Persian 74·9 is well explained, but the others are rather too inexact or far fetched, though quite possible.

CHAPTER XVII

BALANCES.

95. SOME boxes of balances, with or without weights, have been obtained; these weights have been dealt with before in their place, under the Ungia. The means of weighing, apart from the weights, have to be described.

The oldest balance beam is of red limestone. From the nature of the material it is apparently prehistoric. It is 3·35 inches long, 0·16 to 0·20 wide, 0·17 to 0·20 deep (*Prehistoric Egypt,* xlvi, 36). The middle hole for suspension has a short tube rising

from it; hence the centre of motion is far above the suspension of the pans, and the balance is very rigid, so that equality can only be seen by the exact level. There is a difference of 1 in 120 in the arms; and a change of 1 in 500 can be seen by the change of level.

96. After that, there is not here any balance till Roman times. The finest (pl. xvi) is a box, 12·2 × 5·6 × 1·5 inches, with an iron band round one end, studded with iron nails. This retained the end of a wooden tray 10·6 × 4·4 × 0·6 inches. In the box is a balance beam, with suspender-loop and vertical tongue, of very slight make, 9·5 long; and two pans of brass 3·2 diameter. Five brass weights are sunk in square holes fitted to them, all in perfectly fresh condition with original polish. These are nos. 5399–5403, pl. xlvi, from six ounces down to two nomisma, with an average error of 2·4 grains. Also a loose weight marked .I., which does not belong to this series: one empty square pit shows a weight to have been lost. In the tray is a lesser balance beam, 6·8 long, with two pans of 1·75 wide, which fit the tray; also a second pair of pans 2·1 wide. Two round weights of ounce and half ounce are here, two coins slightly ground, and two glass lumps, nos. 5405–5410. The coins of Constantine II and Constans as Caesars, must be between 333 and 337 A.D., and were probably not placed here later than 350. The tray has six square holes, to which nothing fits, and two lids to holes.

Another box, 5·8 × 1·85 × 0·9 inch, contains a beam 3·95 long, with pans 1·2 wide. A lid slips under a catch on one end, and has two hooks projecting to hold studs on the sides of the box. There are two square pits for weights, but none fit in them; four lie loose, nos. 5411–5414. No. 5412 has a faint impress, apparently of a pegasus.

Another box is 8·5 × 2·5 × 1·3, with a lid. A square hole, and a round hole, are cut in the block for weights. Beam 5·7 long, pans 1·6 wide. In it was an odd lot, in which no unit is obvious; white glass bottle stamp, with Eros, 85·0 grains; Ptolemaic coin 76·3; triply forked piece of hard wood, 58·0; a blue glazed melon bead, 41·6; a glass weight of El 'Azyz (975–996 A.D.), 22·8; a slip of blue glass inlay, 9·6; lastly a bone hair pin with scoop end. These seem as if dropped in by a sebakh digger as they turned up.

Box 8·4 × 2·6 × 1·2 inches; lid split in two, drilled for repair. Beam 6·2, pans 1·6 wide and a second

pair 1·85. A square pit has a thin lid, and a scrap of stuff at the bottom; there are two round pits. Three nomisma weights here, are nos. 5300, 5369, 5371. Fourteen cowries of very various sizes, five cone shells, and an iron ring, may all be later additions.

Box 6·75 × 3·0? × 1·2, side broken away. Tray for a balance 5·3 long, and pans 1·6 wide, all lost. In the body 2 large square pits and 8 round: in the tray 2 oblong pits.

Box 6·5 × 2·4 × 0·6. Two square pits. Two pans left, 1·3 wide.

97. Of other countries there are a few examples of scales.

Frankish balance, beam 4·5 long, pans 1·6 wide: no case.

Box, cut in a block with rounded corners, 4·8 × 2·0 × 0·85; lid attached by wire hinges. Beam 3·7 long, round pan 1·05 wide, triangular scale 1·6 wide. Nest of cone weights of XIID, XXXD, VS, of 92·0, 229·2, 457·7 grs., mean value 91·6, mean error 0·3. Round brass weights of George II guinea (128·1), 21S (129·0), 21S (120·5), 13S6D (83·3 grs.). Paper in lid of "proclamation on 24th June last" of limits of light weight allowance on guineas before and after 1771.

Box, constructed, 5·75 × 2·75 × 1·1, lid with wire hinges. Beam 5·1 long, pans 2·0 wide. Paper in lid of standard weights of moidores, £3 12s piece, £1 16s, 18s, 7s, guinea, half guinea, pistole.

Nest of weights, turned in brass. 1 pound down to ¼ ounce. The outer pan is 7·1 grains light, on the mean scale, and apparently worn below. The mean scale of the others is to a pound of 6993·4 grains, or 6·6 grains light. The mean error of the weights is 1·0 grain. Probably late xviiith century.

Chinese balance in a box with two drawers, and upright stand to fit on box. Made for European use, with numerals of style of xviiith century. Box 10·5 × 5·25 × 4·3 high. Beam 8·9 long, pans 3·9 wide. Box ends to beam. Brass weights of native form, of 0·2 tael, 2 to 10 taels, and 20 to 50 taels. Mean scale 579·78 ± 0·06 grains; mean error per tael 0·11 grs.; the error is less on the larger weights, 20 to 50 taels having average error of 0·4 grs. or $\frac{1}{5000}$th of the weight.

CHAPTER XVIII
OTHER COLLECTIONS OF WEIGHTS.
PLS. XLVII–LIII.

As the material is much scattered, it seems desirable to put together, in brief outline, the prin-cipal collections of weights to which reference has been made in describing the College collection.

Naukratis, Defenneh, and Cairo. Pls. XLVII–XLVIII.

98. When I went to excavate Naukratis, there were only a few dozen weights known from Egypt. After two seasons there, and at Defenneh, nearly 1300 were collected and classified. These were all published, and then the collection lay in reserve for some years, and were finally given by the Egypt Exploration Fund to museums in the United States. A few had been selected for the Cairo Museum; these, and others in Cairo to the number of 214, are included in the outline list here issued, pls. xlvii, xlviii. The fuller account of all in this list is in the volumes on *Naukratis I* and *Defenneh* (in *Tanis II*), and the Cairo Museum Catalogue by Weigall. In the present list the less useful material is omitted, such as weights with serious amount of alteration, small weights under 50 grains which are less exact and difficult to attribute, and metal weights which are always the most liable to damage. After the gatherings above named, more weights were found at various sites and bought, and the whole of these were kept for University College, and form the present collection of over 3400 examples.

Gezer. Pl. XLIX.

99. The weights found in the excavation of Gezer by the Palestine Exploration Fund, have all been weighed and published by Prof. STEWART MACALISTER in his *Excavation of Gezer*. These are summarised here in a classified list, pl. xlix. As there does not seem to have been any allowance made for chipping or wear, these amounts are *minima*, and may have been somewhat larger. For remarks upon them, see chapter XI.

Troy. Pl. XLIX.

In 1887 Dr. Schliemann kindly obtained the following particulars of thirty-one weights, from Dr. Krause, keeper of the Völkerkunde Museum, Berlin. He also added details of eight in his own possession. These were all weighed to the nearest decigramme, and they are here reduced to grains to make them comparable with other collections. It is notable that the necef of Syria does not appear there. The limits of the different standards are very distinct.

Weights in the British Museum. Pls. L–LIII.

100. Forty years ago I weighed all the weights in the Graeco-Roman Department of the British Museum, and supplied a list of them, with estimation of gain and loss. As that list has not yet been published, I have here revised it, in view of the later discoveries of the early standards and names, though hardly a single instance of re-attribution proved necessary. This list is a useful appendix to that of the Egyptian weights, as it shows how the early standards were continued in rather varied form in classical times. This material was used for the article *Weights* in the *Encyclopaedia Britannica*, 1890.

The system of this list is as follows. 1st col. the Museum reference, the year, month and day of reception, and the number in the day list. 2nd the material; B, bronze; G, glass; L, limestone; M, marble; P, plumbum, lead; S, serpentine; Sy, syenite. 3rd column the present weight in grains. 4th the total weight of changes estimated. 5th the estimated original weight. 6th the multiple. 7th the resulting unit. 8th the resulting mina. 9th the source, marked A, Athens; Ae, Aegospotamos; B, Budrum; C, Corfu; Cg, Carthage; Co, Corinth; Cr, Crete; Ct, Catania; E, Ephesos; G, Gaul; Ge, Gela; H, Herakleia; K, Knidos; Kl, Kalymnos; Km, Kameiros; Kr, Kyrenaica; Ky, Kyme; L, Lyons; Lk, Lykia; N, Naxos; R, Rhodes; Ro, Rome; S, Smyrna; Sy, Syria. 10th column, the marks or inscriptions; these are usually self-explanatory, or will be readily understood on looking at the multiple.

Daric. After a mixture of Peyem and Daric confused, the second group is of a remarkable class of large rectangular marble weights, with two breasts on the top, sometimes joined by a handle. They belong to the daric and sela standards, see also 3 in Univ. Coll.; 14 come from the temenos of Demeter at Knidos, 2 from the temenos of the Muses at Knidos, 2 from the temple of Diana at Ephesos, others from Budrum (Halikarnassos) and Lycia, 2 from the temple at Jebail (Byblos), 1 from Der el Kalaat, S.E. of Beyrut, and 1 from Cyrenaica. Thus they are mostly, perhaps all, from temples, and therefore sacred standards. It is notable that, though with breasts on them, they do not come from Aphrodite temples or Cyprus. The usual Assyrian mina of 60 shekels or darics was used at Antioch, and at Cyzicus, where it was a stater or double shekel ("tris," tri-stater), and mina

of 30 staters. The third group from Carthage has 3, 6 and 12 as multiples, owing to the mina of 60 shekels being divided by 20, 10 and 5.

Litra. The Italic litra seems to have been a confused group coming from three standards, peyem, daric, and Attic stater.

Stater. The Attic stater and mina is the commonest Greek standard. The marks, H+, are a row of drachma signs ├─├─├─ conjoined. The often blundered inscription ΔΗΜΟ, is for ΔΗΜΟΣΙΟΝ "treasury" standard, or "public" weight. In several marked instances, the standard seems to have been a double mina, *tritē* or $\frac{1}{3}$ is 4587, *tetart* or $\frac{1}{4}$ is 3180, *hemitetart* or $\frac{1}{8}$ is 1796, 1808, 1836, all showing a mina of 100 staters or about 13,600 grains. One weight of Antioch is on the single mina.

The types which appear, whole or halved, are of the following fractions of the mina.

Half crescent, 5 of $\frac{1}{8}$, 1 tetradrachm,

„   „   + star 1 of $\frac{1}{8}$,

Crescent 3 of $\frac{1}{6}$, 2 of $\frac{1}{5}$, 1 of $\frac{1}{4}$,

Crescent + star 3 of $\frac{1}{6}$,

Half tortoise, 8 of $\frac{1}{4}$, 1 of $\frac{1}{6}$,

Tortoise 3 of $\frac{1}{2}$, 1 of $\frac{1}{3}$,

Quarter amphora, 1 of $\frac{1}{8}$,

Half   „   2 of $\frac{1}{3}$, 1 of $\frac{1}{4}$,

Amphora 5 of $\frac{2}{3}$,

Dolphin $\frac{1}{5}$, $\frac{1}{4}$, $\frac{1}{2}$, 5 whole mina.

Though there is some variation in most signs, yet the half sign is in weight a half or two thirds of the whole sign; there seems no distinction between the standards of different signs. They may belong to different families of makers. The obolos seems to have retained some independant position, as the fractions of $\frac{1}{6}$, $\frac{1}{3}$, $\frac{2}{3}$ of a mina, and $\frac{8}{3}$ of a drachma, are the simple numbers of 100, 200, 400 and 16 oboli.

Necef. A few examples of this standard occur, half of them as small weights, others as mina, halves, and quarters.

Khoirīnē. A few examples of this are likewise partly small weights, partly mina and divisions: but usually the mina was taken over in Italy and divided in the familiar way there, into 12 unciae, each of 24 scripula.

Beqa. This standard seems to have been the origin of the Aeginetan and Roman systems. The Aeginetan range is 9060–9960, or 180–199, rather degraded from the low beqa 188–203. The Italic and Roman uncia ranges from 380–420, or 190–210, nearly agreeing with the whole beqa range 188–216.

The types and half types of this system show a method like that of the Attic.

Half crescent 3 of $\frac{1}{10}$ of mina,
Crescent 3 of $\frac{1}{8}$,
Half tortoise $\frac{1}{8}$,
Tortoise $\frac{1}{4}$,
Quarter amphora 2 of $\frac{1}{8}$,
Half amphora $\frac{1}{4}$,
Amphora $\frac{1}{4}$,
Dolphin 2 of whole mina.

The marks on 46.4. 47.3 and 82.5 refer to the obolos, and the latter weight of 5 oboli shows the obolos as independant of the drachma. 282.0 bears a double mark, as 3 Aeginetan drachmae of 93.7 and four Attic drachmae of 70.2. The double standard, or whole beqa, is shown by 752.3 marked Δ, $= 4$. The weight 294.2 can hardly be 20 oboli, and K is probably not a number but an initial. A light, or half, mina is named on 4823.3; and a still lighter, or quarter mina is named on 1159.7 which is called half, this would imply a mina of 10 beqas. In the next section is a litra mina of 12 beqas or unciae, the light Italic litra. Weight 194.4 is double marked as 1 uncia on one side, and with S as half uncia on the other side.

The great series of the Roman libra shows much corruption, the variations extending to a quarter of the whole amount. The median is 4905 and mean variation 100 grains. Even weights of the same nature and period show almost equal irregularity. The early black serpentine weights average for the libra 4956 with a mean variation of 86. The solidus weights average the libra at 4819 m.v. 60. The latest oungia and nomisma weights average 4857 m.v. 122. The weights tested by a single official and certified by him vary from 4362 ot 5625; and those made in a uniform set vary from 4770 to 5168 for the standard. It would have seemed incredible that with the Roman legality, and the fine balances that were made, such gross errors would have been tolerated. On the other hand, sets of small weights, that are less pretentious, show exactitude, as in the set in a scale box at University College. Of the marks on this series there is no uncertainty, Λ for libra; δ or Γo for oungia, uncia; SOL or N for solidus or nomisma; S for semis or solidus; and the usual Greek numerals. The series of scripula from Lyons are fairly made, the average error being only 0.8 grain.

Sela, Phoenician or Alexandrian. For the series of breast weights, see the remarks in the daric series. In three instances the multiples prove that a double mina was used. The general series is mostly Graeco-Roman, on the duodecimal division of the mina into 12 unciae; only one fifth of all belongs to the original Phoenician system of 100 drachmae in the mina. Apparently this standard was much confused with the lighter libra derived from the beqa. The Carthaginian weights are naturally on the Alexandrian system, which was so widely spread by the Ptolemaic coinage. The series of small weights with concave sides has a basis of 12.5 grains; this is like an eighth of the Aeginetan or a quarter of the Alexandrian, but falls between the two.

CHAPTER XIX
THE DIALS AND DRAWINGS.

101. THE Egyptians regularly worked with a dial for measuring the altitude of the sun, by a shadow on a horizontal,—or later a sloping,—surface, with scales for the variation in each month. This form is best explained by the upper figure in pl. xxvi, which is a copy of a dial sold in lot 456 of the Hoffmann sale, 1894. The names of the months are all given. Below this copy is a dial cut in black steatite, the full inscriptions on which are copied in pl. xxv. It was made for Sennu, who held many priesthoods, but the inscription does not relate to the dial itself. At the lower point a mass has been broken off which rose up, doubtless to carry the edge which was to cast the shadow on the slope. The slanting lines on the slope show the place of the shadow for six hours, before and after noon, in different months. On the slope were six spaces, one for each month of spring and of autumn. Down the middle was a strip inlaid for the two months of the equinoxes. The graduation is not exact, and the latitude cannot be deduced from the maximum readings. When the dial was moved about, it was provided with a plumb bob, hanging down the projection which is now lost: this enabled the dial to be set upright.

102. The Greek form of dial, shewing the direction of the sun by the shadow of a polar gnomon, is independent of variation in altitude, but it must be fixed, or adjusted to the north whenever used. Of this form, a concave of a quarter of a sphere, ruled with hour lines, there is half a dial of large

size in the collection, published in *Roman Portraits*, pls. xvi and xxiii. Also half of a small dial in limestone, pl. xxvi here, with the *uzat* eye in relief on the outside.

103. On pl. liv two drawings on papyrus are photographed. They were bought as one roll, broken across the middle, found at Gurob, and therefore probably of the New Kingdom. The papyrus is divided into squares by red lines, averaging 1·3614 inches apart; this has no close connection to any measure, the nearest being $\frac{1}{8}$ of a foot of 10·89 inches which, before contraction of the papyrus by age, might be near the Punic foot of 11·1. The whole roll was 21·7 inches wide, and the two drawings were each 30·3 inches high, before one was broken at the top. The subject of the drawings is a front and side view of a wooden shrine; this was suspended by twisted ropes, from the roof of a framework like a four-poster bed, and it was further secured from swinging by twisted ropes below, attaching it to the basis of the frame. The top of the frame is shaped like the usual lids of Egyptian coffers, sloping gradually up from the back, till it sharply rounds over to the front. There is no obvious use in such a form of lid, but it was copied from the roof of a canopy as shown here. The purpose of the form was highly ingenious; the top was of thin springy board, the sling near the flat end would tend to shorten it when loaded, the sling near the curved end would equally tend to lengthen it. Thus the total length of the spring top would be unchanged, although loaded with weight or unloaded. In this way the spring could act without expanding or contracting the framework in which it was fixed. When we see a shrine being drawn along over a desert road in a funeral scene, we might well wonder how its contents bore the jerks and jolts; this drawing explains the skilful arrangement of spring and slings, to reduce the roughness of the transport. For further detail, see *Ancient Egypt*, 1926, 1.

APPENDICES

Western Standards.

The use of a definite unit of weight in Egypt as early as the use of metal suggests that it is not unlikely that weight standards might be used for precious metals at the same stage of culture in Europe. This is confirmed by the weights in the form of a double axe (with an impossibly small haft hole) found in Germany, Serbia, Switzerland and France; these conform to three main standards, the gold beqa or Aeginetan, the sela or Phoenician, and the necef or Syrian (*Tools and Weapons,* 14).

The collection of gold work of the Royal Irish Academy has been so well published by Mr. E. C. R. Armstrong (1920), that it is a favourable ground for enquiry on weights. Some groups of related objects show that there is good reason to expect the use of standard units. The gold box (371), weighing 467 grains, had in it a gold ring of 467 grs.; another box (372) of 476, had in it a ring of 482 grs.; clearly these are all made to one definite unit. Another box (373) is 290 grs., half the weight of a gold cup (376) of 588 grs.; these numbers are $2\frac{1}{2}$ and 5 units, of which 4 equal each of the other boxes and rings, the unit averaging here 117·6 grs. $\pm$ 0·6. Another group is of six gold balls found together (341–5, 347), which are in the proportions of 10, 8, and 6 of a unit of 113·9 grs., $\pm$ 0·8. Another group is of flat band armlets found together (413–6) which are in the proportion of 6, 7, 8, 9 of a unit of 84·0 to 85·2 grs., average 84·8 $\pm$ 0·2, or half of 169·6. Another group of armlets (193–6) has proportions of 50, 4, 6, 6 of a unit of 166·5 grs. $\pm$ 0·5. Of two remarkable ribbed bracelets, one has 8 grooves, the other 6, and they weigh 8 and 6 of the 100 grain unit.

It is, then, evident that we have here not only regular proportions between objects found together, but also general units, such as 117·6 and 113·9, 169·6 and 166·5, varying a little as they do in all other ancient countries. As different classes of objects are likely to vary in their periods and their sources, the most likely line of enquiry was to set out in diagram the weights of objects of each of the fifteen different classes separately, and then study them to see where clusters of similar weights had any relation one to another. In this way it was found that the most usual unit of three of the classes was about 100 grains, another three classes showed about 113 grains, two other classes showed 129 grains, and four classes agreed on 165 grains. Such were the direct results, and it was only afterwards that I observed that these were the three units of the European double-axe weights, and also the Babylonian daric weight. This may be taken as confirming the probability of these units having been used. After this, the remainder of each class, which did not conform to its most obvious unit already found, was examined;

it proved to be nearly all in conformity with some of the other three units. Fourteen of the residue agree together on a further unit of 145·1 ± 0·6, which is the usual Egyptian standard; and eight are on the khoirīnē unit, 182·9 ± 1·0.

In the following table each class is averaged separately, as this shows what variation existed in various times and places. The upper number of each entry is the number of examples, then the unit in grains, lastly the probable error.

Lunulae		(8) 109·8 ± 0·5	(2) 125·9 ± 0·5		(12) 167·0 ± 3·6		1071 1092
Gorgets	(3) 101·0 ± 0·8		· · ·		(2) 169·6 2·2		
Torques	(1) 101·0	(2) 111·0			(11) 166·3 0·7		
Ribbon torques			(6) 126·5 1·0	(2) 142·8		(1) 189·2	
Slug links	(13) 100·4 0·5	(10) 110·8 0·6	(2) 130·4 0·3	(2) 145·3	(2) 169·0 0·8	(2) 179·5 ± 0·5	
Trumpet links		(2) 109·7 0·3	(14) 131·6 0·7	(1) 145·4			1391
,,			(6) 122·1 0·4				
Trumpet armlets		(6) 113·9 0·6	(6) 132·6 0·7		(16) 165·7 0·8		
Bangles	(27) 101·5 0·6	(8) 114·8 0·9	(7) 127·0 0·3	(1) 145·8	(7) 166·4 0·9	(4) 182·1 1·0	
Armlets	(1) 97·5	(1) 115·2			(4) 162·3 1·5		
Discs	(1) 100	(8) 111·0 1·0		(2) 143·5		(1) 182	52,77
Balls		(6) 113·9 0·8			(1) 162·2		
Boxes, cup-grooved bands		(8) 117·0 0·5					
Bracelets	(5) 100·4 0·4	(1) 112·5	(1) 125·3	(2) 148·6			
,, flat					(5) 168·2 1·0		Residue
Rings			(1) 129·0	(4) 143·2 0·6			
Limits	97·5–101·5	109·7–117·2	125·3–132·6	142·8–148·6	162·2–169·6	179·5–189·2	
Eastern units	2×94—101	2×107—114	125—133	140—148	160—168	177—188	
	Lower beqa	sela	daric	early qedet	higher necef	higher khoirīnē	
	Gold unit	Phoenician	Babylonian	Egyptian	Syrian		

Thus there are only four objects which do not fall in with the units frequently found here, and the range of variation of each unit in different classes agrees with the range of variation found in Egypt, or is rather less than that. Names have been applied to some classes, as those already in use were very long but not descriptive. The small rings, commonly called "ring-money," are not included, as they have no distinct grouping, and cannot therefore indicate any result in their general diffusion.

Notes from Italian Museums.

SOME results obtained when on a photographic tour in 1891 may be worth recording, and the notes on what awaits further examination will be useful for any future students.

Weights. In Bologna, Museo Civico, are 5 large stone weights dome-shaped with iron rings and adjusting pieces; between 1 and 2 cwt. each. Over 100 stone and bronze weights.

In the Capitoline Museum are several large weights.

In the Kircherian Museum are 17 flatted globe weights, 12 edged disc, 6 disc, 22 pendant weights (? for steelyards), 18 small weights.

In Naples Museum are a hundred flatted globe weights (74179 to 74278) from 10 librae to ¼ uncia; a set of 13 bronze edged discs with silver marks, × to ⅛ uncia (74280–92). About 30 pendant weights. A set of corn-shaped weights, 10 librae to ¼ uncia (74293–74305). Lead weights 20 lbs. to 1 lb. (74394–74438).

Steelyards. In Bologna, 5 with hingeing loop reversal and 2 suspensors; 3 with saddle and 3 suspensors. In the New Capitoline are two reversing steelyards, and three rotating.

In Perugia is a rotating steelyard.

In the Kircherian, 3 with 2 suspensors, one with 3 suspensors.

In Naples, 27 with ring at end for reversal and 2 suspensors, 2 with saddle for 2 and for 3 suspensors.

Capacity measures. Two cylindrical bronze vessels (Naples 74600–1) have each an axial rod supporting three radii of bronze which form the top, and define the contents accurately for dry measure. The larger has the whole base dished upward, the smaller has the base dished over rather more than half. This is obviously done to stiffen it, and prevent pressure bulging it. The two crossing diameters were measured at top, mid, and base, and the depth at 9 points. From these measurements the means are,—diameters 10·20 and 7·38 inches, depths 8·72 and 6·66, contents (after allowing for axis and cross arms) 709·7 and 283·5 cubic inches. If these are intended for 20 sextarii and 8 sextarii (½ modius), they result in 35·48 and 35·44 for the sextarius, or 1703 and 1701 cubic inches for the amphora. This is rather higher than the three other standards known. It would be desirable to weigh the contents of water; but one measure has the bottom partly cracked and a bit gone, the other has the bottom patched with solder. It is best to stop all defects with wax when guaging by liquids. On the lesser vessel is pricked by points D. D. P. P. HERC. The axial pin in the lesser vessel has sunk 0·09 inch below the cross arms,

to which it is not attached. If due to sinking of the bottom, the contents may be now an inch or two in excess. Both vessels are turned. There is also a similar vessel of iron (74602) too much rusted to give accurate results.

The celebrated Farnese congius was inspected with a view to its antiquity. There is no true patina upon it, only a little superficial green; what appear to be patches of red oxide are drops of shell lac left when stopping a hole in the edge. The age of it must therefore entirely depend on the style of the inscription. It cannot be guaged by lineal measure.

In Naples (74165) is an ingenious weighing vessel for liquids. The pan has a long handle, with a slit along the middle, at the end of the handle was a counterpoise; a sliding suspensor travelled in the slit, and the vessel balanced at different suspensions according to the amount in the pan. The numbers in the graduation range from I to XII; it would not be difficult to restore the unit by trial. There are also some small bronze mug measures, probably for oil.

Foot measures. In the Capitoline museum are two monuments of architects. The most complete is that of Statilius; among his implements is figured a foot scale, divided in $\frac{1}{16}$ths. This, by the average of all the divisions, gives 11·42 ± 0·04 inches for the foot, but the total length is 11·61. With it is a long rod represented, with widened ends (evidently metal terminals), and a knob which divides the rod in the proportion of 2 : 3. The total is 37·80 ins., with a variation by irregularity of ± 0·06. The knob divided it into 15·13 and 22·67 inches. As $\frac{2}{3}$ of 22·67 is 15·11, the uncertainty of the total length (0·06) far exceeds the difference in the proportion (0·02). The ratio of 2 : 3 looks like the usual one of a foot to a cubit, but no foot of 15·13 is known, nor a cubit of 22·67. There is however a cubit rod mark at 22 digits = 15·2 inches.

The other monument is to M. Aebutius; a foot rule there has two digits and two quarters marked, giving a mean foot of 11·63 ± 0·03. Another slab, known as the Lapis Capponianus, with a foot divided in quarters, gives 11·67 ± 0·03.

In Naples the plain foot measures of bronze are 11·500 (no. 76692), 11·600 (76694), 11·662 (76697). Those divided clearly in half are 5·792 + 5·760, 11·552 (76695); 5·806 + 5·798, 11·604 (76693); 5·801 + 5·803, 11·604 (76696). Two are divided in 12ths; one is very well divided, the mean value being

11·68 ± 0·01, on total 11·64; the other is badly divided and only the total can be trusted, 11·68.

The whole of these foot measures, then, are

Statilian	total length	11·61
Aebutian	mean	11·63
Capponian	mean	11·67
Bronze measures	(76692)	11·50
	(76695)	11·552
	(76694)	11·60
	(76693)	11·604
	(76696)	11·604
		11·64
	(76697)	11·662
		11·68

Thus 11·613 ± 0·01 is the mean. Previous means from measures give 11·616 and from buildings 11·607, with probable errors of about 0·01. From the agreement of all these results it seems that it is unlikely to have been either 11·60 or 11·62.

Balances. The large conical sockets ending with a hook, are usually at Naples set up as supports for balances; but as 16 out of 24 are paired it is probable that they were generally the ends of large wooden balance beams. An observation of the exact position of finding would settle the purpose. The metal balance beams are always tapering; round, square or octagonal, but never deeper than the width. There are 8 examples of a beam divided in 12 for a rider weight. There are no tongues to the beams at Naples. In the Capitoline and New Capitoline are beams with tongues. In Perugia is a beam with both arms hingeing up to the long tongue.

These notes will show what a large amount is waiting to be done, to render the Italic collections of scientific use.

The Cowry as a weight.

On enquiry from Prof. D'ARCY THOMPSON, he quoted several Greek references to the Χοιρίνη, cowry, adding "The Mediterranean species are all small . . . but the larger species from the Red Sea, Indian Ocean, &c., have been articles of trade from time immemorial . . . you want for your hypothesis a cowry of 170 grains, *Cypraea moneta* and its allies (*C. erosa*, &c.), are too small, *C. tigris* and the like are too big."

M. LOUIS GERMAIN in *Les Mollusques recueillis dans les anciens monuments égyptiens,* quotes as having been found in Egypt, *Cypraea annulus, arabica, camelopardalis, caput serpentis, carneola, caurica, erosa, erythraensis, histrio, moneta, pantherina, reticulata, tigris, vitellus.* By the kindness of Dr. Bather, I have received from the principal authority on the species, Mr. COSMO MELVILL, the following :—"Six species of *Cypraea* or cowry shell inhabit the Mediterranean out of a total of 215 recent species. Three of these are very small (of subgenus *Trivia*) and one British species is one of these (*C. Europea*). It weighs 9 to 10 grains only. The remaining three are called *C. spurca, physis* and *lurida.* I have had a fair sized adult specimen of this last weighed, the result 214 grains. *Spurca* and *physis* are both smaller, and would not weigh more than 120 or 130 grains, if that."

Dr. HARMER (British Museum) states that *C. lurida* is the largest species inhabiting the Mediterranean. One from Cape Verde Islands weighs 240 grains, and a smaller from St. Helena 142 grains.

[It is thus evident that the standard of the five syenite cowry weights, 170 grains, may well have its name and form from the known variation of the Mediterranean species *Cypraea lurida.*]

INDEX

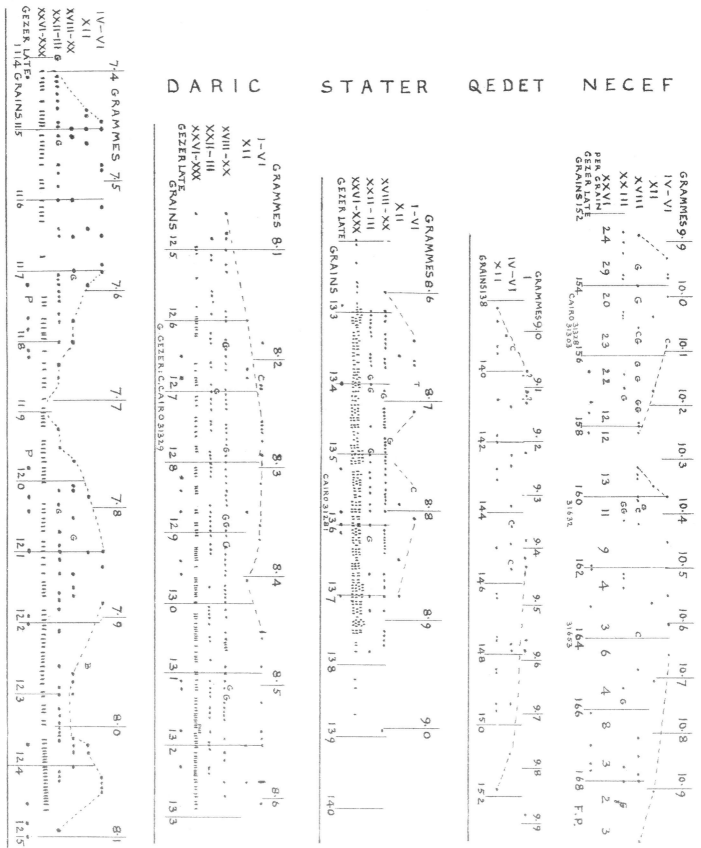

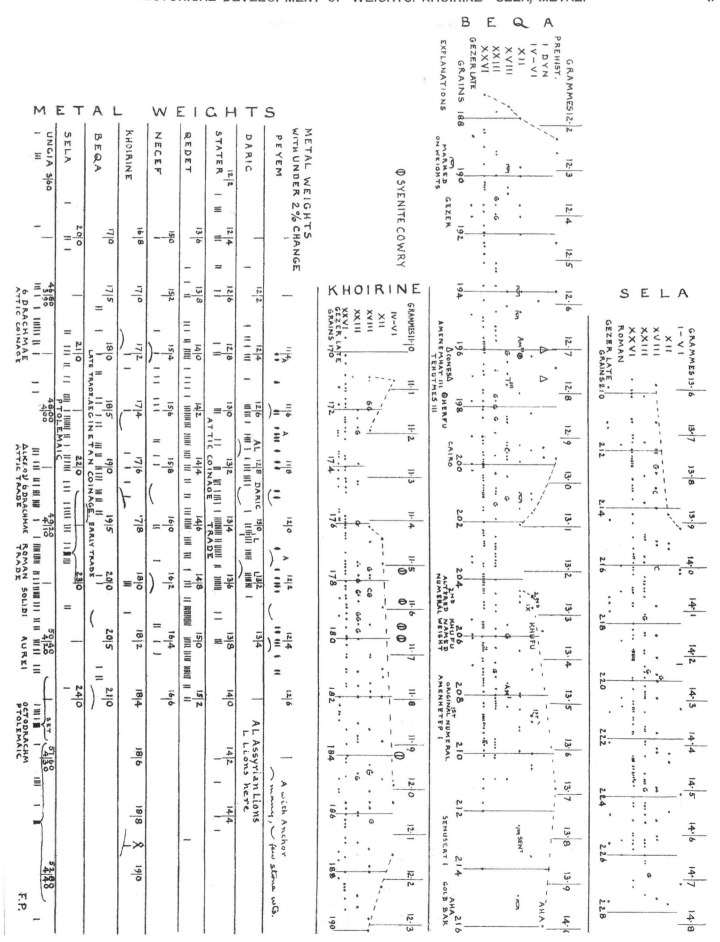

F.P.

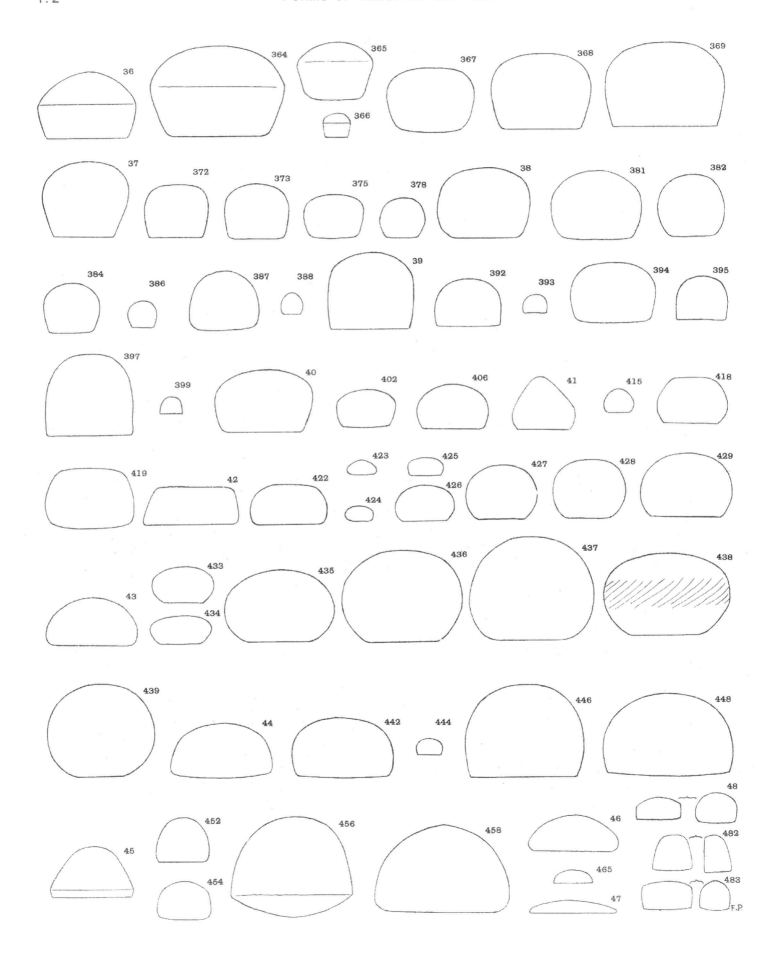

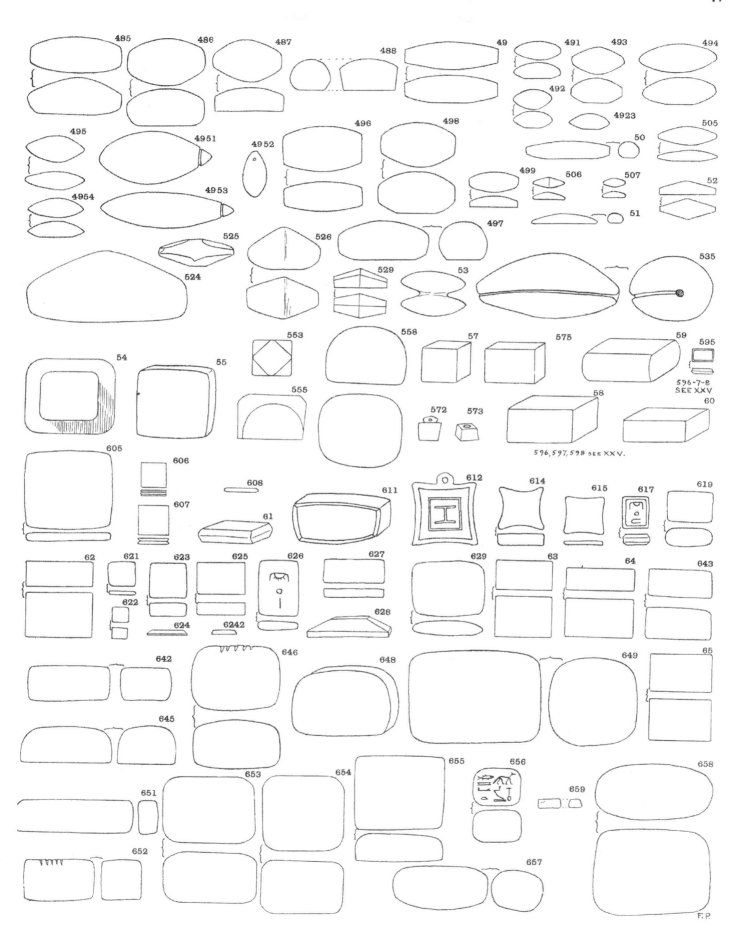

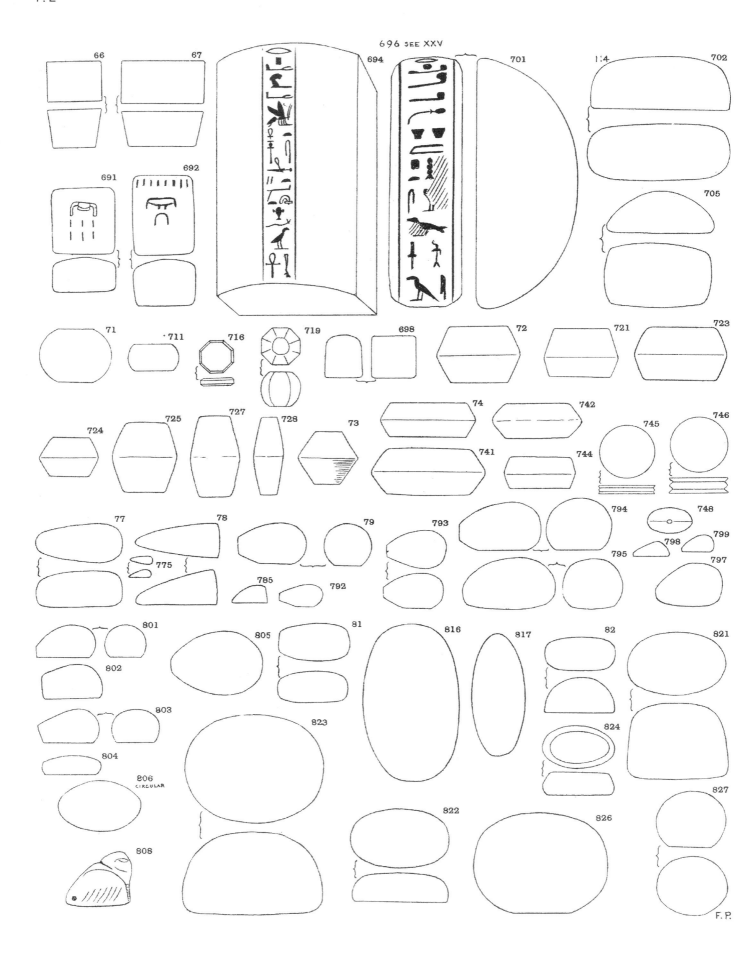

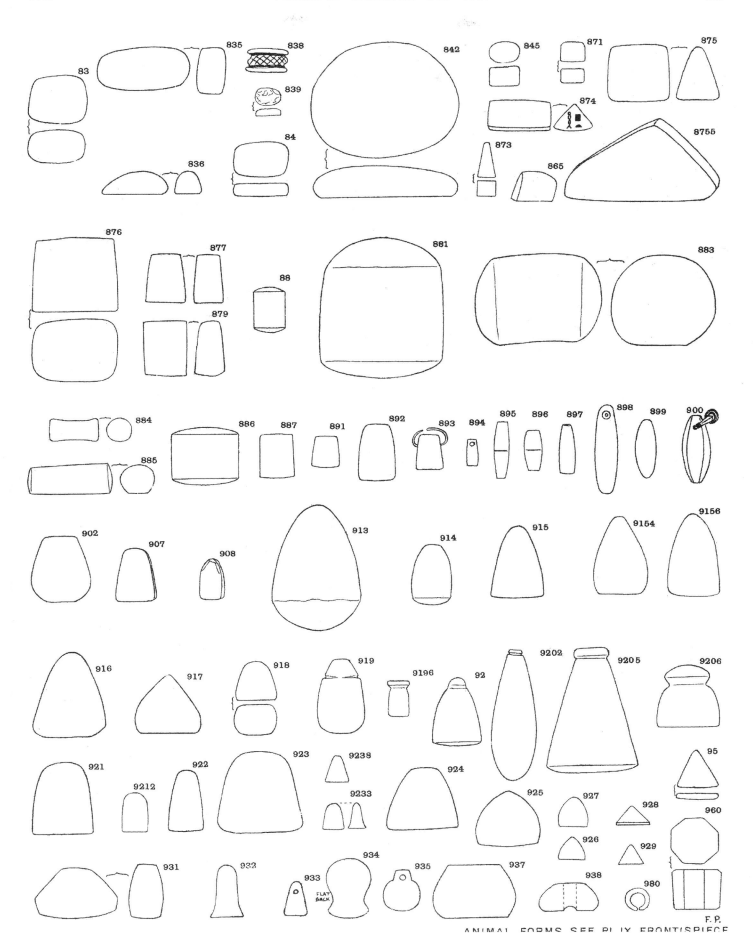

F.P.

ANIMAL FORMS SEE PL.IX FRONTISPIECE

		2308			5141		2705 A		3218		4938		2848		5171	
		3502												2415		
	5120		5050			4917		5034		4626		5145		5195		5163
	4815		5233			4814								5241		5169
		4788														
	5138			5136			4841				4848			5103		5260
	4816				4939			5253				4749		5073		4925
4926																
5149			5329			5130			4801		5121		5259	5127		5109
4920		5119		5258	5186		5245		5264		5083		5146	4775		4913 A
				5154												
	5155 A		4248			5178		5358		4783		4789		4946		3735

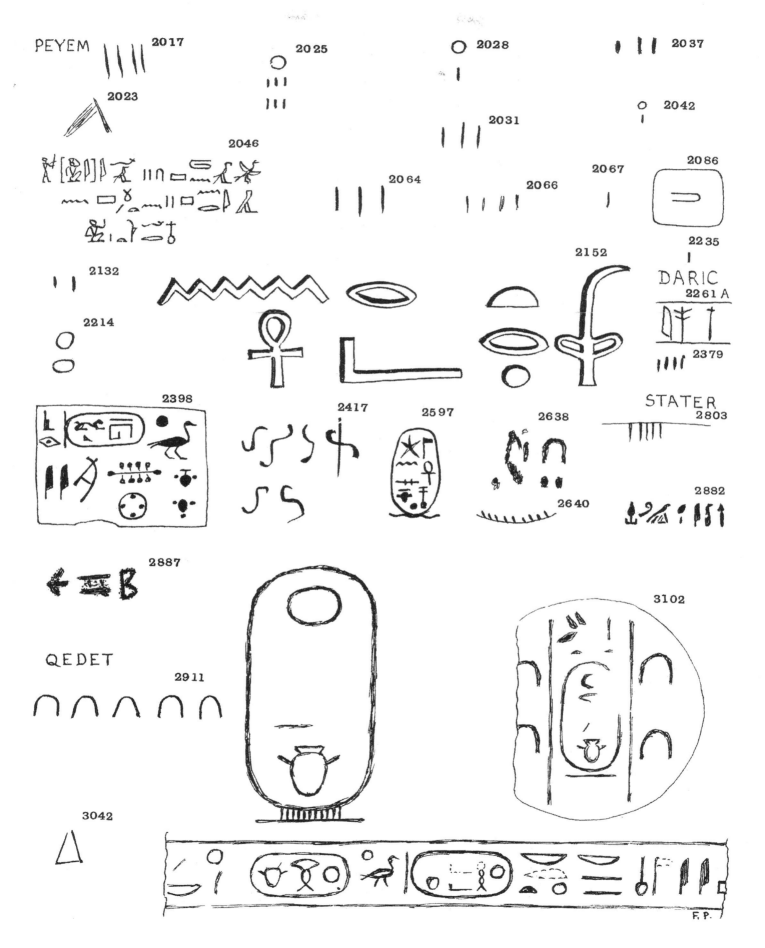

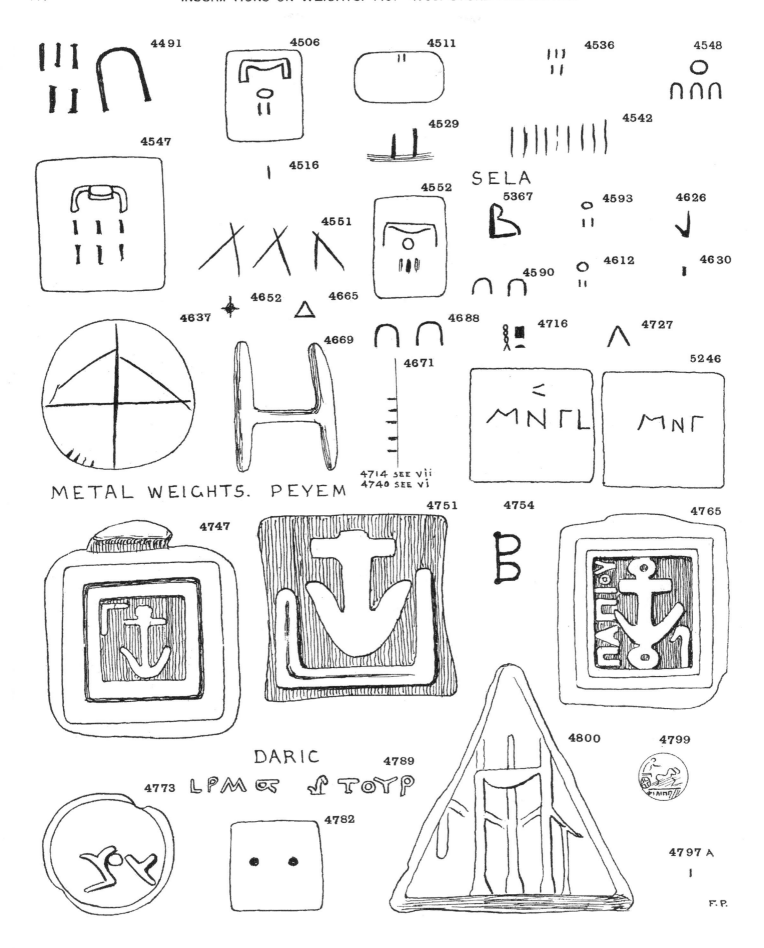

4491   4506   4511   4536   4548

4547   4516   4529   4542

SELA

4552   5367   4593   4626

4551   4590   4612   4630

4637   4652   4665

4669   4688   4716   4727

4671   5246

4714 SEE vii
4740 SEE vi

METAL WEIGHTS. PEYEM

4747   4751   4754   4765

DARIC

4773   LPM   4789   TOYP

4782   4800   4799

4797 A

F. P.

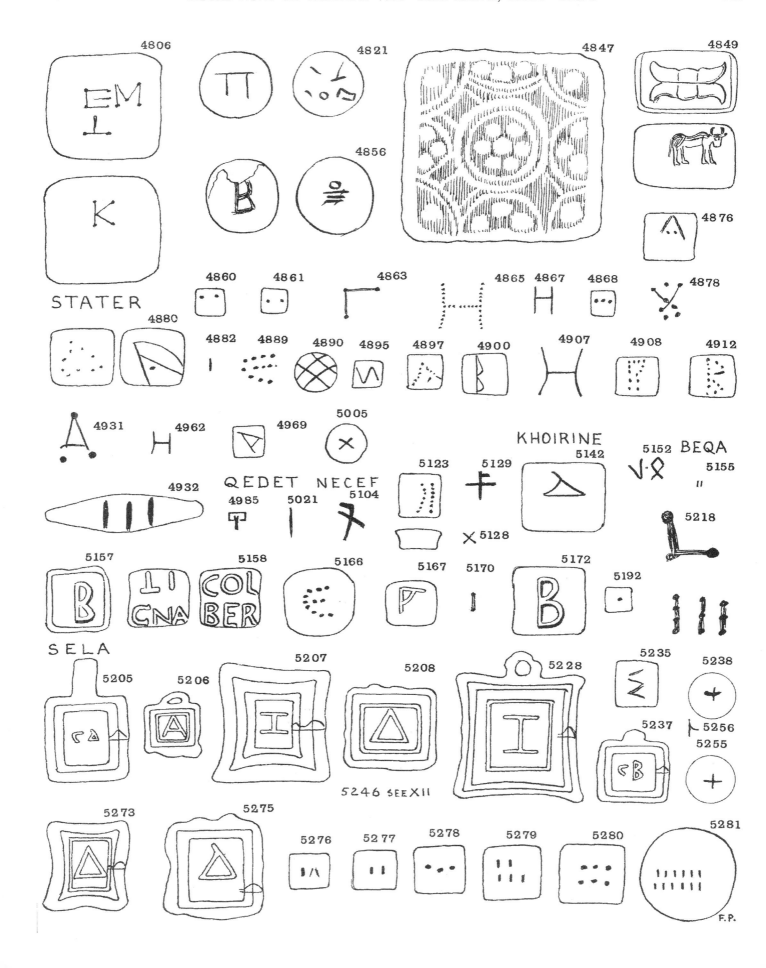

UNGIA

5289

5290

5292

5293

5296

5297

5298

5299

5303

5304
5305

5306

5310

5312

5313

5314
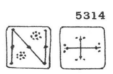

5315

5316

5317

5318
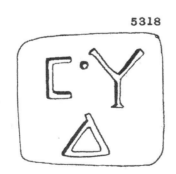

5319

5320

5323

5326

5333

5334

5338

5339
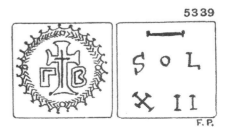

F. P.

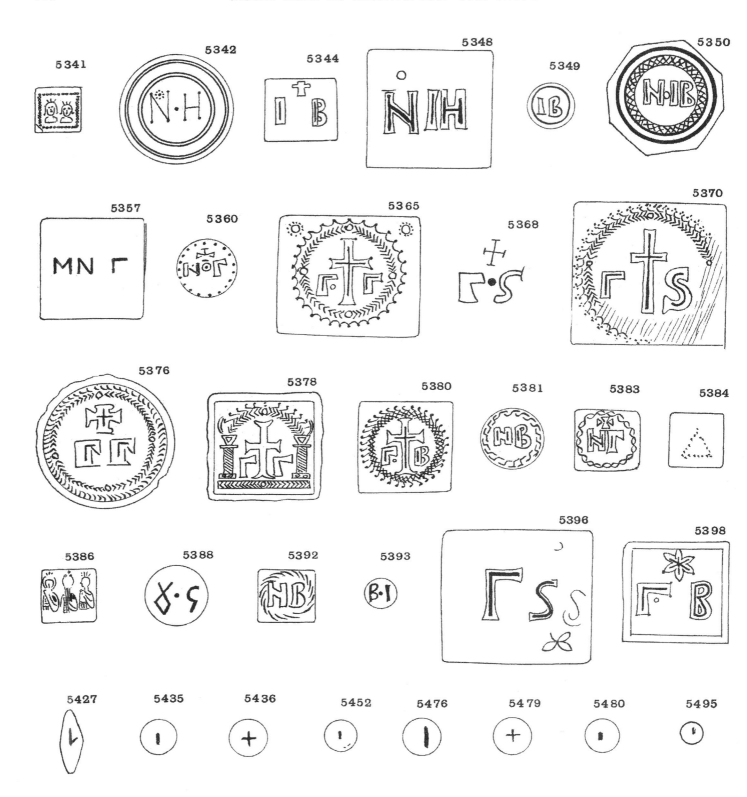

F.P.

CENTRE OF GRAVITY C. G.

HOOKS & SADDLE

4.			.3		.2		.1	b	⊙ h	−1.		−2.		−3. h		−4.
.12	.11	.10	.9	.8	.7	.6 c	−5	.4	.3	T.2	.1	⊙	−1. j	−2.
37.	.35.	. .	. .30	. . .	25.	. . d 20.	. . .	. 15.	. . .	1.0 U	. . k	.5.	. . . ⊙

No2, PSYKHARIDO STEELYARD, DETAIL OF SCALES 6/7 SIZE.

DIMENSIONS, SCALES AND MARKS OF EGYPTIAN STEELYARDS.

No.	GRAINS WEIGHT	TOTAL	INCHES SADDLE TO C.G.	S	T	U	UNIT S	T	U	SCALE VALUES SADDLE TO $=^s h$	$=^T j$	$=^u k$	READINGS ON SUSPENSORS S	T	U	SCALES. C. G. S	T	U
1	12479	19.0	6.79	3.82	2.20	.88	733	.444	.178	5.15	5.00	5.08	+.1	+3.5	+15.9	4.1	13.85	48.5
2	5892	15.5	6.70	3.27	1.84	.75	.909	.526	.224	3.63	3.50	3.41	+.12	+2.08	+8.7	3.92	11.16	35.3
3	4123	15.3	6.42	3.64	2.18	.99	1.044	.650	.273	3.45	3.36	3.6	−.69	+.43	+3.3	1.88	7.0	23.25
4	4187 +x	14 +x	{0 (8.46)	4.80 (3.64)	6.58 (1.9)	LOST (.87)	.86−.94 .91	.484 to .513}	.218	(4.0)	(4.0)	(4.0)	0	+1.72	(+7.6)	4.92	15.15	42.3
5	247	5.7		1.04	.40	.14	.698	.475	.743	1.49	.84	1.0	+.1	+.6	−.5	1.95	4.75	14.0
6	829	8.4	3.36	2.35	1.43	.56	1.67	.876	.352	1.43	1.65	1.61	−.16	+1.75	0(4)	.45	3.9	8.15 (12.15)
7	965	8.3	2.72	1.84	.56	.24	1.30	.448	.154	1.42	1.25	1.56	−.06	+.8	+.85	.57	5.6	16.5
8	5630 +x	14.4	4.38	4.23	2.22	.96	1.156	.586	.248	3.64	3.78	3.84	−.68	+1.35	+7.6	−.55	5.11	20.72
9	7970	16.2	6.20	NONE	2.20	.82	NONE	.57	.212		4.05	3.8		.6	5.7		7.45	31.2
10	3074	14.0	5.30	3.52	1.91	.82	1.0	.546	.25	3.50	3.55	3.42	−.65	+.5	+4.17	1.12	6.76	22.2
11	596	7.9	2.86	2.10	1.18	.33	.0697	.0374	.582	30.	31.5	.566	+4.	+8.	+2.5	15.5	53.	4.7
12	658	8.1	3.13	1.76	.70	.25	.895	.368	.138	1.97	1.91	1.8	0	.45	5.2	1.5	6.75	26.8
13	905	8.1	2.53	2.07	1.18	.42	.0705	.0387	.0138	29.4	30.5	31.2	−4.2	−1.5	+36	2.0	34.	189.
14	3645	14.6		3.36	1.73	.72	.952	.491	.183	3.52	3.50	4.0	−.13	+1.5	+2.5	2.5	9.7	30.3
15	1005	8.1	3.11	2.23	1.07	.32	.0748	.0344	.0100	29.8	31.1	31.9	−2.6	+4.0	−8.4	6.	58	252
16	903 +x	5.5 +x	1.51	1.78	1.36	.86 .36	.524 .0418	.0157	.0112	34.2	32.6	?	31.8	−.72	−.25	?	+16.		

	MARKS	ON	U		T		S	
1	⊦ΠΑΥΛΟϹ⊦	ƎΡƎϤΠƎΟƎϨƎПΕΜ ΜΕΝϨΕΟΕΠΕΡΕ		Ǝ Λ Ǝ Κ	Ι Ǝ Κ		Ǝ	B
2	ΨΥϤΥΑΡΙΔΟΨ	ƎƎΕΝΕΜƎΛΕΚ ΚΕΛΕΜΕΞΞΕ	⊦ΑΤΡΑꟼꟼꟼꟼΟ Ꙅ ⊦ Ǝ Κ Ϩ ⊦ Ζ Κ Ǝ Ϩ ⊦ Ʒ		−⊦	Ǝ	A
3		ΝƎΜ ΕΜ ΚΕΛΕΜ		Ǝ	−⊦ Ǝ		Ǝ	
4		Ν Μ Λ ƎΞ Ε V Μ Ν		⧻ Ι ⧻	−⊦		⊦	⫶⫶
5		X=30 V X=20 V X		X	V ΙΙΙ			
6		Κ ⊦ Ε Κ Ʒ ⊦ Ε Κ		⧻⧻=7 4=◁			Λ=1	
7		Ν V X V X V XX VX		V X	V			
8		ƎΝƎΜƎ V ƎΜƎΝƎ ƎΚ=25		Κ Ι Ε Ϩ Ʒ Ζ			Ǝ	A
9		Ν ⌣⌣⌣ Λ		⫶⫶ ⫶⫶⫶ ⫶⫶⫶				
10		Ν V X V X V XX		X V X V			V	
11	ΑΡΠΟ	A=11 Ι Θ Η Ζ Ϲ ⫽⫽⫽ Δ	ΝΜΑΚΙ ꟼ ꟼ · · ΝΜ ALL + 100			Ο Ξ Ν Μ ⫽⫽⫽ Κ Ι	
12		X V Ν V X V X V XX		V X			V	
13		Ϲ Ε Δ Γ	ꟼ ꟼ Π Ο ⫽⫽⫽ Ν Μ Λ			ΜΕΛΕΚΕΙΕ Α	
14		Ο Ʒ Ǝ Ν Ε Μ Ǝ Ζ Ε Ο ΚΕΛΕΜΕΝ	Ʒ ⊦ Ε Κ Ʒ			−⊦ Ǝ	Λ
15	A=11 Ι Θ Η Ζ Ϲ Ε Α Δ Ʒ Η		ΠΟ Ξ Ν Μ Α Κ Ι ꟼ ꟼ Π Ο Ξ Ν ALL + 100			Ξ Ε Ν Ε Μ Ε Λ Ε Κ Ε Ι Ϲ	
16	ΗΡΨΔΟΥ	Η Ζ Ϲ Ε Δ	⫽⫽⫽⫽⫽⫽ ⫽⫽⫽⫽⫽⫽ Ν Μ			Π Ο Ξ Ν Μ Α Κ	

F.P.

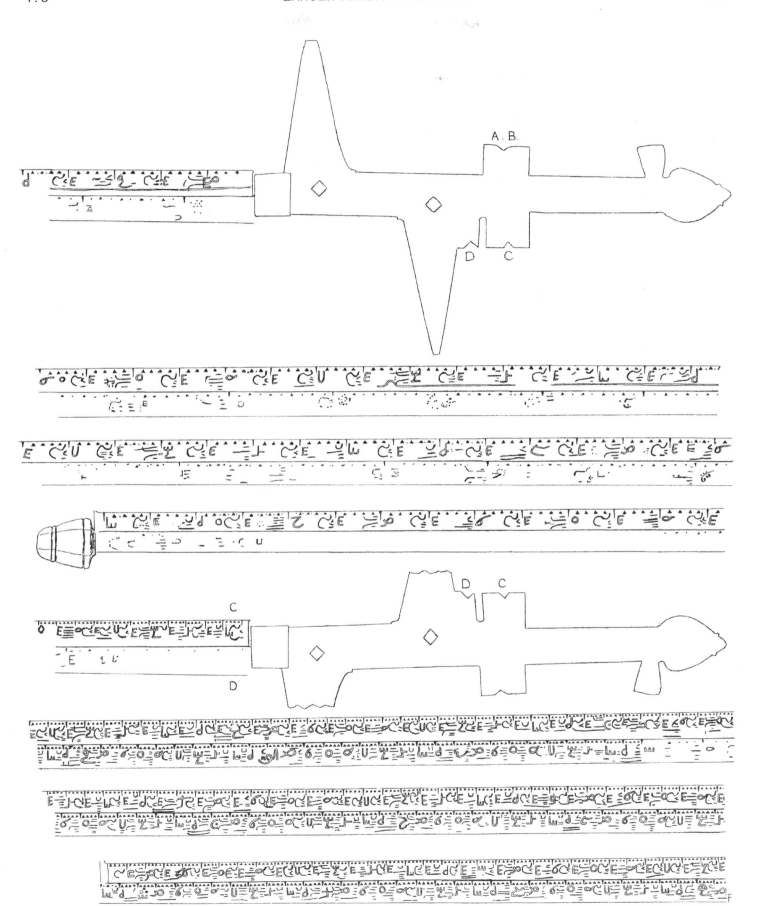

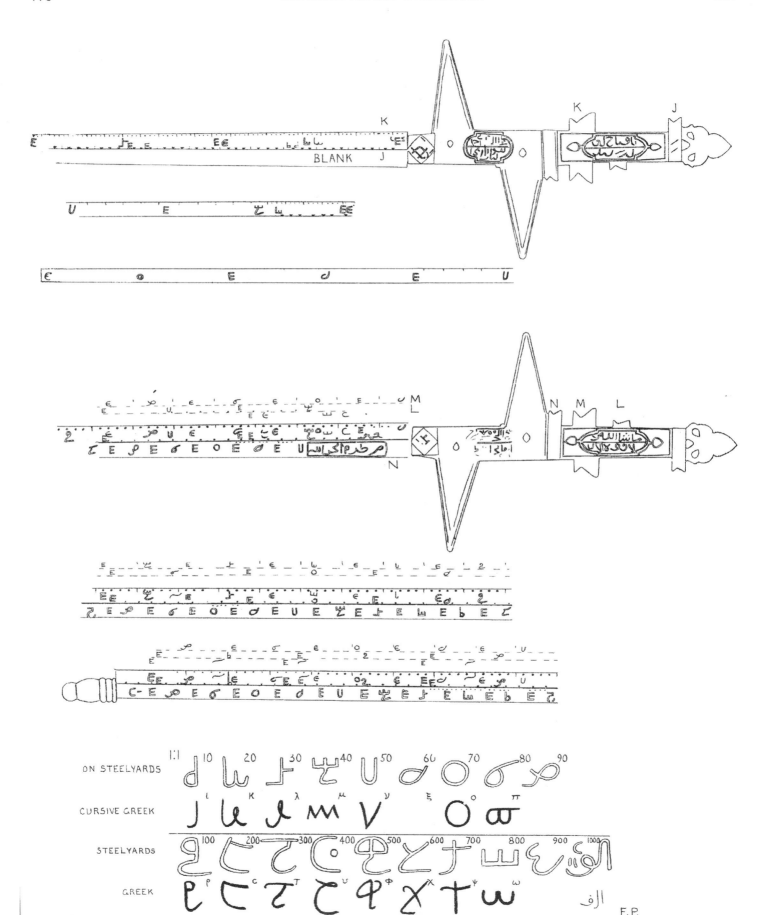

F.P.

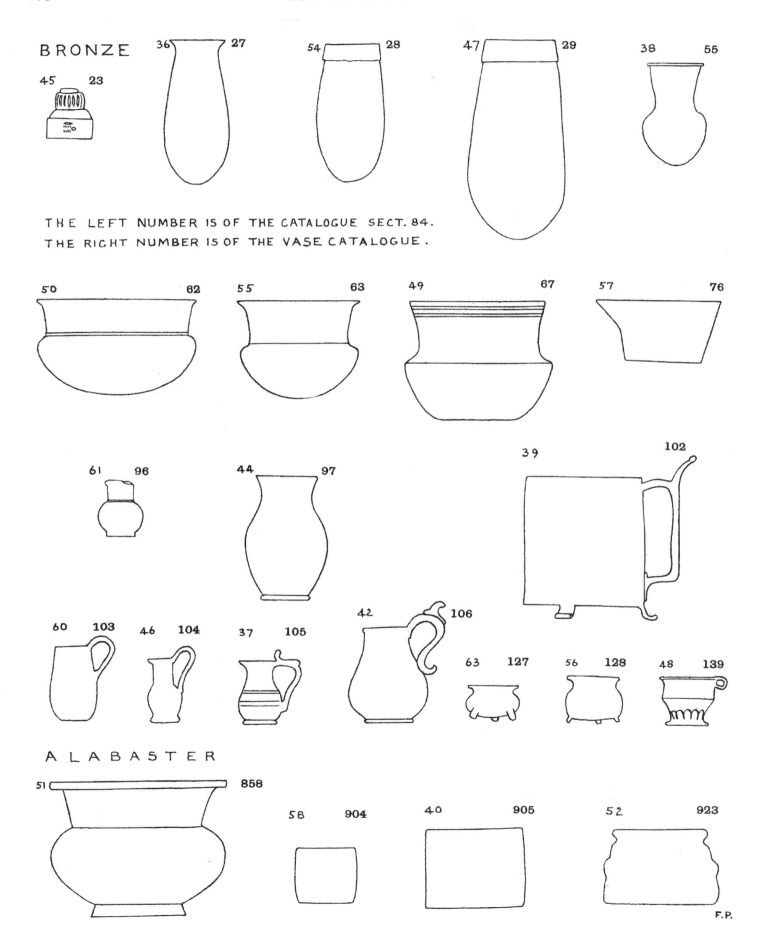

BRONZE

45　　23

36　27　　54　28　　47　29　　38　55

THE LEFT NUMBER IS OF THE CATALOGUE SECT. 84.
THE RIGHT NUMBER IS OF THE VASE CATALOGUE.

50　　　　82　　55　　　　63　　49　　　　67　　57　　　　76

61　96　　44　　97　　39　　　　102

60　103　　46　104　　37　105　　42　　106　　63　127　　56　128　　48　139

ALABASTER

51　　　　858　　58　　904　　40　　　905　　52　　　923

F.P.

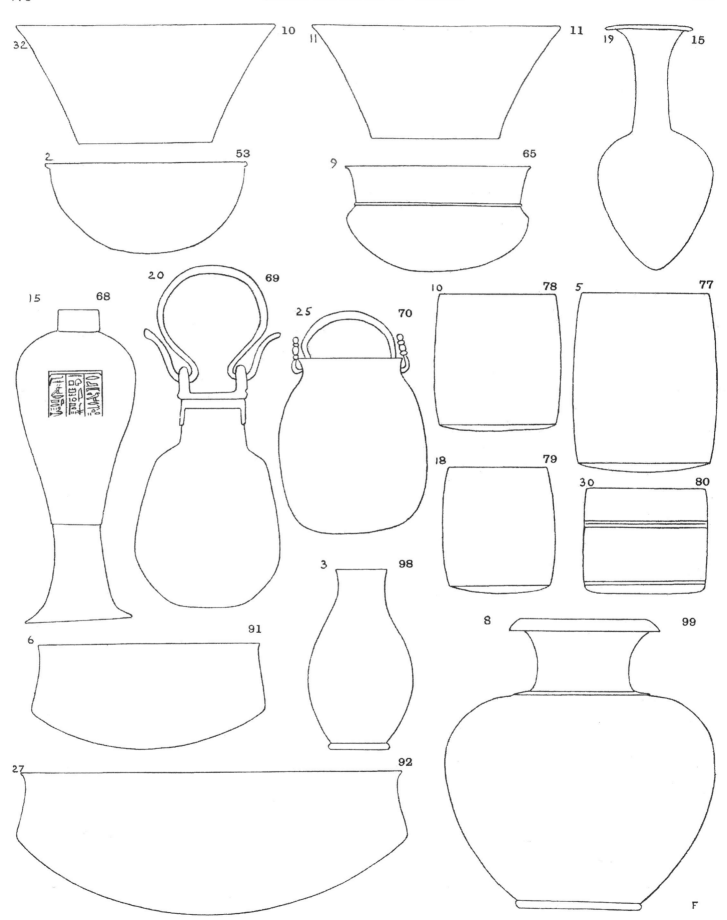

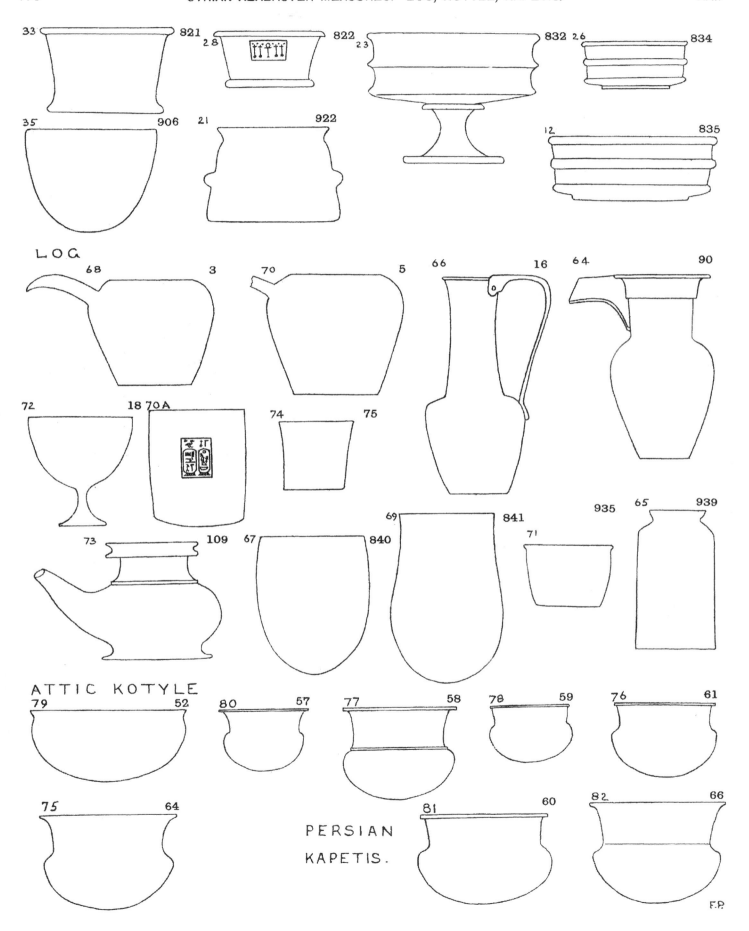

LOG

ATTIC KOTYLE

PERSIAN

KAPETIS.

F.P.

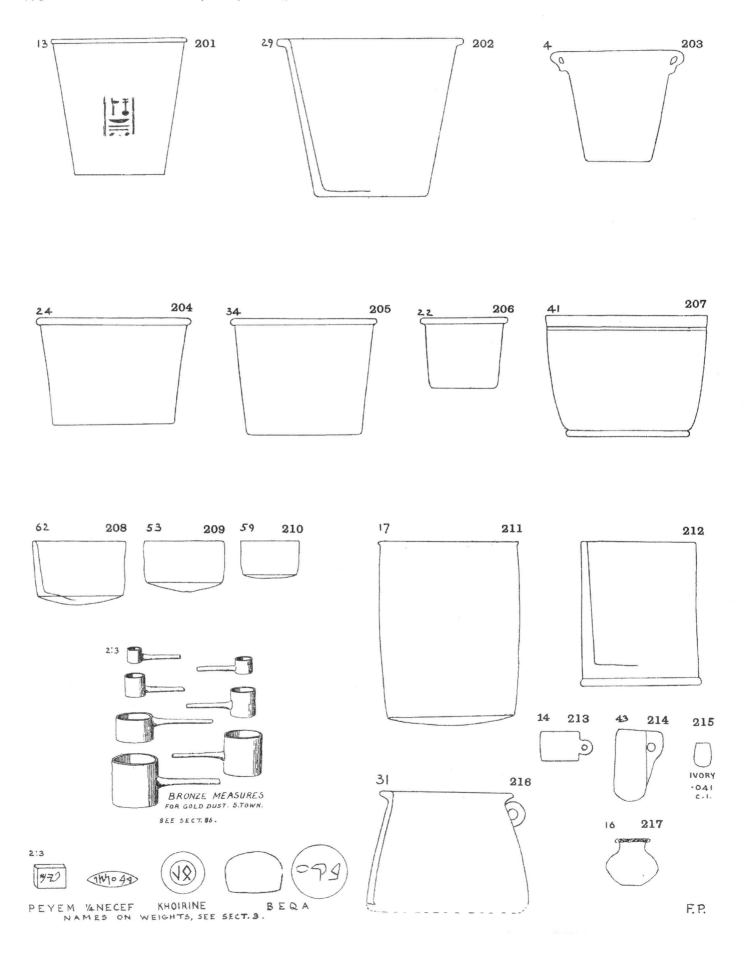

BRONZE MEASURES
FOR GOLD DUST. S.TOWN.
SEE SECT. 86.

2:3

PEYEM ¼ NECEF   KHOIRINE   BEQA
NAMES ON WEIGHTS, SEE SECT. 3.

F.P.

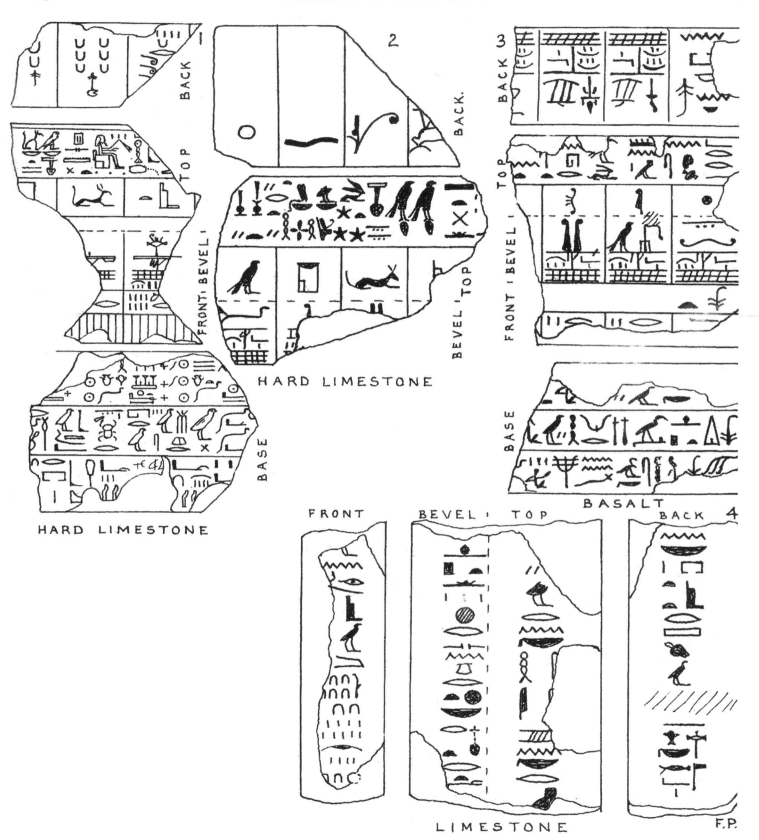

HARD LIMESTONE

HARD LIMESTONE

BASALT

LIMESTONE

F.P.

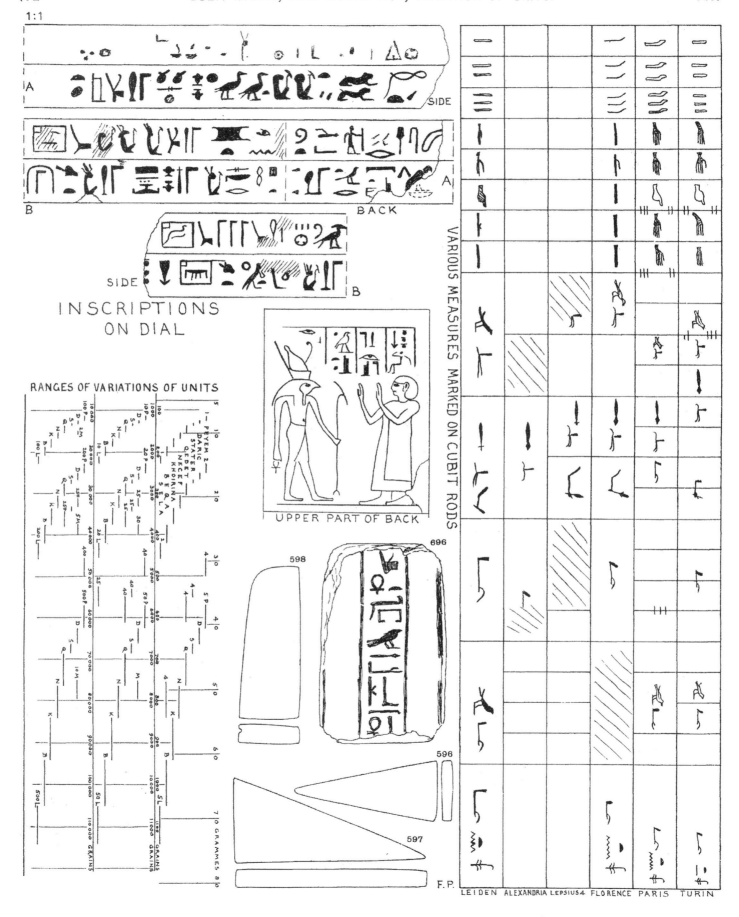

1:1

A SIDE

B BACK A

SIDE B

INSCRIPTIONS
ON DIAL

RANGES OF VARIATIONS OF UNITS

UPPER PART OF BACK

598   696

596

597

F.P.

VARIOUS MEASURES MARKED ON CUBIT RODS

LEIDEN ALEXANDRIA LEPSIUS4 FLORENCE PARIS TURIN

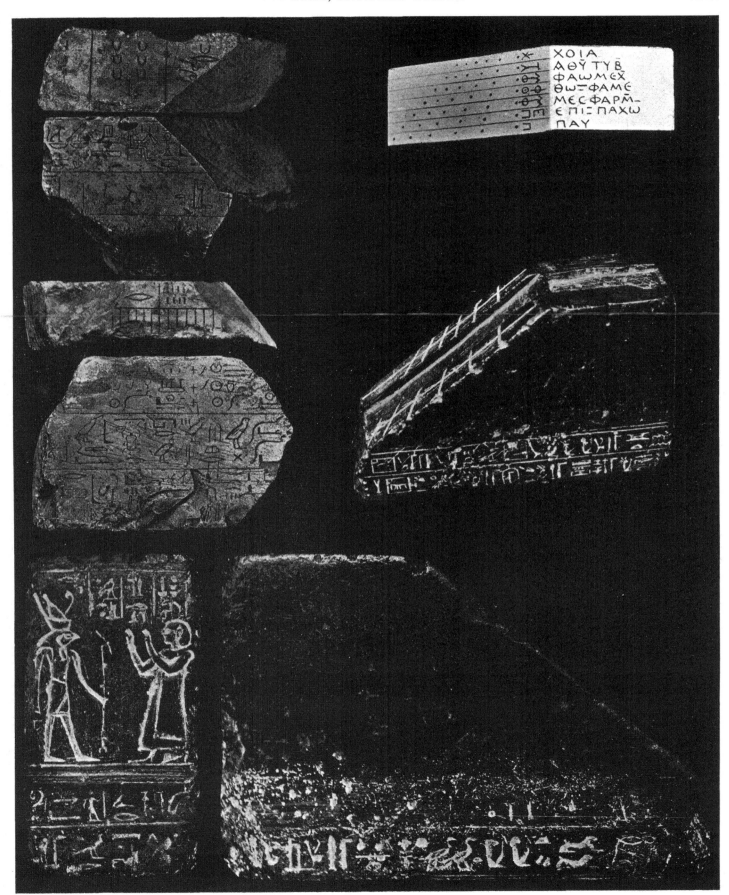

ΧΟΙΑ
ΑΘῩΤΥΒ̄
ΦΑѠΜΕΧ
ΘѠΞΦΑΜΕ
ΜΕΣΦΑΡΜ̄
ΕΠΙΞΠΑΧѠ
ΠΑΥ

PEYEM 112-125 GRS.

NO.	MATERIAL	FORM	GRS.	X	UNIT	DETAIL
2001	CARNEL.	23	28·0	1/4	112·0	PIERCED
2	BK·QTZOSE	9	56865	50	113·7	
3	BK·JASP.	314	28·5	1/4	114·0	PIERCED
4	BK·QTZOSE	659	1369·3	12	·1	
			171200·	1500	·1	SEE K.
5	GY·SY.	238	11416·	100	·2	
6	BK·QTZOSE	2	4571·9	40	·3	
7	GY·QTZOSE	2	4573·2	40	·3	
8	BK·SY.	11	5715·	50	·3	
9	BAS·	33	572·	1/2	·4	
2010	BRECCIA	935	2288·	2	·4	
1	GY·QTZOSE	392	2288·1	20	·4	
2	BK·QTZOSE	2	11445·	100	·4	
3	GY·SY.	9	4580·0	40	·5	
4	BAS.	23	5726·5	50	·5	
5	LIM.	497	57·3	1/2	·6	
6	ALAB.	15	573·1	5	·6	MEM. GLASS
7	BAS.	642	1834·	16	·6	IIII, -10 XII DYN
8	RED GRAN	238	22930·	200	·6	
9	FOS.WOOD	9	4588·0	40	·7	
2020	BAS.	133	28·7	1/4	·8	
1	BAS.	264	57·4	1/2	·8	
2	DURITE	22	2295·8	20	·8	
3	SERP.	558	22964·	20	·8	∧ QU. XII
4	BAS.	258	11485·	100	·8	
5	BAS.	656	1379·3	12	·9	OIIIII V
6	BK·QTZOSE	923	2298·4	20	·9	
7	″ ″	105	5745·8	50	·9	
8	BAS.	65	230·0	2	115·0	O I´ VI
9	HAEM.	497	459·9	4	·0	XVIII
2030	ALAB.	26	575·	5	·0	-15
			5749·3	50	·0	SEE Q
1	LIM. QU.	646	6900·	60	·0	III -450 XII
2	HAEM.	499	2303·	2	·1	
3	GY.SY.	10	46060·	40	·1	
4	BK.QTZITE	313	46054·	400	·1	
5	LIM.	38	115·2	1	·2	
6	BAS.	372	1152·3	10	·2	
7	LIM. QU	64	1382·2	12	·2	III XII
8	BK.QTZOSE	53	1383·0	12	·2	
9	QTZ.	81	230·6	2	·3	MEM.GLASS
			576·7	5	·3	SEE Q
2040	BAS.	254	11533·	100	·3	
			46149	40	·4	SEE K
1	RED SY.	345	5768·2	50	·4	
2	DURITE	618	231·1	2	·5	O I VI
2A	LIM.	916	462·0	4	·5	KOM SULT. VI
3	BAS.	125	1155·0	10	·5	
4	LIM.	26	28·9	1/4	·6	
5	LIM.	422	925·0	8	·6	MEM.GLASS
6	LIM.	BALL	1387·0	12	·6	OIIIII -10
7	GRAN.	11	4630·2	40	·7	
8	BK.QTZOSE	877	463·4	4	·8	
9	GY.SY.	20	1157·7	10	·8	
2050	QTZITE	54	4630·5	40	·8	
1	LIM.	653	6950·	60	·8	III -500
2	Y.LIM.	495	29·0	1/4	116·0	XVIII
3	BK.WT.QTZ	10	4639·0	40	·0	
4	BR.QTZITE	347	46420·	400	·0	
			580·5	5	·1	SEE Q
5	ALAB.	656	1392·0	12	·1	QUFT IV
6	BAS.	11	2322·3	20	·1	
7	BAS	11	23250·	20	·2	
8	RED GRAN.	311	46470·	400	·2	-2
9	BAS	311	4653·1	40	·3	
			582·1	5	·4	SEE Q

No.	MATERIAL	FORM	GRS.	X	UNIT	DETAIL
2060	BK·QTZOSE	7?	46565·	40	116·4	
1	GY·SY.	921	11640·	100	·4	KAHUN
2	Y·LIM.	656	466·1	4	·5	IV
3	BAS.	802	1164·8	10	·5	MEM. XVIII
4	LIM. ABYD.	63	1400·	12	·7	III -15
5	LIM.	267	116·8	1	·8	
6	DIORITE	65	1870·2	16	·9	IIII VI
7	HAEM.	49	117·0	1	117·0	SYRIA XVIII
8	BAS.	653	2339·6	20	·0	MEM. V
9	GY.SY.	2	4685·8	40	·1	
2070	GY.QTZOSE	8	4686·0	40	·1	
1	Y.BK.SERP.	691	469·0	4	·2	ROUGH XII
2	GY.QTZOSE	8	4690·3	40	·2	
3	BAS.	358	11721·	100	·2	
4	BAS.	358	938·3	8	·3	MEM.GLASS
5	BK.QTZ.	10	5863·0	50	·3	
6	GY.SY.	346	4695·0	40	·4	
7	GY.QTZOSE	54	4696·6	40	·4	
8	″ ″	54	4696·9	40	·4	
9	BK. ″	105	23480·	200	·4	-4
2080	BAS.	12	1175·0	10	·5	
1	GY.SY.	54	2352·3	20	·6	
2	HAEM.	492	117·7	1	·7	XVIII
3	BAS.	313	117·7	1	·7	
4	GY.QTZOSE	10	4709·4	40	·7	
5	BAS.	11	5884·	50	·7	
6	CHLORITE	64	117·8	1	·8	⊐
7	GY.QTZOSE	558	5890·	50	·8	GHUROB
8	LIM.	442	235·9	2	·9	
			589·7	5	·9	
9	BAS.	437	1179·1	10	·9	
2090	GY.SY.	31	1179·3	10	·9	
1	HAEM.	49	236·1	2	118·0	-20? XVIII
2	GY.QTZOSE	54	2360·4	20	·0	MERENPT.
3	BK. ″	10	5898·	50	·0	
4	QTZITE	19	1180·4	10	·0	
5	BAS.	442	2366·5	20	·3	
6	BAS.	254	29·6	1/4	·4	MERENPTH.
7	BAS.	BALL	1184·0	10	·4	
8	BK.QTZOS	53	1184·8	10	·5	
9	ALAB.	439	4738·5	40	·5	
2100	BAS.	419	5926·	50	·5	
1	OBSID.	928	59·3	1/2	·6	
			593·2	5	·6	SEE Q
2	BAS.	353	2372·4	20	·6	
3	BAS.	452	5932·	50	·6	
			593·6	5	·7	SEE Q
4	BAS.	367	1187·6	10	·8	
5	BAS.	22	119·0	1	119·0	
6	BAS.	424	1190·2	10	·0	
7	BK.QTZOSE	54	5946·	50	·0	
8	BAS.	313	23800·	200	·0	-180
9	BAS.	326	4763·0	40	·1	
2110	QTZITE	9	4765·8	40	·1	
1	RED GRAN·	63	47700·	400	·2	-270 KAH
			5967·	5	·2	SEE Q
2	BK.QTZOSE	9	5967·	50	·3	
3	HAEM.	399	59·7	1/2	·4	
4	GY.SY.	9	4775·9	40	·4	
5	HAEM·	65	119·5	1	·5	
6	″ ″	482	477·9	4	·5	
			597·7	5	·5	SEE Q
			598·1	5	·6	SEE Q
7	BK.QTZOSE	9	5979·	50	·6	
8	GY.GRAN.	439	47844·	400	·6	
9	LIM.	141	1197·3	10	·7	
2120	BK.SY.	352	4788·0	40	·7	
	BAS.	48	5983·	50	·7	MERNPT.XVIII

No.	MATERIAL	FORM	GRS.	X	UNIT	DETAIL
2122	BAS.	38	1197·9	10	119·8	
3	HAEM.	436	119·9	1	·9	
4	GYPSUM	535	2390·	20	·9	-10
5	BK.QTZOSE	8	5994·	50	·9	
6	ALAB	63	30·0	1/4	120·0	
7	LIM.	265	240·1	2	·0	
8	ALAB	625	240·1	2	·0	MERENPTH
			600·1	5	·0	SEE Q
9	BAS.	20	24003·	20	·0	
2130	HAEM.	491	240·2	2	·1	XVIII
1	ALAB.	496	600·4	5	·1	AMARNA ″
2	″	63	481·0	4	·2	II XII
3	BK.SY.	125	481·2	4	·3	
4	BK.QTZOSE	55	2405·3	20	·3	
5	BAS.	314	30·1	1/4	·4	
6	ALAB.	264	60·2	1/2	·4	
			6019·	50	·4	SEE Q
7	BK.QTZOSE	558	6019·	50	·4	
8	HAEM.	874	120·5	1	·5	ROUGH
*9	ALAB.	203	120·6	1	·6	
2140	BAS.	237	4825·5	40	·6	
1	BK.QTZOSE	54	2413·2	20	·7	
2	GY.SY.	54	4829·0	40	·7	
			604·0	5	·8	SEE Q
*3	LIM.	63	2417·0	20	·8	RETABEH
4	GY.MARB.	32	604·3	5	·9	
5	BR.QTZITE	26	24190·	200	·9	-4
6	BAS.	31	1209·6	10	121·0	MERENPTH.
7	BAS.	351	1210·2	10	·0	
8	CHLORITE	646	2420·	20	·0	-20 XII
9	ALAB.	654	2420·	20	·0	-2 VI
2150	LIM.	442	2422·3	20	·1	
1	BK.QTZOSE	54	2422·4	20	·1	
2	BK.SY.	27	48476·	400	·2	RAONKH IV
3	Y.LIM.	498	242·6	2	·3	GEBLEYN XVIII
4	GN.QTZOSE	11	4853·5	40	·3	
5	BAS.	328	24260·	200	·3	
6	BAS.	327	243·0	2	·5	
7	LIM.	16	486·0	4	·5	QUFT
8	BRECCIA	80	1215·1	10	·5	XVIII
9	ALAB.	313	2430·3	20	·5	
2160	BR.QTZITE	14	24300·	200	·5	-40
1	BONE	46	152·	1/8	·6	
			607·9	5	·6	
2	ALAB.	483	1215·8	10	·6	AMARNA,XVIII
3	BK.QTZOSE	56	1216·0	10	·6	
4	LIM.	56	12160·	100	·6	-9
5	BAS.	652	608·7	5	·7	VI
6	BK.SY.	12	4872·7	40	·8	
			6088·2	50	·8	SEE B
7	BK.QTZOSE	10	6092·9	50	·8	
8	BAS.	102	61·0	1/2	122·0	
9	BAS.	436	244·0	2	·0	
2170	HAEM.	425	122·1	1	·1	MARATHUS
1	GY.PORPHY	8	4885·4	40	·1	
2	BK.SERP.	261	61·1	1/2	·2	
3	BAS.	256	122·2	1	·2	
4	BR.QTZITE	435	24450·	200	·2	-30
5	BR.LIM.	358	489·4	4	·3	
6	BAS.	348	12228·	100	·3	
7	BK.QTZOSE	31	15·3	1/8	·4	
8	Y.LIM.	38	122·5	1	·5	
9	GN.PORPHY	311	612·4	5	·5	TARTUS
2180	BAS.	64	4900·	40	·5	-35
1	BK.SY.	12	4901·6	40	·5	
2	BAS.	367	6131·	50	·6	
*3	GY.QTZOSE	10	6132·	50	·6	
4	SERP.	12	1227·	10	·7	-2

ABBREVIATIONS
BASalt (Grown) | BRown | CHALCedony | GLazed | GRANite | JASPer | LT. Light
ABydos | BK. black | BRS breasts | DK. dark | GLS. Glass | GY. gray | KA hun | MARBle
ALABaster | BLue | CARNelian | FOSsil | GN. green | HAEMatite | LIMestone | MEMphis

No.	MATERIAL	FORM	GRS.	X	UNIT	DETAIL
2185	RED QTZITE	558	1227·3	10	122·7	AMARNA XVIII
6	BAS.	325	6133·	50	·7	
7	GY.SY.	237	12268·	100	·7	MERNPTAH
8	BAS.	254	122·8	1	·8	
9	GY.SY.	367	6143·	50	·9	
2190	BK.STEA·	232	123·0	1	123·0	
1	BK.PORPHᵧ	11	6150·	50	·0	
2	BR.QTZITE	367	24600	200	·0	−20
2A	GY.LIM.	497	1231·0	10	·0	24·V·21
			6153·	50	·1	SEE B
3	BAS.	262	154·	1/8	·2	
4	BAS.	203	61·6	1/2	·2	
5	BAS.	261	61·6	1/2	·2	
6	BAS.	131	123·2	1	·2	
7	LIM.	920	493·0	4	·2	
8	ALAB.	12	1232·1	10	·2	
·9	GY.SY.	9	6158·	50	·2	KAHUN XII
2200	GY.SY.	9	6167·	50	·3	" XII
1	HAEM.	452	617·	1/2	·4	MARATHUS
2	LIM.	916	617·	5	·4	−2
3	BK.QTZOSE	11	6168·	50	·4	
4	BAS.	367	2467·4	20	·4	
5	BAS.	54	24697·	20	·5	
6	BK.QTZOSE	10	4941·3	40	·5	
7	HAEM.	484	123·6	1	·6	XVIII
8	BR.SY.	10	4946·0	40	·6	
9	ALAB.	801	123·7	1	·7	XVIII
2210	DIORITE	64	123·7	1	·7	XII
1	BK.QTZOSE	14	618·8	5	·7	
2	BAS.	40	1236·7	10	·7	MERNPTAH
3	GY.QTZITE	384	123700	1000	·7	−800
4	CHLORITE	652	495·4	4	·8	○○ XII
5	HAEM.	399	619·0	5	·8	MARATHUS
6	" RED	493	619·	5	·8	−7
7	BAS.	372	619·2	5	·8	
8	BAS.	392	1237·6	10	·8	
9	WT.QTZITE	364	24760	200	·8	
2220	BAS.	358	2479·0	20	·9	
1	CHLORITE	805	31·0	1/4	124·0	
2	BAS.	33	15·5	1/8	·0	
3	LIM.	482	620·2	5	·0	KARNAK XVIII
3A	GY.LIM.	797	372·2	3	·1	24·V·21
4	BAS.	336	1241·5	10	·1	
5	ALAB.	894	2483·0	20	·1	
6	BK.QTZOSE	10	4962·5	40	·1	
7	"	54	4964·4	40	·1	
8	BAS.	352	6206·	50	·1	
9	GY.GRAN.	422	49660·	400	·1	−20
2230	LIM.	65	620·8	5	·2	QUFT VI
0A	DK·GY·LIM.	498	621·0	5	·2	24·V·21
1	LIM.	40	621·3	5	·2	
2	HARD LIM.	652	1242·5	10	·2	ABYD. VI
3	BK.QTZOSE	54	4967·1	40	·2	
4	BAS.	358	12420·	100	·2	−700
5	BAS.	656	2487·	2	·3	I IV
6	BAS.	653	24868·	20	·3	GHUROB IV
*7	LIM.	254	124·4	1	·4	
8	ALAB.	38	248·9	2	·4	
9	BAS.	265	1243·7	10	·4	
2240	BAS.	33	2488·	20	·4	−2
1	LIM.	881	2488·0	20	·4	MERNPTAH
2	BAS.	18	2488·5	20	·4	
3	BR.SY.	313	4974·7	40	·4	
4	BAS.	367	1246·2	10	·6	
5	LIM.	913	498·7	4	·7	
6	GY.SY.	10	4996·8	40	·9	MERENPTAH
7	ALAB.	802	31·3	1/4	125·2	MERENPTAH

DARIC 124–133 GRS M=MINA

No.	MATERIAL	FORM	GRS.	X	UNIT	DETAIL
2248	BAS.	446	7465·	M	124·4	−5
9	SERP.	26	41·5	1/3	·5	
2250	ALAB.	805	3112·0	25	·5	−·4 XVIII
1	SARD	628	10·4	1/12	·8	
2	HAEM.	493	41·6	1/3	·8	XVIII
3	BAS.	803	3745·0	30	·8	XVIII
4	GY.SY.	8	6242·	50	·8	KAHUN, XXIII
5	HAEM.	2	624·6	5	·9	MERNPTAH
6	GN.SERP.	33	62·5	1/2	125·0	
7	LIM.	364	62·5	1/2	·0	
8	HAEM.	107	62·5	1/2	·0	GHUROB
9	"	482	125·0	1	·0	XVIII
2260	BAS.	426	1250·0	10	·0	
*1	LIM.	192	1250·2	10	·0	
2	BAS.	331	3751·4	30	·0	
3	BK QTZOSE	63	2501·8	20	·1	XXIII
4	GY.SY.	54	3128·1	25	·1	XXIII
5	ALAB.	802	31·3	1/4	·2	MERNPTAH
6	HAEM.	895	125·2	1	·2	TARTUS, XVIII
			3758·7	30	·2	SEE B
7	ALAB.	795	626·4	5	·3	QUFT, XVIII
8	CHLORITE	649	3133·9	25	·3	
			3760·	30	·3	SEE B
9	LIM.	263	20·9	1/6	·4	
2270	ALAB.	264	125·4	1	·4	QUFT
1	LIM.	16	2508·	20	·4	MEM·GLASS,−15
2	PINK LIM.	38	1253·9	10	·4	QUFT
3	BR.SERP.	922	502·0	4	·5	
4	BK.QT ZOSE	54	6279·	50	·6	XXIII
5	BK.SY.	5	6280·	50	·6	XXIII
6	BK QTZOSE	653	12560·	100	·6	−140 XXIII
			1864·8	15	·6	SEE K
7	CHLORITE	165	41·9	1/3	·7	
8	BAS.	54	1256·8	10	·7	
			2011·8	16	·7	SEE B
9	BAS.	54	2550·3	20	·7	
2280	GN.SERP.	891	629·1	5	·8	
1	ALAB.	192	629·3	5	·8	
2	BAS.	422	12585·	10	·8	
3	BAS.	358	6290·	50	·8	−20
4	BRECCIA	79	629·8	5	·9	XVIII
5	HARD LIM	797	2518·8	20	·9	QUFT XVIII
6	BK.SY.	9	3146·6	25	·9	XXIII
			3776·3	30	·9	SEE K
7	LIM.	26	21·0	1/6	126·0	
8	DURITE	65	21·0	1/6	·0	XII
9	BAS.	356	42·0	1/3	·0	
2290	BAS.	265	42·0	1/3	·0	
1	HAEM.	402	63·0	1/2	·0	
1A	ALAB.	494	126·	1	·0	MEM−15
1B	"	433	126·	1	·0	MEM −2
2	BAS.	356	629·9	5	·0	
3	ALAB.	937	2519·2	20	·0	
4	LIM.	436	126·1	1	·1	
5	ALAB.	352	252·2	2	·1	
6	BAS.	38	2521·8	20	·1	
			3783·5	30	·1	SEE K
			3783·5	30	·1	SEE B
			3784·6	30	·1	SEE B
7	ALAB.	423	126·	1	·2	DELTA
8	HAEM.	143	252·5	2	·2	MERNPTAH
9	BK.STEA.	64	505·	4	·2	−5 XII
2300	LIM.	353	1261·9	10	·2	
1	BAS.	63	1262·	10	·2	−12 XXIII
2	BAS.	352	2523·2	20	·2	
3	BK QTZOSE BALL		3786·0	30	·2	XXIII

No.	MATERIAL	FORM	GRS.	X	UNIT	DETAIL
2304	BAS.	192	631·8	5	126·3	−·2
5	BRECCIA	801	631·8	5	·3	HOLED XVIII
5A	LIM.	916	1263·0	10	·3	KoM SULTAN,VI
6	BK.QTZOSE	54	2526·0	20	·3	XXIII
7	HAEM.	483	1263·9	10	·4	TARTUS, XVIII
			31600·	250	·4	SEE N
8	HAEM.	49	632·8	5	·5	ΦIX XVIII
9	BAS.	23	42·2	1/3	·6	
2310	GN.SERP.	31	42·2	1/3	·6	OVAL
1	HAEM. ABYD	496	633·2	5	·6	AOHMES I
2	BK.QTZOSE	54	3164·8	25	·6	XXIII
3	FLINT	9	3796·2	30	·6	XXIII
3A	RED LIM.	488	380·0	3	·7	
4	BAS.	238	2534·0	20	·7	
			3801·	30	·7	SEE B
5	BAS.	369	7600·	M	·7	−8
6	GY.SY.	165	12674·	100	·7	
7	LIM. KAHUN	63	25350·	200	·7	−150 XII
			30400·	4M	·7	SEE Q
			30402·	4M	·7	SEE Q
8	LIM.	458	253·6	2	·8	MEM.
9	ALAB.	427	253·7	2	·8	
2320	Y.BK.SERP.	63	507·1	4	·8	XII
1	BRECCIA	378	6340·	5	·8	
2	BK.SY.	428	12682·	10	·8	
3	BAS.	238	25368·	20	·8	
4	GY.GRAN.	33	76100·	10M	·8	
5	ALAB.	22	423·	1/3	·9	
6	"	33	423·	1/3	·9	
7	BK.JASP.	529	126·9	1	·9	KARNAK
7A	LIM.	9156	507·6	4	·9	KoM SULTAN,VI
8	BK.QTZOSE	55	2537·8	20	·9	XXIII
9	BAS.	357	38069·	30	·9	
9A	SANDST.	59	6347·	50	·9	ZET, ABYD.601
2330	Y.LIM.	493	127·0	1	127·0	XVIII
1	ALAB.	498	1270·	10	·0	−2·2
2	GY.QTZOSE	10	3174·0	25	·0	XXIII
3	GN.QTZ.	146	15240·0	2M	·0	−30
4	HAEM.	49	127·1	1	·1	XVIII
5	LIM.	442	127·1	1	·1	
5A	BAS.	165	127·1	1	·1	MEM.
6	BAS.	19	635·5	5	·1	
7	BAS.	339	635·5	5	·1	
8	BK.SY.	422	635·5	5	·1	PEBBLE BORED
9	GY.SERP.	426	6356·	5	·1	
2340	LIM.	40	1270·9	10	·1	
1	DIORITE	9	3178·6	25	·1	XXIII
			30510·	4M	·1	SEE N
2	GY.GRAN.	331	76272·	10M	·1	
2A	AMAZONITE	448	21·2	1/6	·2	
3	HAEM.	646	127·2	1	·2	XVIII
4	GY.SERP.	493	127·2	1	·2	XVIII
5	BAS.	367	6362·	5	·2	
6	FOS·WOOD	9	3178·8	25	·2	XXIII
7	QTZITE	10	3816·1	30	·2	XXIII
			7633·	M	·2	SEE N
8	BAS.		7634·	M	·2	
			3820·	30	·3	SEE B
9	BK.QTZOSE	448	7639·	M	·3	
			30545·	4M	·3	SEE N
2350	ALAB.	63	509·6	4	·4	ABYD VI
1	BAS.	352	1274·2	10	·4	
2	BAS.	357	6370·	5D	·4	−15
3	BAS.	427	7642·	M	·4	−3
4	BAS.	446	7646·	M	·4	−3
5	BAS.	446	7647·	M	·4	−12
6	HAEM.	895	127·5	1	·5	TARTUS, XVIII
7	ALAB.	238	127·5	1	·5	

MERNPTH. XIX　　NAQada　　PEBble　　QUft　　SCHST. schist　STEAtite　　VN veined　　GRS. original
dyn palace Mem. NUM mulitic　PORPH yry　ROman　　SERP entine　SYenite　　VOLcanic ash　weight of stone
METAMorphic　OBSIDian　QTZ quartz　SANDSTone　SILICate　　VARiegated White　　−n loss of stone
m 2308 &c, ΦIX = photograph in pl. IX (frontispiece), and similarly ΦXVI and XXVI.

No.	MATERIAL	FORM	GRS.	X	UNIT	DETAIL
2358	BRECCIA	802	255·0	2	127·5	
9	ALAB.	496	637·5	5	·5	AMARN-7 »
2360	LIM.	63	637·6	5	·5	MEM. VI
1	BAS.	422	2550·0	20	·5	
2	BAS.	54	2550·3	20	·5	XXIII
3	BK·QTZOSE	54	3187·1	25	·5	XXIII
4	BAS.	439	6374·	50	·5	
5	GY.SY.	357	6376·	50	·5	
6	LIM.	649	15300	2M	·5	-320
7	GY.SILIC.	415	127·6	1	·6	
8	ALAB.	426	637·8	5	·6	KARNAK
9	BAS.	378	1275·8	10	·6	
			3828·	30	·6	SEE B
2370	QTZITE	14	6380·	50	·6	MERNPT. -50
1	LIM.	38	6380·	50	·6	-12
			31900	250	·6	SEE N
2	HAEM.	52	127·7	1	·7	XVIII
3	HAEM.	48	255·5	2	·7	XVIII
4	BAS.	656	1277·0	10	7	IV
5	LIM.	314	21·3	1/6	·8	
6	ALAB.	38	639·1	5	·8	MERNPTH
7	BAS.	368	1278·5	10	·8	
8	BAS.	448	6390·	5D	·8	
9	HAEM.	493	85·3	4/6	·9	IIII
2380	ALAB.	426	127·9	1	·9	MERNPTH
1	BAS.	14	639·7	5	·9	
2	QTZITE	9	3196·8	25	·9	XXIII
3	BK·QTZOSE	9	3198·4	25	·9	XXIII
4	"	54	3836·5	30	·9	XXIII
4A	" SKEW	63	46040·	36	·9	Z. ABYD,510
5	HAEM.	526	128·0	1	128·0	XVIII
5A	"	49	256·	2	·0	-20
6	BAS.	427	1280·3	10	·0	
7	LIM.	916	1279·8	10	·0	KAHUN XII
8	BAS.	238	2559·6	20	·0	
9	BK·QTZOSE	16	3839·0	30	·0	XXIII
2390	HAEM.	499	128·1	1	·1	XVIII
1	BAS.	33	256·2	2	·1	
2	BAS.	352	2560·8	20	·1	
3	BK·QTZOSE	54	3542·1	30	·1	RIQQEH XXIII
4	"	54	6407·	50	·1	XXIII
5	ALAB.	358	128·2	1	·2	MEM.
6	BAS.	237	640·8	5	·2	
7	ALAB.	790	641·1	5	·2	XVIII
8	BR·SERP.	64	1282·	10	·2	TAHARQA -10
9	LIM.	925	3846·	30	·2	MALTA
2400	BK.BAS.	314	25650·	200	·2	-150
1	HAEM.	439	513·2	4	·3	MARATHUS
2	BAS.	426	641·4	5	·3	MEM.
3	LIM.ROUGH	922	1283·0	10	·3	
4	BK·QTZOSE	875	6418·	50	·3	ZET ABYD,121
5	ALAB.	30	64·2	1/2	·4	
6	BAS.	395	128·4	1	·4	
★7	ALAB.	802	128·4	1	·4	QUFT XVIII
8	"	426	642·2	5	·4	
9	BAS.	365	1284·1	10	·4	
2410	BAS.	364	12840·	100	·4	-40
1	BK.STEA.	898	128·5	1	·5	TYRE XVIII
2	HAEM.	499	128·5	1	·5	MEM. XVIII
3	LIM.	931	514·2	4	·5	
4	LIM.	5	25700	200	·5	φIX -40 SPARTA XVIII
5	HAEM.	DUCK	2571·2	20	·6	
6	BAS.	14	2572·7	20	·6	MERNPTH
7	CHLORITE	65	2571·7	20	·6	S

No.	MATERIAL	FORM	GRS.	X	UNIT	DETAIL
2417A	BK.QTZOSE	54	6434·	5D	128·6	
8	Y.BK.SERR	149	42·9	1/3	·7	
9	BAS.	269	42·9	1/3	·7	
2420	GY.SIL.	63	257·4	2	·7	
1	BAS.	355	257·5	2	·7	
2	LIM.	393	643·4	5	·7	SAIS
3	ALAB.	14	643·7	5	·7	
			3859·7	30	·7	SEE B
4	BK·QTZOSE	10	6434·	50	·7	XXIII
			38600·	5M	·7	SEE B
5	BK·Y·SERP.	252	64·4	1/2	·8	
6	BAS.	20	644·1	5	·8	
7	BAS.	20	1287·8	10	·8	
8	BK·QTZOSE	55	1288·0	10	·8	XXIII
9	BAS.	427	1288·1	10	·8	
			3865·	30	·8	SEE B
2430	BK·QTZOSE	436	6438·	5D	·8	XXIII
1	BAS.	254	257·8	2	·9	
2	SERP.	428	644·6	5	·9	
3	BAS.	33	644·7	5	·9	
4	BK·QTZOSE	55	1288·8	10	·9	
4A	LIM.	646	3223·7	25	·9	ZET, ABYD,601
5	BAS.	38	6448·	5D	·9	
6	PINK GRAN	20	15467·	2M	·9	
7	LIM.	328	64·5	1/2	129·0	-2·
8	ALAB.	425	129·0	1	·0	
9	GY·QTZOSE	429	258·0	2	·0	
2440	ALAB.	339	258·1	2	·0	
1	BAS.	352	645·0	5	·0	
2	BAS.	802	1290·	10	·0	-1·4
3	PINK LIM.	436	1290·5	10	·0	XVIII
			1548·8	12	·0	SEE N
4	BK·QTZOSE	11	2579·8	20	·0	XXIII
5	ALAB.	12	2580·1	20	·0	
6	QTZITE	9	3224·8	25	·0	XXIII
7	BAS.	356	12900·	100	·0	-40
8	ALAB.	22	3227·0	25	·1	
			7745·	M	·1	SEE B
8A	PORPHY	653	9685·	75	·1	ZET, ABYD,510
9	PINK LIM.	797	646·0	5	·2	XVIII
2450	BK·QTZOSE	54	3229·2	25	·2	XXIII
1	QTZITE	54	3876·1	30	·2	XXIII
2	BAS.	237	6459·	50	·2	
3	BAS.	238	6460·	50	·2	-55
4	GY.VOLC.	265	431·	1/3	·3	
5	BAS.	368	129·3	1	·3	
6	BAS.	38	646·4	5	·3	
7	HAEM.	498	1293·0	10	·3	XVIII
8	BAS.	367	2587·1	20	·3	
			3233·3	25	·3	SEE N
9	GY.SY.	10	6466·	50	·3	XXIII
2460	RED GRAN	367	25870·	200	·3	-50
1	WT.QTZITE	5	93100·	12M	·3	-300
2	BR·SERP.	20	3882·	3	·4	·
3	BAS.	12	1293·8	10	·4	QUFT
4	BRECCIA	795	1294·2	10	·4	KARN. XVIII
			31065·	4M	·4	SEE N
5	GY.SERP.	494	647·4	5	·5	XVIII
6	"	494	647·5	5	·5	XVIII
7	Y.SANDST.	339	1295·0	100	·5	-90
8	QTZ	DUCK	162·	1/8	·6	XVIII
9	Y.BK.SERP.	263	432·	1/3	·6	
2470	BK.PORPHY	26	432·	1/3	·6	
1	BK.SERP.	887	259·1	2	·6	

No.	MATERIAL	FORM	GRS.	X	UNIT	DETAIL
2472	BR·QTZITE	452	77800·	10M	129·6	MEM. -800
3	BK·WT.PORP.	65	259·5	2	7	XII
4	BAS.	38	1297·3	10	·7	DELTA
5	BAS.	351	3892·0	30	7	
6	RED GRAN	328	64830·	500	7	
7	BK·QTZITE	452	77800·	10M	·7	-800
8	BAS.	265	64·9	1/2	·8	
9	GN.SILIC.	795	64·9	1/2	·8	XVIII
2480	BAS.	33	129·8	1	·8	
1	LIM.	356	259·6	2	·8	
2	Y. LIM.	79	649·3	5	·8	GEBELEYN,XVIII
3	GY.SILIC.	10	32458·	25	·8	
			7788·	M	·8	SEE B
4	BK.BAS.	12	64904·	500	·8	
5	HAEM.	899	259·9	2	·9	SYRIA,XVIII
6	RED LIM.	427	389·7	3	·9	KARNAK XVIII
7	BAS. poor	26	1299·0	10	·9	
8	BAS.	372	1299·5	10	·9	
9	BAS.	356	2597·4	20	·9	
2490	BAS.	20	2598·7	20	·9	
1	BAS.	254	260·0	2	130·0	
2	HAEM.	483	390·1	3	·0	TARTUS XVIII
3	BAS.	428	1299·7	10	·0	
4	GY.SY.	165	6500·	50	·0	
5	BAS.	438	6501·	50	·0	
6	GY. LIM.	427	3904·	3	·1	
7	BAS.	215	650·5	5	·1	
8	BAS.	428	1301·0	10	·1	
9	BAS.	19	2603·2	20	·1	
2500	BK·QTZOSE	10	3253·1	25	·1	XXIII
1	GY.SY.	10	3902·5	30	·1	XXIII
2	BK·WT·SY.	10	3903·5	30	·1	XXIII
			7807·	M	·1	SEE N
3	HAEM.	505	21·7	1/6	·2	MEM.
4	SARD	839	21·7	1/6	·2	XVIII
5	GY.SERP.	424	65·1	1/2	·2	
6	BAS.	415	65·1	1/2	·2	
7	HAEM.	328	130·2	1	·2	
8	ALAB.	23	390·7	3	·2	
9	BAS.	382	1302·0	10	·2	
2510	BK·QTZOSE	11	6508·	50	·2	XXIII
1	NUM.LIM.	314	7810·	M	·2	
2	LIM.	38	2607·2	2	·3	MEM.
3	GY·QTZOSE	406	651·6	5	·3	
4	LIM.	426	1303·3	10	·3	
5	LIM.	79	1303·3	10	·3	MERNPTH
6	BK·QTZOSE	10	3257·9	25	·3	XXIII
			7821·	M	·3	SEE B
7	ALAB.	339	652·	1/2	·4	
8	HAEM.	49	86·9	2/3	·4	XVIII
9	BAS.	38	260·8	2	·4	
2520	BAS.	261	260·9	2	·4	
1	BAS.porous	879	521·6	4	·4	ABYD. 1ST
2	LIM.	426	652·1	5	·4	
3	BAS.	20	3260·0	25	·4	
4	GY.SY.	314	6519·	50	·4	
5	BK·QTZOSE	238	6521·	50	·4	
6	HAEM.	896	130·5	1	·5	TARTUS,XVIII
7	BK·QTZOSE	21	130·5	1	·5	
8	ALAB.	38	261·0	2	·5	
9	BAS.	352	261·0	2	·5	
2530	BAS.	372	2609·7	20	·5	
1	BK·QTZOSE	60	2610·	20	·5	-10 XXIII
2	"	9	3261·8	25	·5	XXIII

No.	MATERIAL	FORM	GRS.	X	UNIT	DETAIL
2533	Y.LIM.	65	6525·	50	130·5	−50 V
4	ALAB.	238	39150·	5M	·5	
5	ALAB.	238	130·6	1	·6	
6	LIM.	498	391·8	3	·6	XVIII
7	ALAB.	801	653·2	5	·6	XVIII
8	PINK LIM.	483	1306·	10	·6	KARN,−6,XVIII
9	BAS.	318	2613·1	20	·6	
2540	PORPHY	313	261·4	2	·7	
*1	LIM.	931	522·8	4	·7	
2	HAEM.	50	43·6	1/3	·8	XVIII
3	BAS.	125	65·4	1/2	·8	
4	BAS.	37	1308·2	10	·8	MEM.
5	BAS.	8	2616·7	20	·8	MERNPTH
6	BAS.	351	6540·	50	·8	−75
7	BAS.	351	13082·	100	·8	−20
8	RED GRAN.	333	157000·	20M	·8	−300
9	ALAB.	484	873·	2/3	·9	XVIII
9A	LIM.	915	327·3	2½	·9	KOM SULTAN VI
2550	BAS.	442	1309·5	10	·9	
OA	ALAB.	437	65·5	1/2	131·0	−4
1	BRECCIA	79	131·	1	·0	−2·
2	BAS.	254	131·0	1	·0	MEM.
3	BAS.	827	1310·2	10	·0	
4	BAS.	235	2619·8	20	·0	
5	BAS.	352	2620·7	20	·0	
6	BAS.	238	3929·2	30	·0	
7	GY.GRAN.	351	26200	200	·0	−45
8	,,	3	39300	5M	·0	−250
9	,,	23	78602	10M	·0	AMARN, XVIII
2560	HAEM.	498	437·	1/3	·1	XVIII
1	BAS.	397	131·1	1	·1	
2	LIM.	931	262·2	2	·1	
3	BAS.	435	3932·9	30	·1	
4	GY.SY.	9	3934·2	30	·1	XXIII
5	BK.SY.	40	6553·	50	·1	
6	BAS.	165	6556·	50	·1	
7	BAS.	367	6557·	50	·1	
8	BAS.	33	262·4	2	·2	
9	BAS.	313	2624·	2	·2	
2570	BAS.	33	656·0	5	·2	
1	GY.LIM.	801	1311·6	10	·2	XVIII
2	ALAB.	83	1311·9	10	·2	
3	BK.QTZOSE	558	2623·3	20	·2	XXIII
4	GY. ,,	54	2626·2	20	·3	XXIII
5	BK. ,,	10	3282·8	25	·3	XXIII
6	BR.QTZITE	422	6558·	50	·3	
7	GY.SERP.	265	43·8	1/3	·4	
8	BAS.	33	43·8	1/3	4	MEM.
9	BAS.	33	262·9	2	·4	
2580	LIM.	11	657·2	5	·4	
1	BAS.	498	1313·8	10	·4	XVIII
2	BAS	65	2627·8	20	·4	VI
			7886·	M	·4	SEE N
3	ALAB.	192	263·1	2	·5	
4	LIM.	931	394·4	3	·5	
5	Y.LIM.	498	657·5	5	·5	
6	PINK LIM.	494	657·6	5	·5	XVIII

No.	MATERIAL	FORM	GRS.	X	UNIT	DETAIL
2587	BAS.	426	1314·8	10	131·5	
8	BAS.	347	1315·3	10	·5	
9	BAS.	238	2629·2	20	·5	
2590	BK.QTZOSE	11	2629·5	20	·5	XXIII
1	BAS.	429	3945·5	30	·5	
2	GY.QTZOSE	54	3945·9	30	·5	XXIII
3	BAS.	333	13150·	100	·5	−7
4	LIM.	422	26300·	200	·5	−40
5	Y.LIM.	802	131·6	1	·6	XVIII
6	BAS.	384	131·6	1	·6	
7	BAS.	33	657·8	5	·6	
						ONKHNESRANEFERAB
8	ALAB.	80	658·	5	·6	−3·8 XVIII
9	BAS.	427	2631·3	20	·6	XXIII
2600	LIM.	351	2631·5	20	·6	
1	BAS.	235	2633·2	20	·6	
			3290·2	25	·6	SEE N
2	Y.BK.SERP.	33	43·9	1/3	·7	
3	BAS.	33	263·4	2	·7	
4	BAS.	192	658·4	5	·7	
5	BAS.	38	658·5	5	·7	
6	BK.SY.	315	658·6	5	·7	
7	ALAB.	23	1317·	10	·7	−8
			3950·	30	·7	SEE B
8	GY.SY.	373	6584·	50	·7	
9	LIM.	31	131·8	1	·8	
2610	BAS.	339	131·8	1	·8	
1	ALAB.	364	263·6	2	·8	
2	LIM. Tough	918	263·7	2	·8	
3	QTZITE	54	2635·8	20	·8	GHUROB XXIII
4	BAS.	64	2636·0	20	·8	VI
5	BAS.	356	2636·8	20	·8	
6	BAS.	333	6591·2	50	·8	
6A	LIM.	452	1055·5	8	·9	KOM SULTAN
7	LIM.	456	1319·3	10	·9	PREHIST.?
*8	HARD LIM.	498	1319·5	10	·9	XVIII
*9	BAS. Tough	356	2637·7	20	·9	
2620	BAS.	38	2638·1	20	·9	
1	BAS.	235	2638·3	20	·9	
2	BAS.	33	6592·	50	·9	SAIS
3	ALAB.	25	44·0	1/3	132·0	
4	DURITE	65	44·0	1/3	·0	VI
5	BAS.	202	132·0	1	·0	
6	BK.STEA.	62	264·0	2	·0	XII
7	LIM.	916	660·	5	·0	−4
8	BAS.	23	660·1	5	·0	
9	BAS.	315	660·1	5	·0	
2630	BAS.	38	1319·8	10	·0	
1	BAS.	358	1319·8	10	·0	
2	GN.SY.	59	2639·7	20	·0	XXIII
3	BK.PORPH	9	3961·3	30	·0	XXIII
4	GY.SY.	7	6598·	50	·0	XXIII
5	GY.GRAN.	254	66000·	500	·0	−400
6	BAS.	265	264·2	2	·1	
7	BK.QTZOSE	10	6605·	50	·1	
8	BAS. DUCK		31700·	4M	·1	−1400 XVIII
			31700·	4M	·1	SEE N

No.	MATERIAL	FORM	GRS.	X	UNIT	DETAIL
2639	BAS.	392	264·4	2	132·2	
9A	GY.LIM.	797	661·3	5	·2	24·V·21
2640	BK.SY.	325	1321·9	10	·2	III III III
1	LIM.	38	1322·0	10	·2	
2	BK.QTZOSE	372	2643·6	20	·2	
3	ALAB.	16	3306·1	25	·2	
4	BUFF.LIM.	368	3967·0	30	·2	XVIII?
5	BAS.	422	6610·	50	·2	
6	ALAB.	26	264·6	2	·3	
7	BAS.	428	661·3	5	·3	
8	BR.SERP.	496	661·5	5	·3	
9	BAS.	373	1322·8	10	·3	
2650	GY.SY.	11	2645·7	20	·3	XXIII
1	BAS.	238	2647·0	20	·3	
2	GY.SY.	422	26490	20	·3	
3	BAS.	235	3308·1	25	·3	
4	BAS.	314	264·9	2	·4	
5	BAS.	378	662·1	5	·4	
6	GY.SY.	442	2649·0	20	·4	
7	BK.SY.	54	3971·2	30	·4	XXIII
8	BAS.	313	6621·	50	·4	
9	BAS.	368	7945·	M	·4	−40
2660	BAS.	364	132·5	1	·5	
1	GY.SY.	378	1325·	1	·5	
2	LIM.	495	132·5	1	·5	MERNPTH
3	MALACHITE	495	132·5	1	·5	ZER,−2·5 1
4	BK.SY.	64	662·6	1	·5	XII
5	BRECCIA	498	2650·8	20	·5	XVIII
6	BAS.	33	22·1	1/6	·6	
7	BAS.	429	1325·6	10	·6	
8	ALAB.	21	1325·9	10	·6	
9	BK.SY.	11	1325·9	10	·6	
2670	QTZITE	38	2653·0	20	·6	
			3979·1	30	·6	SEE B
			6629·	50	·6	SEE S
1	LIM.	406	2655·	2	·7	
2	ALAB.	484	398·0	3	·7	AMARNA XVIII
			398·2	3	·7	SEE S
3	BAS.	352	663·6	5	·7	
4	BAS.	428	1327·0	10	·7	
5	GY.SERP.	265	1327·	10	·7	−10
6	BAS.	436	2654·8	20	·7	
7	GY.SY.	442	6635·	50	·7	
8	BK.QTZOSE	9	26542·	200	·7	
9	BAS.	33	66·4	1/2	·8	
2680	BAS.	232	66·4	1/2	·8	
1	BAS.	63	663·8	5	·8	VI
2	BAS.	238	1327·7	10	·8	
3	BR.SY.	356	6640·	50	·8	
4	BUFF.LIM.	33	44·3	1/3	·9	
			31900·	4M	·9	SEE N
			39890·	5M	·9	SEE B
5	HAEM.	507	88·8	2/3	133·3	
6	LIM.	918	133·3	1	·3	
7	LIM.	931	564·1	4	141·0	

STATER 132-138 GRS.

No.	MATERIAL	FORM	GRS.	X	UNIT	DETAIL
2688	BK·STEA	144	22·0	1/6	132·0	DEFENNEH
8A	HARD LIM.	497	1320·	10	·0	24·V·21 -5
9	BK·BAS.	351	26400·	4M	·0	-60
2690	PINK GRAN.	351	132020·	20M	·0	
1	BK·BAS.	25	132330	20M	·3	-2
2	ALAB.	885	66·3	1/2	·6	SMYRNA
3	GY·SY.	38	6629·	M	·6	
4	LIM.	79	398·2	3	·7	
5	GY·GRAN	40	132700·	20M	·7	-20
6	BL·GL·SCHST	406	132·9	1	·9	
7	BAS.	352	2658·0	20	·9	
8	BAS.	313	66·5	1/2	133·0	
9	HAEM.	498	133·0	1	·0	TARTUS XVIII
2700	WT·LIM.	406	133·0	1	·0	
1	ALAB.	256	133·0	1	·0	
2	BAS.	254	133·0	1	·0	
3	LIM.	31	133·0	1	·0	-1·1
4	Y·LIM.	498	399·1	3	·0	KARNAK XVIII
*5	ALAB.	79	665·0	5	·0	MERN PTH
6	BAS.	372	2660·0	20	·0	»
7	BAS.	26	2661·0	20	·0	
8	BAS.	314	26600·	4M	·0	-800
9	HAEM.	499	133·1	1	·1	SYRIA XVIII
2710	BAS.	254	133·1	1	·1	
1	BR·HAEM.	45	266·3	2	·1	
2	BAS.	458	665·6	5	·1	
3	BAS.	439	2661·4	20	·1	
4	BAS.	358	2662·4	20	·1	
5	GY·SY.	54	6655·	M	·1	XXIII
6	BK·SY.	429	6655·	M	·1	
7	GY·VOLC.	165	6657·	M	·1	XXIII
8	ALAB.	252	33·3	1/4	·2	
9	BAS.	110	444·	1/3	·2	
9A	SY.	4952	133·2	1	·2	PIERCED
2720	BAS.	355	666·2	5	·2	
1	LIM.	452	1331·9	10	·2	
2	BAS.	358	2663·6	20	·2	
3	BAS.	238	2664·0	20	·2	
			3329·0	25	·2	SEE N
4	BAS.	238	6661·	M	·2	DRILL CAP
5	BAS.	267	133·3	1	·3	
6	BAS.	265	133·3	1	·3	
7	BAS.	352	133·3	1	·3	
8	ALAB.	27	266·7	2	·3	
9	Y·LIM.	38	666·5	5	·3	XVIII
2730	BAS.	356	2666·3	20	·3	
1	BAS.	149	3331·6	25	·3	XXIII
2	BK·SY.	11	6665·	M	·3	XXIII
3	BAS.	26	66·7	1/2	·4	
4	LT·BL·GLASS	12	66·7	1/2	·4	
5	ALAB.	256	266·9	2	·4	
6	WT·LIM.	498	400·2	3	·4	XVIII
7	BK·SY.	643	533·7	4	·4	VI?
8	BAS.	367	666·9	5	·4	
9	BAS.	494	1333·8	10	·4	XVIII
2740	BAS.	262	1334·3	10	·4	
1	WT·LIM.	433	1334·4	10	·4	
2	BAS.	368	2667·7	20	·4	
			3334·5	25	·4	SEE N
3	ALAB.	265	44·5	1/3	·5	
4	WT·LIM.	429	400·5	3	·5	
5	Y·LIM.	435	667·5	5	·5	
6	BAS.	25	1334·8	10	·5	
7	BAS.	354	1335·1	10	·5	
8	BAS.	235	2669·2	20	·5	

No.	MATERIAL	FORM	GRS.	X	UNIT	DETAIL
2749	BAS.	313	667·8	5	133·6	
2750	BAS.	358	2671·7	20	·6	
1	BAS.	115	3340·0	25	·6	XXIII
2	LIM.	60	3340·	25	·6	KAHUN,-24,XII
3	BAS.	264	6679·	M	·6	
4	BK·QTZOSE	11	6681·	M	·6	XXIII
5	WT·LIM.	436	133·7	1	·7	
6	BAS.	254	534·8	4	·7	
7	DIORITE	64	534·9	4	·7	
8	BAS.	435	668·5	5	·7	MERN PTH
9	DIORITE	54	1336·9	10	·7	VI or XXIII
2760	Y·LIM.	794	1337·0	10	·7	GEBELEN, XVIII
1	BAS.	368	1337·0	10	·7	
2	BAS.	802	1337·5	10	·7	XVIII
3	WT·LIM.	46	13374·	2M	·7	RETABEH
4	BUFF LIM.	265	66·9	1/2	·8	
5	BAS.	265	133·8	1	·8	
6	BAS.	333	133·8	1	·8	
7	BAS.	256	669·2	5	·8	
8	BAS.	27	1338·3	10	·8	
9	Y·BK·SERP.	331	267·8	2	·9	
2770	GY·SY.	256	669·6	5	·9	
1	BAS.	354	1338·8	10	·9	
2	BAS.	356	2677·4	20	·9	
3	BAS.	236	13388·	2M	·9	
4	GY·QTZOSE	16	67·0	1/2	134·0	
5	BAS.	364	67·0	1/2	·0	
6	BAS.	406	670·1	5	·0	MERN PTH
7	LIM.	382	1339·7	10	·0	
7A	HAEM.	4953	1340·0	10	·0	END GROOVE 24·V·21
8	BAS.	312	2679·8	20	·0	
9	BAS.	352	2680·6	20	·0	
2780	LIM.	436	2681·0	20	·0	
1	BAS.	352	2681·8	20	·0	
2	RED GRAN.	11	20100·	3M	·0	-60
3	BAS.	429	6705·	5	·1	
4	BAS.	801	1340·7	10	·1	MEM. XVIII
5	GY·SERP.	725	1341·0	10	·1	
*6	BAS.	238	2683·0	20	·1	
7	BAS.	2	671·2	5	·2	
8	BAS.	312	1342·4	10	·2	
9	BAS.	352	2684·6	20	·2	
2790	BAS.	235	6708·	M	·2	
1	GY·SY.	26	6709·	M	·2	
2	GY·SY.	33	134·3	1	·3	
3	BAS.	365	671·7	5	·3	
4	ALAB.	9206	1075·0	8	·3	
5	BAS.	368	1343·5	10	·3	
6	BAS.	33	268·8	2	·4	
7	BAS.	254	268·9	2	·4	
8	BAS.	498	671·8	5	·4	XVIII
9	ALAB.	267	672·0	5	·4	
2800	BAS.	33	672·0	5	·4	
1	BAS.	347	672·0	5	·4	MEM.
2	ALAB.	79	672·2	5	·4	LAHUN, XVIII
3	GY·MARB	65	2687·4	5	·4	IIIII V
4	GY·SY.	10	26882·	20	·4	
5	ALAB.	9205	3226·6	24	·4	
6	BAS.	352	33595·2	25	·4	
7	HAEM.	493	134·5	1	·5	MEM. XVIII
8	LIM.	802	134·5	1	·5	XVIII
9	BAS.	415	134·5	1	·5	
2810	GY·SERP.	498	4035·	3	·5	XVIII
1	LIM.	429	672·4	5	·5	
2	BAS.	27	672·6	5	·5	
3	BAS.	338	672·7	5	·5	
4	HAEM.	493	1344·7	10	·5	TARTUS, XVIII

No.	MATERIAL	FORM	GRS.	X	UNIT	DETAIL
2815	FLINT PEB.		2690	20	134·5	-10
6	BK·BAS.	339	134500·	20M	·5	-2000
7	BAS.	267	134·6	1	·6	
8	ALAB.	226	134·6	1	·6	
9	GY·SERP.	364	134·6	1	·6	
2820	BAS.	338	673·0	5	·6	
1	BAS.	367	673·1	5	·6	
2	BK·QTZOSE	2	1345·6	10	·6	MERN PTH
3	BAS.	311	1345·8	10	·6	
4	HAEM.	WOLF HEAD	1345·8	10	6	=4938
5	BAS.	392	44·9	1/3	·7	
6	BR·SERP.	254	134·7	1	·7	
7	BAS.	254	673·7	5	·7	
8	BAS.	384	1347·4	10	·7	
9	BAS.	482	67·4	1/2	·8	XVIII
2830	BAS.	256	134·8	1	·8	
1	BAS.	237	134·8	1	·8	
2	BRECCIA	496	1347·6	10	·8	XVIII
3	BAS.	333	6740·	M	·8	
4	ALAB.	254	269·8	2	·9	
5	ALAB.	436	269·9	2	·9	
6	BAS.	237	269·9	2	·9	
7	BAS.	79	674·6	5	·9	XVIII
8	BAS.	358	1348·7	10	·9	
9	BAS.	352	1349·3	10	·9	
2840	HAEM.	DUCK	2698·4	20	·9	XVIII
1	BAS.	368	2698·9	20	·9	
2	ALAB.	494	22·5	1/6	135·0	rough XVIII
3	BAS.	25	450·	1/3	·0	
4	BAS.	33	67·5	1/2	·0	
5	BAS.	256	270·0	2	·0	
6	BAS.	256	270·0	2	·0	
7	BAS.	313	270·0	2	·0	
8	HAEM.	DUCK	270·1	2	·0	TARTUS XVIII
9	BAS.	435	674·8	5	·0	...IX
2850	WT·LIM.	40	675·0	5	·0	
1	BAS.	448	675·1	5	·0	
2	BRECCIA	797	1350·	10	·0	-15, XVIII
3	BAS.	444	1350·0	10	·0	
4	WT·LIM.	406	1350·4	10	·0	
5	BAS.	268	2699·2	20	·0	
6	BK·QTZOSE	10	3374·3	25	·0	XXIII
7	HAEM.	496	1350·7	10	·1	XVIII
8	RED LIM.	79	1350·8	10	·1	XVIII
9	BK·QTZOSE	10	3378·6	25	·1	XXIII
2860	RED HAEM.	802	67·6	1/2	·2	XVIII
1	BAS.	382	67·6	1/2	·2	
2	BAS.	27	270·4	2	·2	
3	BAS.	33	270·4	2	·2	
4	BR·SERP.	452	676·0	5	·2	
5	ALAB.	256	676·0	5	·2	
6	BAS.	33	1351·8	10	·2	
7	BAS.	382	1352·2	10	·2	
8	BAS.	438	6760·	M	·2	-20
9	BAS.	237	451·	1/3	·3	
2870	BK·SY.	17	135·3	1	·3	
1	BAS.	254	135·3	1	·3	MEM.
2	ALAB.	256	135·3	1	·3	MEM.
3	RED PORPH.	26	270·6	2	·3	
4	WT·LIM.	790	676·5	5	·3	-10 XVIII
5	BAS.	256	676·5	5	·3	
6	BAS.	338	1353·0	10	·3	
7	BAS.	312	2707·1	20	·3	
8	GN·PORPH.	10	3382·1	25	·3	
			3382·8	25	·3	SEE N
9	BK·QTZOSE	11	3383·0	25	·3	
2880	BAS. rough	33	406·3	3	·4	

No.	MATERIAL	FORM	GRS.	X	UNIT	DETAIL
2881	BAS.	429	676·8	5	135·4	
2	BAS.	384	676·9	5	·4	"ATA"
3	Y.BK.LIM.	367	677·1	5	·4	
4	LIM.	79	1354·	10	·4	−1·3 XVIII
5	BAS.	33	1354·1	10	·4	
6	MALACHITE	422	2708·	20	·4	−10
7	FLINT PEB.		3385·8	25	·4	INSCRIBED
8	LIM.	452	6771·0	10M	·4	
9	BAS.	33	271·0	2	·5	RIQQEH
2890	ALAB.	498	406·5	3	·5	EHNASYA,XVIII
1	BAS.	369	677·6	5	·5	
2	BAS.	352	1355·2	10	·5	
3	SY.	10	3388·0	25	·5	
4	ALAB.	22	6774·	M	·5	MERNPTH
5	BR.QTZITE	185	27034·	4M	·5	
6	ALAB	491	22·6	1/6	·6	
7	BUFF LIM.	266	45·2	1/3	·6	
8	BK.SY.	17	135·6	1	·6	OVAL
9	BRECCIA	802	406·8	3	·6	XVIII
2900	BAS.	254	678·2	5	·6	
1	BAS	452	1356·1	10	·6	
2	GY.SERP.	494	2712·0	20	·6	XVIII
3	ALAB.	254	1357·	1	·7	
4	BAS	33	271·4	2	·7	
5	Y.BK.LIM.	27	271·4	2	·7	
6	BAS.	803	407·0	3	·7	XVIII
7	BAS.	313	678·5	5	·7	
8	BAS	352	1356·8	10	·7	
9	BK.QTZOSE	55	2713·5	20	·7	XXIII
2910	BAS.	358	2715·0	20	·7	
1	Y.LIM.	63	13566·	2M	·7	mmmm QU. XII
2	Y.BK.LIM.	206	67·9	1/2	·8	
3	GN.SILIC.	26	67·9	1/2	·8	
4	BAS.	448	135·8	1	·8	
5	BAS.	44	135·8	1	·8	
6	LIM.	801	271·6	2	·8	
7	BAS.	27	271·7	2	·8	
8	BAS.	235	1358·2	10	·8	
9	BK.QTZOSE	55	3396·0	25	·8	XXIII
2920	RED GRAN.	345	13581·	2M	·8	
1	Y.SANDST.	368	13583·	2M	·8	
2	BAS.	33	135·9	1	·9	
3	BAS.	436	271·8	2	·9	
4	HAEM.	645	679·7	5	·9	VI
5	BAS.	336	1359·0	10	·9	
6	BAS.	352	1359·2	10	·9	
			3397·0	25	·9	SEE N
7	HAEM.	50	68·0	1/2	136·0	SYRIA XVIII
8	BK.SERP.	908	68·0	1/2	·0	
9	HAEM.	439	68·0	1/2	·0	
2930	BK.STEA.	323	68·0	1/2	·0	
1	BAS.	256	679·9	5	·0	
2	DIALLAGE	435	680·0	5	·0	−20
3	BAS.	368	680·0	5	·0	
4	BAS.	313	1360·1	10	·0	
5	BK.QTZOSE	39	2720·5	20	·0	XXIII
6	BAS.	33	136·1	1	·1	
7	BAS.	338	272·2	2	·1	
8	BAS	795	272·3	2	·1	XVIII
9	HAEM.	803	680·7	5	·1	XVIII
2940	BAS.	352	1360·8	10	·1	
1	BAS.	352	1361·4	10	·1	
2	BAS.	352	2722·3	20	·1	MEM.
			3401·8	25	·1	SEE K
3	BAS.	38	6805·	M	·1	
4	BAS.	339	6806·	M	·1	
6945	Y.BK.SERP.	26	45·4	1/3	136·2	
6	BRECCIA	498	68·1	1/2	·2	XVIII
7	BAS.	446	272·5	2	·2	
8	GY.LIM.	498	408·6	3	·2	XVIII
9	BAS.	368	680·8	5	·2	
2950	BAS.	395	680·9	5	·2	
1	BAS.	454	681·1	5	·2	
2	BAS.	27	681·2	5	·2	
3	BAS.	354	1361·8	10	·2	
4	HAEM.	DUCK	1362·2	10	·2	XVIII
5	BK.SY.	235	6811·	M	·2	
6	GY.SERP.	498	1363·	1	·3	BORED, XVIII
7	BAS.	79	681·5	5	·3	XVIII
8	GY.SERP.	436	1363·3	10	·3	
9	HAEM.	499	68·2	1/2	·4	XVIII
2960	BAS.	392	68·2	1/2	·4	
1	BAS.	33	68·2	1/2	·4	
2	ALAB.	206	136·4	1	·4	DELTA
3	BAS.	333	681·8	5	·4	
4	BAS.	331	681·8	5	·4	
5	BAS.	33	681·8	5	·4	
6	BAS.	428	681·9	5	·4	
7	BAS.	338	682·1	5	·4	
8	BAS.	165	682·2	5	·4	
9	BAS.	331	1363·6	10	·4	
2970	BAS.	39	1364·2	10	·4	
1	BK.LIM	20	136·5	1	·5	
2	BAS.	372	682·4	5	·5	
3	BAS.	26	273·0	2	·5	−1·5
4	ALAB.	SLAB	2729·2	20	·5	XII
5	QTZITE	369	13650·	2M	·5	
6	BAS.	331	68·3	1/2	·6	
7	BAS.	33	136·6	1	·6	
8	ALAB.	141	136·2	1	·6	
9	GY.SERP.	12	273·3	2	·6	MEM.
2980	BAS.	436	409·8	3	·6	
1	BAS.	428	682·9	5	·6	
2	ALAB.	338	683·2	5	·6	
3	BAS.	336	2731·5	20	·6	
4	BAS.	312	2732·2	20	·6	
5	BAS.	352	2732·0	4M	·6	−3
6	ALAB.	26	136·7	1	·7	
7	GY.SERP.	436	410·1	3	·7	
8	HAEM.	483	410·2	3	·7	XVIII
9	BAS.	38	683·6	5	·7	
2990	BAS.	429	1366·9	10	·7	
1	BK.QTZOSE	9	3417·6	25	·7	XXIII
2	BAS.	206	68·4	1/2	·8	
3	BAS.	79	136·8	1	·8	MEM. XVIII
4	WT.LIM.	38	273·6	2	·8	
5	BAS.	433	684·0	5	·8	
6	BAS.	354	1368·4	10	·8	
7	BAS.	406	1368·5	10	·8	
8	BAS.	33	136·9	1	·9	
9	BAS.	44	136·9	1	·9	
3000	BAS.	369	273·8	2	·9	
1	BAS.	268	684·3	5	·9	
2	BAS.	498	684·7	5	·9	XVIII
3	BAS.	33	684·8	5	·9	
4	BAS.	352	1368·6	10	·9	
5	BAS.	422	1369·0	10	·9	
6	BAS.	352	1369·	10	·9	−1·8
7	BAS.	262	1369·2	10	·9	
8	BK.SY.	268	2737·4	20	·9	
9	BAS.	436	6847·	M	·9	
3010	GY.SY.	32	68·5	1/2	137·0	DEFENNEH
3011	ALAB.	206	68·5	1/2	137·0	
2	BAS.	406	137·0	1	·0	MERNPTH
3	BK.SERP.	263	685·0	5	·0	−·6
4	BAS.	312	685·1	5	·0	
5	BAS.	352	1370·0	10	·0	
6	BAS.	795	1370·0	10	·0	XVIII
7	BAS.	12	1370·4	10	·0	
8	BK.SY.	10	2739·7	20	·0	
9	BK.BAS.	618	2740·	20	·0	−40 XII
3020	GY.SY.	264	13708·	2M	·0	
1	BAS.	265	137·1	1	·1	
2	BAS.	27	274·2	2	·1	
3	Y.LIM.	435	685·3	5	·1	
4	LIM.	311	1370·6	10	·1	
5	BAS.	352	1371·0	10	·1	
6	BAS.	235	2743·1	20	·1	
7	BAS.	33	68·6	1/2	·2	
8	ALAB.	39	137·2	1	·2	
9	BAS.	802	274·4	2	·2	XVIII
3030	BAS.	265	274·5	2	·2	
1	BAS.	27	274·5	2	·2	
2	BAS.	433	685·8	5	·2	
3	BAS.	356	685·8	5	·2	
4	BAS.	238	1371·8	10	·2	
5	BAS.	238	1372·2	10	·2	
6	FOS. WOOD	10	2745·1	20	·2	XXIII
7	BAS.	347	6863·	M	·2	
8	GY.SERP.	406	274·7	2	·3	OVAL
9	BK.QTZOSE	82	1372·9	10	·3	
3040	GY.SY.	406	137·4	1	·4	
1	BAS.	435	274·6	2	·4	
2	BAS.	265	274·8	2	·4	DELTA
3	BK.SERP.	33	274·8	2	·4	
4	BAS.	334	687·2	5	·4	
5	BAS.	448	687·2	5	·4	
6	BAS.	40	1373·6	10	·4	
7	BAS.	428	1373·7	10	·4	
8	BAS.	428	2749·0	20	·4	
9	BAS.	312	2749·0	20	·4	
3050	BAS.	264	6870·	M	·4	−66
1	BAS.	364	6871·	M	·4	
2	BAS.	314	45·5	1/3	·5	
3	BAS.	33	137·5	1	·5	
4	BAS.	12	137·5	1	·5	
5	BRECCIA	795	412·4	3	·5	XVIII
6	BAS.	354	687·4	5	·5	
7	BAS.	237	1375·1	10	·5	
8	BAS.	40	1375·4	10	·5	
9	BK.SERP.	48	3438·7	25	·5	MERNPTH
3060	RED.LIM.	802	68·8	1/2	·6	XVIII
1	ALAB.	484	412·7	3	·6	XVIII
2	ALAB.	79	413·0	3	·7	XVIII
3	WT.LIM.	826	6884·	M	·7	
4	BAS.	368	6885·	M	·7	
5	BAS.	452	45·6	1/3	·8	
6	BK.STEA.	232	457·	1/3	138·1	
7	BAS.	33	457·	1/3	·1	
8	BAS.	263	457·	1/3	·1	
9	BAS.	415	414·5	3	·2	
3070	LIM.	38	46·1	1/3	·3	
1	BAS.	38	23·1	1/6	·6	
2	Y.BK.SERP.	14	23·1	1/6	·6	
*3	BAS.	434	416·0	3	·7	
*4	WT.LIM.	427	416·7	3	·9	
5	BAS.	79	420·9	3	1403·	

Q E D E T 137–152 GRS.

No.	MATERIAL	FORM	GRS.	X	UNIT	DETAIL
3076	LIM.	919	542·	4	135·5	−2
7	BAS.	33	275·1	2	137·5	
8	BAS.	324	137·6	1	·6	
9	BAS.	393	137·6	1	·6	
3080	DURITE	268	137·6	1	·6	
1	GY.MARB.	32	1376·0	10	·6	
2	GY.SERP.	373	1375·7	10	·6	
3	BAS.	358	2752·0	20	·6	
			3440·1	25	·6	SEE K
4	GY.SY.	9	6878·	50	·6	GHUROB
5	HAEM.	422	6878·	50	·6	
6	BK.QTZOSE	439	13761·	100	·6	
7	BAS.	258	45·9	1/3	·7	
8	BAS.	262	137·7	1	·7	
9	BAS.	487	1377·0	10	·7	XVIII
3090	BAS.	406	1377·4	10	·7	
1	BAS.	422	1376·6	10	·7	
2	GY.QTZOSE	384	13770·	100	·7	−27
3	BK.JASP.	364	68·9	1/2	·8	
4	QTZITE	347	2754·5	20	·8	
			3445·4	25	·8	SEE K
5	„	344	13776·	100	·8	
6	BAS.	792	137·9	1	·9	XVIII
7	BAS.	32	137·9	1	·9	
8	BAS.	264	275·8	2	·9	
9	BAS.	313	275·8	2	·9	
			3447·0	25	·9	SEE K
3100	DURITE	324	46·0	1/3	138·0	
1	BAS.	380	1380·0	10	·0	
2	BR.QTZITE	442	55200·	400	·0	nnnn −6600 HAA·AB·RA
3	ALAB.	373	690·7	5	·1	
4	BAS.	794	1380·7	10	·1	XVIII
5	BAS.	141	1381·1	10	·1	
6	BK.SY.	18	138·2	1	·2	
7	LIM.	334	276·5	2	·2	
8	BAS.	368	276·5	2	·2	
9	BAS.	352	276·5	2	·2	
3110	SERP.	803	691·2	5	·2	KARNAK XVIII
1	BAS.	356	1381·6	10	·2	
2	BK.QTZOSE	394	2763·3	20	·2	
3	„	55	2763·5	20	·2	
4	BAS.	64	2764·7	20	·2	XII
5	RED GRAN	353	27650·	200	·2	−10
6	GY.SY.	26	46·1	1/3	·3	
7	Y.BK.SERP.	254	46·1	1/3	·3	
8	BAS.	31	138·3	1	·3	
9	ALAB.	427	691·4	5	·3	
3120	SERP.	493	691·7	5	·3	XVIII
1	BAS.	382	1383·5	10	·3	
2	BR.SY.	38	2766·5	20	·3	
3	BK.SY.	40	2766·6	20	·3	
4	BAS.	345	276·8	2	·4	
5	LIM.	14	276·8	2	·4	KAHUN
6	BAS.	498	692·0	5	·4	XVIII
7	BAS.	448	692·1	5	·4	
8	BAS.	232	1384·0	10	·4	
9	BK.QTZOSE	54	2768·3	20	·4	XXIII
3130	BAS.	37	6919·	50	·4	
			20758·	15	·4	nnnn SEE B
1	BAS.	356	277·	2	·5	−2
2	BAS.	256	692·6	5	·5	
3	RED GRAN	346	69250·	500	·5	−170
4	GY. „	356	69250·	500	·5	−10
5	RED „	314	138500·	1000	·5	−70
6	BK.WT.SY	334	46·2	1/3	·6	
3137	ALAB.	16	69·3	1/2	138·6	
8	BAS.	207	69·3	1/2	·6	
9	BAS.	254	277·3	2	·6	
3140	BAS.	338	693·2	5	·6	
1	DIORITE	646	2080·	30	·6	nnn ABYD.XII
2	BAS.	368	2771·1	20	·6	
3	DURITE	267	1387·	1	·7	
4	HAEM.	499	138·7	1	·7	XVIII
5	DURITE	40	138·7	1	·7	
6	BAS.	333	277·5	2	·7	
7	HAEM.	454	138·8	1	·8	
8	BAS.	333	138·8	1	·8	
9	LIM.	803	1388·0	10	·8	−4
3150	BAS.	367	1388·2	10	·8	
*1	GY.SY.	419	6942·	50	·8	
2	BAS.	262	138·9	1	·9	MEM.GLASS
3	GY.QTZOSE	57	1388·9	10	·9	XXIII
4	LIM.	426	1389·1	10	·9	JERUSALEM
5	BAS.	39	2778·3	20	·9	
6	BK.QTZOSE	327	69·5	1/2	139·0	
*7	HAEM.	494	69·5	1/2	·0	SMYRNA, XVIII
8	BK.QTZ	32	139·0	1	·0	
9	BAS.	344	278·1	2	·0	
3160	BAS.	448	694·9	5	·0	
QA	BK.QTZ	651	695·6	5	·0	QAU X
1	BAS.	368	1390·0	10	·0	
2	BAS.	402	6949·	50	·0	
3	SY.	202	139·1	1	·1	
4	BAS.	378	2782·	2	·1	
5	BAS.	428	278·2	2	·1	
6	LIM.	395	695·7	5	·1	
7	BAS.	57	695·7	5	·1	
8	BAS.	345	1391·5	10	·1	
			3478·2	25	·1	SEE K
9	BK.BAS.	256	27820·	200	·1	−13
3170	LIM.	203	55650·	400	·1	−35
1	BK.LIM.		69·6	1/2	·2	
2	DURITE	425	139·2	1	·2	
3	BAS.	429	139·2	1	·2	
4	ALAB.	338	695·9	5	·2	
5	LIM.	913	2785·	20	·2	NAQ.461,−6 PRE
6	BR.SY.	9	3480·9	25	·2	
7	„	439	6962·	50	·2	
8	DURITE	64	139·3	1	·3	QU."1/2" XII
			1392·8	10	·3	SEE P
9	GY.SY.	369	6964·	50	·3	
3180	BK.SY.	348	6965·	50	·3	
1	GY.SY.	353	13932·	100	·3	
2	LIM.	BULL	27866·	200	·3	φXVI
3	BR.QTZITE	426	69630·	500	·3	
4	ALAB.	256	69·7	1/2	·4	
5	ALAB.	78	139·4	1	·4	
6	BAS.	312	278·9	2	·4	
7	ALAB.	28	278·9	2	·4	
8	GY.QTZOSE	406	1393·8	10	·4	
9	BR.SY.	387	6969·	50	·4	
9A	BAS.	79	46·5	1/3	·5	
3190	HAEM.	499	46·5	1/3	·5	
1	ALAB.	262	139·5	1	·5	
2	BAS.	63	558·2	4	·5	XII
3	BK.BAS.	497	697·4	5	·5	XVIII
4	ALAB.	185	1395·5	10	·5	MEM.
5	BAS.	348	27900·	200	·5	
6	WT.QTZITE	18	27900·	200	·5	
7	BK.QTZOSE	312	69·8	1/2	·6	
8	BK.BAS.	395	69·8	1/2	·6	
9	BAS.	344	139·6	1	·6	
3200	BAS.	364	697·9	5	·6	MEM.
3201	BAS.	381	2791·3	20	139·6	
2	BAS.	656	2792·2	20	·6	
3	BAS.	266	139·7	1	·7	
4	BK.QTZ.	392	139·7	1	·7	
5	BAS.	314	1397·1	10	·7	
6	BK.BAS.	795	2794·	20	·7	−18
			3491·5	25	·7	SEE K
7	GY.SY.	235	13969·	100	·7	
8	BAS.	397	46·6	1/3	·8	
9	BK.BAS.	33	69·9	1/2	·8	
3210	BK.STEA.	4	139·8	1	·8	
1	BAS.	262	279·7	2	·8	
2	GY.SY.	312	279·7	2	·8	
3	BAS.	265	699·0	5	·8	
4	BAS.	373	699·0	5	·8	
5	LIM.	203	699·0	5	·8	
6	BAS.	190	1397·6	10	·8	
7	BAS.	264	1398·4	10	·8	
8	HAEM. HIPPO HEAD		1398·4	10	·8	NUBT XVIII φIX
9	QTZITE	368	6988·	50	·8	
3220	GY.QTZOSE	21	139·9	1	·9	
1	BAS.	254	279·8	2	·9	
2	QTZITE	237	13988·	100	·9	
3	BK.Y.SERP	265	70·0	1/2	140·0	
4	BAS.	446	140·0	1	·0	
5	ALAB.	395	140·0	1	·0	
6	BAS.	63	559·8	4	·0	−1·6
			1400·	10	·0	SEE P
7	BAS.	336	2799·3	20	·0	
8	BAS.	202	2801·0	20	·0	
9	RED PORPH	465	140·1	1	·1	
3230	BAS.	369	280·2	2	·1	
1	BAS.	428	1401·0	10	·1	
2	BAS.	263	2802·4	20	·1	
3	HAEM.	149	2802·9	20	·1	
4	ALAB.	386	70·1	1/2	·2	
5	RED HAEM.	802	140·2	1	·2	XVIII
6	ALAB.	144	2803·8	20	·2	
7	BAS.	328	2804·1	20	·2	
8	BAS.	71	14018·	100	·2	
9	LIM.	RAM	21277·	150	·2	φXVI
3240	BAS.	344	701·5	5	·3	
1	ALAB.	368	701·6	5	·3	
2	BAS.	482	701·7	5	·3	XVIII
3	BAS.	482	1402·8	10	·3	XVIII
4	BAS.	392	1403·0	10	·3	
5	HAEM.	498	280·8	2	·4	XVIII
6	ALAB.	331	280·8	2	·4	
7	BAS.	334	280·9	2	·4	
8	BK.SY.	384	7022·	50	·4	
9	GY.SY.	429	14039·	100	·4	
3250	HAEM.	657	140·5	1	·5	XVIII
1	BAS.	27	281·0	2	·5	
2	BAS.	27	281·0	2	·5	
3	BAS.	406	281·1	2	·5	MEM.
4	BAS.	192	1405·0	10	·5	
5	LIM.	525	1405·5	10	·5	
6	LIM.	442	28100·	200	·5	−150
7	BK.JASP.	465	140·6	1	·6	
	BAS.	795	703·2	5	·6	
9	BAS.	263	1405·8	10	·6	
3260	BAS.	395	1406·0	10	·6	IIIII
1	BAS.	352	2812·7	20	·6	
2	BAS.	425	281·5	2	·7	
3	BAS.	452	281·5	2	·7	
4	RED-QTZITE	11	28135·	200	·7	
5	BK.STEA.	617	70·4	1/2	·8	−·1

No.	Material	Form	Grs.	X	Unit	Detail
3266	BAS.	33	281.7	2	140.8	
7	BAS.	356	563.4	4	.8	MEM.
8	BK.QTZ	11	2816.2	20	.8	
9	BR.QTZITE	18	28160.	200	.8	-5
3270	ALAB.	275	140.9	1	.9	
1	BAS.	429	7044	5	.9	
2	ALAB.	915	845.3	6	.9	TARKHAN 1
			3522.8	25	.9	SEE K
3	BAS.	144	47.0	1/3	141.0	
4	Y.BK.SERP.	197	47.0	1/3	.0	
5	Y.LIM.	49	47.0	1/3	.0	
6	BAS.	57	70.5	1/2	.0	V
7	JADEITE	933	70.5	1/2	.0	
8	BAS.	258	282.0	2	.0	
9	ALAB.	406	282.1	2	.0	
3280	LIM.	486	564.1	4	.0	
1	BK.QTZOSE	13	705.	5	.0	-13
2	ALAB.	264	282.2	2	.1	
3	BK.QTZOSE	654	1410.9	10	.1	GHUROB, XXIII
4	GY.SILIC.	394	2821.3	20	.1	
5	HAEM.	429	70.6	1/2	.2	
6	HAEM.	499	70.6	1/2	.2	
7	HAEM.	505	70.6	1/2	.2	MERNPTH
8	HAEM, LEAD	493	282.5	2	.2	XVIII
9	HAEM.	499	282.5	2	.2	TARTUS, XVIII
3290	BAS.	268	7059	5	.2	
1	LIM.	937	5646.6	40	.2	
2	BAS.	312	47.1	1/3	.3	
2A	BAS.	368	47.1	1/3	.3	MEM.
3	GY.BAS.	393	141.3	1	.3	
4	BAS.	418	1413.1	10	.3	
5	ALAB.	402	1413.5	10	.3	MERNPTH
5A	GRNSTONE	64	4238.	30	.3	ZET, ABYD, 121 -20
6	BK.SY.	458	7066.	50	.3	
7	BAS.	267	70.7	1/2	.4	
8	HAEM.	487	141.4	1	.4	
9	BAS.	358	706.8	5	.4	
3300	BAS.	23	707.2	5	.4	MEM.
1	BAS.	38	707.3	5	.4	
2	BAS.	419	2828.8	20	.4	
3	GY.SY.	2	2828.9	20	.4	
4	"	392	2829.0	20	.4	MEM.
5	BAS.	497	5655.0	40	.4	IIII XVIII
6	BK.QTZOSE	426	141.5	1	.5	
7	BAS.	328	707.4	5	.5	
8	GY.SY.	11	14146.	10	.5	
9	BK.BAS.	316	28300.	200	.5	-17
3310	GY.GRAN.	38	28300.	200	.5	-40
1	BAS.	313	70.8	1/2	.6	
2	HAEM.	494	283.2	2	.6	XVIII
3	GY.SY.	442	1415.9	10	.6	-.4
4	BAS.	331	1416.0	10	.6	
5	BAS.	435	1416.1	10	.6	GHUROB
6	LIM.	16	1416.3	10	.6	
7	BAS.DRILL CAP	359	7078.	50	.6	
8	BAS.	368	7080.	50	.6	
9	GY.BAS.	333	35400.	250	.6	-2
3320	BR.QTZITE	261	56650	400	.6	-80
1	BAS.	264	283.5	2	.7	
2	GY.QTZOSE	418	1417.4	10	.7	
3	BK.SY.	237	7083.	50	.7	
4	PINK GRAN.	238	28350.	200	.7	-150
5	GY.MARB.	426	567.1	4	.8	
5A	HAEM.	8985	708.9	5	.8	PIERCED
6	BAS.	369	709.1	5	.8	
7	BAS.	11	709.1	5	.8	
8	BAS.	442	709.1	5	.8	
3329	BR.SY.	378	1418.5	10	141.8	
3330	LIM.	498	1418.3	10	.8	KARNAK XVIII
1	GY.QTZOSE	10	3545.8	25	.9	XXIII
2	BK. "	17	141.9	1	.9	XVIII
3	GN.MARB.	692	283.9	2	.9	QUFT XII
4	BK.SY.	422	709.5	5	.9	
5	BR.FLINT	428	709.6	5	.9	
6	BR.SERP.	655	1418.8	10	.9	
7	SY.	256	2839.0	20	.9	
7A	BAS.	331	71.0	1/2	142.0	
8	LIM.	33	284.0	2	.0	
9	BAS.	393	284.1	2	.0	
3340	BAS.	358	710.1	5	.0	
1	GY.SY.	406	710.1	5	.0	
2	ALAB.	358	1419.7	10	.0	
			3549.0	25	.0	SEE K
			3549.6	25	.0	"
3	PINK LIM.	653	5680.	40	.0	∩∩ QUFT.
4	SANDST.	629	7102.	50	.0	XII
5	BAS.	436	7102.	50	.0	
6	HAEM.	494	710.7	5	.1	XVIII
7	ALAB.	649	5683.	40	.1	GHUROB, XVIII
7A	ALAB.	311	23.7	1/6	.2	MEM.
8	BAS.	263	47.4	1/3	.2	
9	ALAB.	397	71.1	1/2	.2	
3350	GY.QTZ.	426	71.1	1/2	.2	
1	BAS.	426	142.2	1	.2	
2	ALAB.	265	284.5	2	.2	
3	BAS.	324	284.5	2	.2	
4	BAS.	225	710.8	5	.2	
5	BK.JASP.	126	711.1	5	.2	
6	BAS.	262	711.2	5	.2	
7	BAS.	20	1422.5	10	.2	
8	LIM.	265	2843.5	20	.2	
			5686.5	40	.2	SEE P
9	ALAB.	801	284.6	2	.3	GHUROB, XVIII
3360	BK.SY.	2	1422.8	10	.3	
0A	HARD LIM.	597	1423.5	10	.3	ZET.ABYD.329
1	BK.SY.	333	7113.7	50	.3	
2	GY.QTZOSE	315	7116.	50	.3	
3	GY.SY.	642	71.2	1/2	.4	V
4	BK.BAS.	287	142.4	1	.4	
5	ALAB.	428	142.4	1	.4	
5A	ALAB.	797	3560.6	25	.4	
6	BK.QTZOSE	25	7120.	50	.4	
7A	ALAB.	23	47.5	1/3	.5	
8	BAS.	264	142.5	1	.5	MERNPTH
9	GY.SY.	245	14252	10	.5	
3370	FLINT	54	3563.2	25	.5	XXIII
1	HAEM.	524	7126.	50	.5	XVIII
2	BAS.	33	71.3	1/2	.6	
3	BAS.	232	71.3	1/2	.6	
4	BAS.	402	285.2	2	.6	
5	GY.SY.	422	285.2	2	.6	
6	BAS.	311	285.3	2	.6	
7	BAS.	350	713.0	5	.6	
8	BAS.	328	713.1	5	.6	
9	BK.GY.LIM.	23	1425.7	10	.6	
3380	GY.QTZOSE	653	28522.	20	.6	RIQQEH XII
1	BK. "	55	2852.4	20	.6	XXIII
2	GY. "	351	71310.	500	.6	-20
3	BAS.	268	1427.	1	.7	
4	BAS.	339	285.4	2	.7	
5	HAEM.	887	713.4	5	.7	XVIII
6	BAS.	207	1426.8	10	.7	
7	BR.QTZOSE	821	2855.4	20	.7	
8	3K. "	558	3567.1	25	.7	XXIII
3389	BK.STEA.	63	71.4	1/2	142.8	XII
3390	BAS.	202	285.7	2	.8	
1	GY.SY.	254	714.2	5	.8	
2	ALAB.	605	1428.5	10	.8	NUBT
3	QTZITE	329	2856.0	20	.8	MEM.
4	BAS.	245	2856.6	20	.8	
5	BR.QTZITE	44	71400.	500	.8	-550
6	BAS.	442	285.9	2	.9	
7	BK.SY.	203	14290.	10	.9	
8	BAS.	331	2857.6	20	.9	
			5715.	40	.9	SEE P
9	GY.QTZ.	444	71.5	1/2	143.0	
3400	BRECCIA	801	1430.	10	.0	-31
1	GY.SY.	317	2861.0	20	.0	
2	GY.SY.	165	7152.5	50	.0	
3	HAEM.	5	143.1	1	.1	
4	GY.SY.	245	2862.2	20	.1	
			3577.6	25	.1	SEE K
5	BAS.	392	286.5	2	.2	
6	BAS.	203	715.8	5	.2	
7	BAS.	141	2863.1	20	.2	
			5726.	40	.2	SEE P
8	HAEM.	497	143.3	1	.3	XVIII
9	ALAB.	338	286.7	2	.3	
3410	HAEM.	498	1432.6	10	.3	XVIII
1	SY.	352	2866.0	20	.3	
2	LIM.	842	28667.	20	.3	
3	BAS.	264	143.4	1	.4	
4	BAS.	386	286.8	2	.4	
5	BK.JASP.	19	717.2	5	.4	
6	GY.SY.	264	143.5	1	.5	
7	BAS.	349	143.5	1	.5	
8	BAS.	442	287.0	2	.5	
9	BAS.	235	5741.	40	.5	
3420	BK.GRAN.	313	28700.	20	.5	-30
1	BR.QTZITE	264	28710.	20	.5	-7
2	BAS.	394	71740.	50	.5	-30
3	ALAB.	254	71.8	1/2	.6	
4	GN.BK.LIM.	165	71.8	1/2	.6	
5	BAS.	381	2872.7	20	.6	
			5745.	40	.6	SEE P
6	GY.SY.	359	7184	50	.6	
7	LIM.	33	47.9	1/3	.7	
8	BAS.	262	47.9	1/3	.7	
9	BAS.	338	287.5	2	.7	
3430	BAS.	21	574.7	4	.7	
1	GY.SY.	54	5749.	25	.7	KAHUN
2	BAS.	265	143.8	1	.8	
3	BAS.	428	143.8	1	.8	
4	HAEM.	497	719.2	5	.8	XVII.
5	GY.METAM.	486	1438.1	10	.8	XVIII
6	BAS.	356	1438.4	10	.8	
7	ALAB.	426	28753.	20	.8	
8	LIM.	65	2877.2	20	.8	KAHUN
9	BK.QTZOSE	558	3596.0	25	.8	XXIII
3440	BAS.	822	28770.	200	.8	V
1	GY.QTZOSE	265	143.9	1	.9	
2	BAS.	324	287.8	2	.9	
3	BAS.	406	287.8	2	.9	
4	BK.WT.SERP	448	287.8	2	.9	
5	LIM.	913	1439.1	10	.9	KAHUN XVIII
6	LIM.	497	1439.4	10	.9	XVIII
7	BK.WT.SY.	33	48.0	1/3	144.0	
8	GY.QTZOSE	20	72.0	1/2	.0	
9	HAEM.	486	144.0	1	.0	XVIII
3450	LIM.	498	144.0	1	.0	-.1
1	BAS.	344	144.0	1	.0	

No.	MATERIAL	FORM	GRS.	X	UNIT	DETAIL
3452	BAS.	373	288·1	2	144·0	
3	LIM.	63	576·	4	·0	|||| −1·8
4	HAEM.	397	719·9	5	·0	GHUROB
5	BAS.	272	719·9	5	·0	
6	BAS.	369	720·1	5	·0	
7	GY.SY.	33	720·2	5	·0	
8	GY.PORPH	245	719·6	50	·0	
9	QTZITE.	207	14402	100	·0	
3460	BAS.	32	144·1	1	·1	
1	BAS.	366	288·3	2	·1	
2	GY.QTZOSE	55	2882·3	20	·1	MERNPTH
3	QTZITE.	382	7206·2	50	·1	
4	LIM.	9	14415·	100	·1	
5	BAS.	336	72·1	1/2	·2	−·3
6	BK.STEA.	22	144·2	1	·2	
7	BAS.	338	288·4	2	·2	
8	BAS.	314	576·7	4	·2	
9	BAS.	83	721·2	5	·2	MERNPTH
3470	RED SY.	345	5768·	40	·2	
1	BAS.	254	48·1	1/3	·3	
2	BAS.	26	144·3	1	·3	
3	HAEM.	498	1442·8	10	·3	XVIII
4	BAS.	265	72·2	1/2	·4	
5	BAS.	202	72·2	1/2	·4	
6	GY.SY.	33	72·2	1/2	·4	
7	BK.QTZOSE	32	72·2	1/2	·4	
8	SERP.	271	144·4	1	·4	
9	BAS.	265	288·9	2	·4	
3480	BAS.	44	288·9	2	·4	
1	Y.SERP.	32	721·8	5	·4	
2	BAS.	446	722·1	5	·4	
3	QTZITE	372	2888·4	20	·4	
4	BAS.	653	5775·	40	·4	∩∩ QUFT V
5	GY.SY.	261	72200·	500	·4	−20
6	BK.QTZOSE	335	289·1	2	·5	
7	LIM.	452	722·7	5	·5	
8	RED GRAN	256	72250·	500	·5	
9	BK.SERP.	487	723·	1/2	·6	
3490	BAS.	33	289·3	2	·6	
1	GY.QTZOSE	387	1446·2	10	·6	
2	BAS.	37	1446·4	10	·6	
3	BAS.	314	2892·	20	·6	−6
4	GY.SY.	317	28930·	200	·6	−3
5	BAS.	262	289·4	2	·7	
6	BAS.	393	289·4	2	·7	
7	BAS.	33	1446·9	10	·7	
8	BK.QTZOSE	82	7237·	50	·7	
9	ALAB.	9156	144·8	1	·8	TARKHAN I
3500	BK.QTZ.	496	144·8	1	·8	BORED, XVIII
1	GY.SY.	33	723·9	5	·8	
2	HAEM.	498	1447·7	10	·8	φIX. XVIII
3	BAS.	245	28964	20	·8	
			3621·4	25	·8	SEE K
4	QTZITE.	315	14484	100	·9	
5	ALAB.	314	483·	1/3	·9	
6	SERP.	23	144·9	1	·9	
7	BAS.	315	289·8	2	·9	
8	GY.QTZOSE	265	289·8	2	·9	
9	BAS.	324	289·9	2	·9	
510	BK.QTZ	879	724·8	5	·9	XXIII
1	BK.QTZOSE	702	1449·0	10	·9	V
2	QTZITE	82	14489·	100	·9	
3	GY.QTZOSE	352	72450·	500	·9	−20
4	GN.LIM.	265	72·5	1/2	145·0	
5	RED HAEM.	81	290·0	2	·0	XVIII
6	BAS.	397	290·1	2	·0	MEM.GLASS
7	BAS.	110	2899·6	20	·0	

No.	MATERIAL	FORM	GRS.	X	UNIT	DETAIL
3518	LIM.	57	58000·	400	145·0	∩∩, KAHUN XII −900
9	GY.QTZOSE	264	145·1	1	·1	
3520	BAS.	346	145·1	1	·1	
1	ALAB.	338	290·3	2	·1	
2	BK.QTZ.	545	2902·7	20	·1	
3	BAS.	338	48·4	1/3	·2	
4	GY.SY.	33	48·4	1/3	·2	
5	BAS.	328	290·4	2	·2	
6	BAS.	202	290·4	2	·2	
7	BK.QTZ.	369	2905·3	20	·2	
8	BAS.	348	72600·	500	·2	
9	BRECCIA	801	1452·6	10	·3	MERNPTH
9A	HARD LIM.	598	1453·5	10	·3	ZET, ABYD, 329
3530	BAS.	33	1453·5	10	·3	
			3632·7	25	·3	SEE K
1	GY.SY.	823	7266·	50	·3	
2	" "	386	1454·	1	·4	
3	BAS.	337	726·8	5	·4	
4	GY.SY.	262	1453·6	10	·4	
5	" "	33	1453·7	10	·4	
6	BK.SY.	333	1453·8	10	·4	
7	" "	386	291·1	2	·5	
8	ALAB.	206	291·0	2	·5	−1·6
9	LIM.	215	291·1	2	·5	MEM.
3540	GY.MARB.	314	582·1	4	·5	
1	ALAB.	9154	872·8	6	·5	TARKHAN I
2	GY.GRAN.	264	29100·	200	·5	−8
3	GY.SY.	33	728·	1/2	·6	
4	BAS.	203	145·6	1	·6	
5	HAEM.	645	727·8	5	·6	XVIII
6	BAS.	406	728·3	5	·6	
7	BAS.	624	1165·0	8	·6	|||| V
8	DIORITE	727	2911·8	20	·6	
			3641·0	25	·6	SEE K
9	BAS.	263	7280·5	50	·6	
3550	BAS.	316	72830·	500	·6	−50
1	GY.SY.	331	145·7	1	·7	
2	LIM.	915	583·	4	·7	KAHUN −1·5 XII
3	BK.QTZOSE	351	29150·	200	·7	−5
4	BR.QTZITE	314	72860·	500	·7	
5	BAS.	328	291·6	2	·8	
6	BAS.	206	291·7	2	·8	
7	BAS.	422	728·8	5	·8	
8	BAS.	33	1457·8	10	·8	
9	BAS.	33	1458·5	10	·8	
3560	HAEM.	493	291·8	2	·9	XVIII
1	BAS.	324	291·8	2	·9	
2	BAS.	442	291·9	2	·9	
3	BAS.	429	1458·8	10	·9	
4	BAS.	333	73·0	1/2	146·0	
5	BAS.	323	73·0	1/2	·0	
6	AMAZONITE	341	73·0	1/2	·0	THEBES
7	LIM.	497	73·0	1/2	·0	KARNAK XVIII
8	GY.STEA.	285	146·0	1	·0	
9	BAS.	393	146·0	1	·0	
3570	BAS.	261	146·0	1	·0	
1	GY.SY.	287	146·0	1	·0	
2	BRECCIA	801	292·0	2	·0	KARNAK, XVIII
3	BAS.	312	292·0	2	·0	
4	ALAB.	885	729·7	5	·0	THEBES, XVIII
5	LIM.	336	729·8	5	·0	
6	GY.VOLC.	33	730·2	5	·0	
7	BAS.	265	1460·	10	·0	? K −1·2
7A			3651·3	25	·0	
8	RED SY.	265	146,000	1000	·0	
9	BAS.	271	146·1	1	·1	
3580	BAS.	446	73057	50	·1	
1	RED SY.	32	14610	100	·1	

No.	MATERIAL	FORM	GRS.	X	UNIT	DETAIL
3582	ALAB.	335	73·1	1/2	146·2	
3	BAS.	262	146·2	1	·2	
4	BAS.	344	292·4	2	·2	DEFENNEH
5	BAS.	426	292·5	2	·2	
6	MALACHITE	352	585·	4	·2	−4·5
7	BAS.	422	730·9	5	·2	
8	BAS.	258	731·2	5	·2	MEM.GLASS
9	GY.SY.	426	731·1	5	·2	
3590	LIM.	397	29250·	200	·2	−70
1	BAS.	254	146·3	1	·3	
2	GY.STEA.	657	292·7	2	·3	QUFT XII
3	GY.SY.	393	292·7	2	·3	
4	BAS.	11	438·9	3	·3	∧
5	BAS.	337	1463·3	10	·3	
6	DURITE	425	29254·	20	·3	
7	BAS.	393	73·2	1/2	·4	
8	GLZD QTZ.	384	73·2	1/2	·4	
9	BAS.	126	732·2	5	·4	QUFT
3600	BAS.	338	2928·2	20	·4	
1	BK.QTZ.	55	2928·4	20	·4	
2	GY.SY.	642	7319·7	50	·4	XII
3	BK.LIM.	267	732·5	5	·5	−·5
4	BAS.	265	2930·1	20	·5	
5	GY.SY.	392	7323·	50	·5	
6	GY.BAS.	328	29300·	200	·5	
7	GY.SY.	16	73·3	1/2	·6	
8	BAS.	254	293·2	2	·6	
9	GY.SY.	353	733·0	5	·6	
3610	BK.QTZOSE	8	36656	25	·6	XXIII
			5863·	40	·6	SEE P
1	QTZITE	364	14656·	100	·6	
2	RED GRAN	256	73300·	500	·6	
3	BR.HAEM.	494	146·7	1	·7	SYRIA XVIII
4	BAS.	425	146·7	1	·7	
5	BAS.	334	293·5	2	·7	THEBES
6	GY.SY.	321	293·5	2	·7	
7	" "	333	733·6	5	·7	
8	BAS.	329	733·7	5	·7	
			3668·5	25	·7	SEE K
9	HAEM.	51	73·4	1/2	·8	XVIII
3620	HAEM.	368	73·4	1/2	·8	
1	BK.JASP.	12	293·7	2	·8	
2	BK.SY.	331	1468·1	10	·8	
3	BAS.	422	2935·7	20	·8	
			3670·2	25	·8	SEE K
4	HAEM.	49	146·9	1	·9	XVIII
5	BR.SERP.	338	146·9	1	·9	QUFT
6	BAS.	313	293·9	2	·9	
7	LIM.	369	1468·6	10	·9	
8	LIM.	674	1469·0	10	·9	
9	BR.SY.	316	2939·0	20	·9	
3630	JADE	28	49·0	1/3	147·0	DEFENNEH
* 1	BAS.	262	73·5	1/2	·0	
2	HAEM.	803	73·5	1/2	·0	XVIII
3	BAS.	275	294·1	2	·0	
4	BAS.	373	294·1	2	·0	
5	BAS.	203	1470·4	10	·0	
6	GY.QTZOSE	372	2939·8	20	·0	
7	BAS.	329	7351·	50	·0	
8	QTZITE	358	7352·	50	·0	
3640	ALAB. rude	657	58800	400	·0	−10
1	BAS.	315	73520	500	·0	−40
2	HAEM.	12	147·1	1	·1	
3	BAS.	262	294·2	2	·1	
4	BAS.	336	294·2	2	·1	
5	BAS.	252	2941·4	20	·1	

No.	MATERIAL	FORM	GRS.	X	UNIT	DETAIL
3646	BAS.	33	2942.7	20	147.1	
7	BK.QTZOSE	333	2943.0	20	.1	
8	GY.SY.	331	73.6	1/2	.2	
8A	GOLD	RING	147.2	1	.2	
9	BAS.	261	147.2	1	.2	
3650	BAS.	275	735.9	5	.2	MEM.
1	BAS.	498	1471.6	10	.2	XVIII
2	BR.QTZITE	55	2944.3	10	.2	
			5890.	40	.2	SEE P
3	LIM.	262	7360.	50	.2	
4	BAS.	33	1473.4	10	.3	
5	BR.SY.	429	2945.2	20	.3	
6	ALAB.	256	73.7	1/2	.4	
7	GY.SY.	331	147.4	1	.4	
8	HAEM.+LEAD	493	294.9	2	.4	TARTUS, XVIII
9	GY.SY.	275	294.9	2	.4	
3660	GY.SY.	369	1474.4	10	.4	
1	BAS.	265	2948.3	20	.4	
			5898.	40	.4	SEE P
2	BK.QTZOSE	9	7368.	50	.4	
3	BK.BAS.	256	29475.	200	.4	-2
4	BAS.	428	147.5	1	.5	
5	BAS.	344	295.0	2	.5	
6	GY.SY.	57	737.3	5	.5	QUFT XII
7	BAS.	387	1474.6	10	.5	
8	BK.QTZOSE	375	14753.	100	.5	
9	BAS.	264	49.2	1/3	.6	
3670	BAS.	328	147.6	1	.6	
1	GY.SY.	325	1476.0	10	.6	
2	BAS.	27	1476.2	10	.6	
2A	LIM.	645	2214.3	15	.6	ZET,ABYD,309
3	ALAB.	653	2952.4	20	.6	IIII KAHUN
4	ALAB.	33	295.4	2	.7	
5	GY.BAS.	422	295.4	2	.7	
6	BK.JASP.	698	591.0	4	.7	V
7	HAEM.	885	738.6	5	.7	MARATHUS
8	BAS.	350	1477.1	10	.7	
9	BAS.	368	2954.9	20	.7	
			3691.4	25	.7	SEE K
3680	RED SY.	261	59100.	400	.7	
1	BAS.	338	739.2	5	.8	
			3694.5	25	.8	SEE K
2	HAEM.	499	295.8	2	.9	XVIII
3	BAS.	265	295.9	2	.9	
4	BAS.	448	295.9	2	.9	
5	BK.SY.	285	295.9	2	.9	
6	DIORITE	82	1479.6	10	.9	GIZEH V
7	BK.QTZOSE	63	5918.	40	.9	XXIII
7A	"	611	7396.	50	.9	ZET,ABYD,461
8	BAS.	331	74.0	1/2	148.0	
9	BAS.	314	296.0	2	.0	
3690	BAS.	11	740.0	5	.0	
1	BAS.	261	740.1	5	.0	
2	ALAB.	406	740.2	5	.0	
3	BAS.	285	1480.3	10	.0	
4	BAS.	802	2959.9	20	.0	
4A	WT.LIM.	692	2960.	20	.0	AMENEMHAT -500
5	GY.QTZOSE	11	148.1	1	.1	
6	Y.BK.SERP.	263	1481.0	10	.1	
			5926.5	40	.1	SEE P
7	GY.BAS.	314	29620.	200	.1	
8	GY.BAS.	271	29615.	200	.1	-3
9	BAS.	252	74.1	1/2	.2	
3700	BK.PORPHY	8	148.2	1	.2	
1	BK.SY.	393	148.2	1	.2	
2	GY.SY.	327	296.5	2	.2	
3	BAS.	202	593.2	4	.3	

No.	MATERIAL	FORM	GRS.	X	UNIT	DETAIL
3704	BAS.	338	741.7	5	148.3	
5	GY.SY.	363	1483.0	10	.3	
6	BAS.	446	296.8	2	.4	
7	BAS.	331	296.9	2	.4	
8	ALAB.	64	593.6	4	.4	XII
9	QTZITE	356	5939.2	40	.4	
3710	GY.SY.	262	49.5	1/3	.5	
1	BAS.	264	49.5	1/3	.5	
2	BK.QTZOSE	89	297.0	2	.5	XII
3	GY.SY.	263	742.8	5	.5	-.6
4	GY.SY.	33	297.2	2	.6	
5	BR.LIM.	373	2971.8	20	.6	
			5946.0	40	.6	SEE P
6	GY.SY.	315	1487	1	.7	
7	BAS.	328	74.4	1/2	.8	
8	BAS.	165	74.4	1/2	.8	
9	BAS.	285	148.8	1	.8	MEM.
3720	HAEM.	387	297.7	2	.8	
1	BAS.	3255	1487.6	10	.8	
2	PORPH.	MACE	2975.5	20	.8	
			3719.4	25	.8	SEE K
3	HAEM.	493	297.8	2	.9	XVIII
4	BAS.	11	1489.0	10	.9	
5	QTZITE	33	14890.	100	.9	
6	BAS.	262	74.5	1/2	149.0	
6A	SY.	9238	149.	1	.0	-1.9
7	BK.SY.	21	745.1	5	.0	
8	BAS.	8	1489.8	10	.0	
9	ALAB.	256	149000.	1000	.0	-1400
3730	BAS.	350	149.1	1	.1	
1	GY.SY.	262	149.1	1	.1	
2	BAS.	369	745.3	5	.1	
3	BK.SY.	338	1491.1	10	.1	
4	BAS.	19	7453.	50	.1	IX
5	CHALCEDONY	DUCK	74.6	1/2	.2	JERUSALEM
6	BAS.	482	298.5	2	.2	MEM.
7	GY.SY.	312	596.7	4	.2	
8	BAS.	258	1491.7	10	.2	
			5967.	40	.2	SEE P
9	GY.SY.	18	29850.	200	.2	-80
3740	BK.BAS.	346	29840.	200	.2	
1	FLINT	9	2986.8	20	.3	
2	BAS.	392	298.8	2	.4	
3	GY.SY.	32	298.9	2	.4	
4	BR.ALAB.	692	597.7	4	.4	GEBELEYN,XII
5	LIM.	344	747?	5	.4	
6	LIM.	642	14947	10	.4	IIIIIIII -V
7	BAS.	254	2988.5	20	.4	
			5979.	40	.4	SEE P
8	BAS.	19	7470.	50	.4	-90
9	RED SY.	32	59750.	400	.4	
3750	BAS.	33	149.5	1	.5	
1	BAS.	46	149.5	1	.5	
2	BAS.	32	598.1	4	.5	
3	BAS.	337	747.3	5	.5	
4	GY.QTZOSE	422	29900.	200	.5	
5	BAS.	442	74.8	1/2	.6	
6	BAS.	384	74.8	1/2	6	
7	BK.QTZOSE	125	149.6	1	.6	
8	HAEM.	496	299.3	2	.6	XVIII
9	GY.SY.	295	747.8	5	.6	
3760	GY.QTZOSE	55	2991.3	20	.6	
			3740.0	25	.6	SEE K
1	BAS.	382	2991.7	20	.6	
2	LIM.	7	7479.	50	.6	
3	BAS.	264	14958.	100	.6	
4	BK.BAS.	326	29912.	200	.6	

No.	MATERIAL	FORM	GRS.	X	UNIT	DETAIL
3765	BAS.	33	49.9	1/3	149.7	
6	BAS.	23	299.4	2	.7	
7	GY.SY.	373	748.5	5	.7	
8	LIM.	428	1496.8	10	.7	
9	GY.SY.	60	5990.	40	.7	XXIII
3770	GY.QTZOSE	315	7486.3	50	.7	
1	QTZITE	328	7487.	50	.7	tough.
2	ALAB.	384	749.	1/2	.8	
3	GN.SERP.	203	149.8	1	.8	
4	BR.MARB	32	149.8	1	.8	
5	BAS.	429	1498.2	10	.8	
			3745	2.1/2	.8	SEEK
6	ALAB.	386	149.9	1	.9	
7	BAS.	448	149.9	1	.9	
8	BAS.	446	299.8	2	.9	
9	BAS.	429	1499.5	10	.9	
			5994.	40	.9	SEE P
3780	LIM.	342	5997.	40	.9	
1	ALAB.	436	50.0	1/3	150.0	
2	BAS.	356	300.0	2	.0	
3	GY.SERP.	11	600.1	4	.0	
4	BAS.	428	750.1	5	.0	
5	BAS.	372	1500.2	10	.0	
5A	GN.GLZ.	696	7500.	50	.0	-230
6	GY.SY.	692	15000.	100	.0	-40
7	BAS.	426	150.1	1	.1	
8	BAS.	12	150.1	1	.1	DEFENNEH
9	GY.SY.	33	300.2	2	.1	
3790	GY.QTZOSE	265	751.	1/2	.2	DEFENNEH
1	BK. "	235	751.1	1/2	.2	
1A	BAS.	31	150.2	1	.2	MEM.
2	BAS.	333	150.2	1	.2	
3	ALAB.	627	150.3	1	.3	XVIII
4	BAS.	424	150.3	1	.3	DEFENNEH
5	GY.SY.	MACE	1503.5	10	.3	MEROE
6	BAS.	33	1503.5	10	.3	
7	RED SY.	245	30062.	20	.3	
8	ALAB.	265	75.2	1/2	.4	
9	BAS.	263	300.8	2	.4	
3800	BAS.	33	300.8	2	.4	
1	BAS.	338	751.8	5	.4	
2	BAS.	372	752.0	5	.4	MERNPTH
3	BK.JASP.	57	1503.7	10	.4	XXIII
4	GY.SY.	311	15044.	10	.4	
5	GY.SY.	215	15040.	100	.4	
6	BAS.	238	150400.	1000	.4	-10
7	GY.SY.	262	150.5	1	.5	
8	BAS.	213	150.5	1	.5	
9	ALAB.	262	150.5	1	.5	
3810	BAS.	344	301.0	2	.5	
1	BAS.	427	752.5	5	.5	
2	ALAB.	155	3010.7	20	.5	
3	BAS.	351	6019.	40	.5	XXIII
4	Y.RED LIM.	498	301.2	2	.6	QUFT XVIII
5	QTZITE	356	1506.4	10	.6	
6	SANDSTN.	337	7529.	50	.6	
6A	GOLD	SHELL	150.7	1	.7	TA.AA SCARABS XXIII
7	BK.SY	197	753.7	5	.7	
8	GY.QTZOSE	11	30150.	200	.7	
9	BAS.	335	754.1	1/2	.8	
3820	BAS.	314	753.9	5	.8	
1	BAS.	497	754.0	5	.8	XVIII
2	BAS.	654	754.0	5	.8	V
3	LIM.	375	754.0	5	.8	
4	QTZITE	27	754.2	5	.8	
5	GY.SILIC.	262	50.3	1/3	.9	
6	BK.SY.	446	754.4	5	.9	MEM.

No.	MATERIAL	FORM	GRS.	X	UNIT	DETAIL
			6043	4	151·0	SEE P
3827	ALAB.	803	604·0	4	·0	GEBELEYN
8	BAS.	427	302·3	2	·1	
			3776·3	25	·1	SEE K
9	RED SY.	314	30220	200	·1	rough
3830	BAS.	268	75·6	1/2	·2	
1	QTZ.CRYST.	33	75·6	1/2	·2	
2	BK.QTZ.	373	1511·8	10	·2	
3	RED QTZITE	558	3023·6	20	·2	
4	GY.QTZOSE	437	3023·8	20	·2	
5	ALAB.	483	302·6	2	·3	XVIII
6	BAS.	165	756·3	5	·3	
7	BK.QTZ.	DRILL CAP	3027·4	20	·3	
			3783·5	25	·3	SEE K
8	Y.LIM.	653	22700·	300	·3	∩∩∩ KAHUN −600 XII
9	BAS.	265	302·8	2	·4	
3840	BAS.	271	757·1	5	·4	
1	SY.	364	1514·2	10	·4	
2	GY.SY.	353	75720·	500	·4	
3	HAEM.	1	151·5	1	·5	
4	"	493	151·5	1	·5	XVIII
5	FLINT	486	151·5	1	·5	XVIII
6	RED SY.	258	6060·	40	·5	
7	ALAB.	152	151·6	1	·6	KAHUN
8	BAS.	265	151·7	1	·7	
9	BAS.	425	758·6	5	·7	
3850	BK.STEA.	295	1517·0	10	·7	
1	LIM.	465	60680	400	·7	rough
2	BAS.	331	303·6	2	·8	
3	ALAB.	258	303·6	2	·8	
4	BR·MARB.	744	303·6	2	·8	A
5	BAS.	337	151·9	1	·9	
6	HAEM.	494	303·9	2	·9	TARTUS XVIII
7	BAS.	275	303·9	2	·9	
8	GY.PORPH.	10	759·5	5	·9	
9	BAS.	426	3038·4	20	·9	
3860	BAS.	263	3039·3	20	·9	
1	BAS.	238	6078·	40	·9	
2	BAS.	11	607·9	4	152·0	
3	RED SY.	33	30400·	200	·0	
4	GY.SY.	323	30402·	200	·0	
5	ALAB.	313	304·2	2	·1	
6	GY.SY.	33	76·1	1/2	·2	
7	BAS.	331	152·2	1	·2	
7A	ALAB.	4952	913·0	6	·2	
			608·7	4	·2	SEE P
8	GY.ST.EA.	653	1522·	10	·2	−4 VI
9	GY.SY.	33	76100·	500	·2	
3870	SERP.	65	1522·7	10	·3	−4·4 XII
			6093·	40	·3	SEE P
1	GY.SY.	33	50·8	1/3	·4	
2	GY.SY.	191	6097·	40	·4	
2A	SANDSTN	605	305·0	2	·5	DEN, ABYD. 248
3	BAS.	395	305·1	2	·5	
4	GY.SY.	334	76272·	500	·5	
5	RED SY.	12	6121·	40	153·0	
6	Y.LIM. LEAD PLUG	803	6140·	40	·5	HELIOPOLIS −140

NECEF 152—169 GRS.

No.	MATERIAL	FORM	GRS.	X	UNIT	DETAIL
3877	BAS.	38	762·1	5	152·4	
8	BAS.	33	152·5	1	·5	
9	BAS.	27	152·5	1	·5	
3880	Y.BK.LIM.	202	152·5	1	·5	
1	BAS.	392	305·1	2	·5	
2	BAS.	33	305·1	2	·5	
3	BAS.	256	305·1	2	·5	
4	BAS.	446	1524·7	10	·5	
5	BK.QTZOSE	8	1525·5	10	·5	
6	"	4	3050·8	20	·5	XXIII
7	RED GRAN	11	30510·	200	·5	
8	HAEM.	493	76·3	1/2	·6	
9	GY.QTZOSE	19	152·6	1	·6	
3890	BAS.	254	305·3	2	·6	
1	BAS.	27	762·9	5	·6	
2	BAS.	27	1527	1	·7	
3	LIM.	446	1527·2	10	·7	
4	BAS.	33	1527·5	10	·7	
5	BAS.	352	3053·4	20	·7	
6	BAS.	25	7633·	50	·7	
			7634·	50	·7	SEE D
7	WT.QTZITE	328	30545	200	·7	
8	BAS.	33	76·4	1/2	·8	
9	DIORITE	364	152·8	1	·8	
3900	BAS.	334	152·8	1	·8	
1	GN.QTZOSE	10	3056·0	20	·8	
			7643·	50	·8	SEE D
2	BAS.	338	152·9	1	·9	
3	BAS.	33	305·9	2	·9	
4	BAS.	335	76·5	1/2	153·0	
5	Y.BK.LIM.	728	153·0	1	·0	
6	BAS.	36	153·0	1	·0	ΦXVI
A	LIM.	728	306·0	2	·0	
7	BAS.	254	306·1	2	·0	
			15300·	100	·0	−320, SEE D
8	BAS.	33	153·1	1	·1	
9	BAS.	202	153·1	1	·1	
3910	BK.QTZOSE	19	1530·7	10	·1	
1	QTZITE	9	3062·2	20	·1	XXIII
2	BR.JASP.	646	766·	5	·2	−6 VI
3	BAS.	33	765·8	5	·2	
4	BAS.	33	765·8	5	·2	"KHENT"
5	BAS.	338	766·0	5	·2	
6	BAS.	19	1533·3	10	·3	
7	BAS.	27	306·8	2	·4	
8	DIORITE	334	766·7	5	·4	
9	GY.SY.	265	767·0	5	·4	SINAI
	SANDST.		30679·	200	·4	
3920	BAS.	33	153·5	1	·5	
1	BAS.	39	307·0	2	·5	
2	BK.QTZOSE	24	9·6	1/16	·6	
3	PINK LIM.	31	19·2	1/8	·6	
4	BL.GLASS	57	153·6	1	·6	
5	BAS.	33	153·6	1	·6	
6	BAS.	38	768·3	5	·6	
7	LIM.	62	307·5	2	·7	⊃ V
8	BAS.	82	307·5	2	·7	V?
9	BAS.	314	768·7	5	·7	
3930	BAS.	338	1537·0	10	·7	
1	BK.QTZ	5	3074·1	20	·7	MERNPTH
2	BAS.	331	76·9	1/2	·8	
3	BR.MARB.	44	153·8	1	·8	

No.	MATERIAL	FORM	GRS.	X	UNIT	DETAIL
3934	BAS.	314	153·8	1	153·8	
5	BAS.	454	307·6	2	·8	MERENPTH
6	BAS.	365	1538·2	10	·8	
7	BAS.	202	153·9	1	·9	
8	BAS.	368	3079·0	20	·9	
9	HAEM.	487	38·5	1/4	154·0	"1/4"
3940	HAEM.	845	154·0	1	·0	
1	BAS.	27	154·0	1	·0	
2	BK.QTZOSE	81	308·0	2	·0	XVIII
3	BAS.	27	769·8	5	·0	
3A	BRECCIA	MACE?	924·0	6	·0	MEROE ΦXVI
4	BAS.	428	3079·2	20	·0	
5	BAS.	27	308·2	2	·1	
6	BAS.	33	308·2	2	·1	
7	BAS.	338	308·3	2	·1	
8	GY.SILIC.	384	770·4	5	·1	
9	GY.SY.	144	154·2	1	·2	
3950	BAS.	19	1541·9	10	·2	
1	GY.SY.	365	1543·3	10	·3	
2	BAS.	338	1543·	10	·3	−6
3	BAS.	63	3086·7	20	·3	V
4	BAS.	27	309·1	2	·5	
	BK.W.SYN	37	6179·5	40	·5	HIERAKON P.
5	BAS.	262	154·6	1	·6	
6	BAS.	344	154·6	1	·6	
7	BK.W.QTZOSE	19	773·2	5	·6	KARNAK
8	BAS.	256	1545·7	10	·6	
			15467·	100	·7	SEE D
9	GY.SERP.	31	38·7	1/4	·8	
3960	RED SY.	8	3096·3	20	·8	XXIII
1	BK.QTZOSE	12	3096·9	20	·8	XXIII
2	BK.STEAT.	64	154·9	1	·9	⊃ XII
3	LIM.	42	154·9	1	·9	
4	BAS.	19	1548·8	10	·9	
5	BK.QTZOSE	141	3099·1	20	·9	XXIII
6	BAS.	406	77·5	1/2	155·0	
7	ALAB.	657	310·	2	·0	−12
8	BAS.	202	155·1	1	·1	
9	SARD.	728	9·7	1/16	·2	GHUROB, XVIII
3970	BAS.	33	310·4	2	2	
1	BAS.	315	3106·	20	·3	
2	GY.GRAN.	37	31065·	200	·3	
3	GY.SY.	27	77·7	1/2	·4	
4	RED SHELL MARBLE	33	155·4	1	·4	−1·3
5	BAS.	38	310·8	2	·4	
6	BAS.	33	310·9	2	·4	
7	BK.W.PORPH.	8	311·1	2	·5	
8	BAS.	5	777·4	5	·5	irregular
9	BAS.	345	3109·6	20	·5	
3980	BAS.	435	3110·2	20	·5	
1	BAS.	265	77·8	1/2	·6	
2	BAS.	27	777·8	5	·6	
3	BAS.	256	1555·6	10	·6	
			77800·	500	·6	SEE D
4	BAS.	328	778·3	5	·7	
5	BAS.	33	77·9	1/2	·8	
6	BAS.	352	778·8	5	·8	
7	BAS.	338	779·4	5	·8	
8	BAS.	45	155·9	1	·9	
9	GY.LIM.	25	311·8	2	·9	
3990	BAS.	338	779·5	5	·9	
*1	BAS.	33	78·0	1/2	156·0	
2	BAS.	33	312·0	2	·0	

No.	MATERIAL	FORM	GRS.	X	UNIT	DETAIL
3993	BAS.	313	780·1	5	156·0	
4	LIM.	352	780·6	5	·1	
5	BAS.	33	780·6	5	·1	
6	BAS.	265	7807·0	50	·1	
7	BAS.	33	78·1	1/2	·2	
8	BAS.	364	78·1	1/2	·2	
9	BAS.	33	781·2	5	·2	
4000	QTZITE	38	3124·5	20	2	
1	BAS.	33	781·6	5	·3	
2	BAS.	446	312·8	2	·4	
3	BAS.	446	312·9	2	·4	
4	BR.QTZITE	643	1564·2	10	·4	RETABEH
			3128·1	20	·4	SEE D
5	BAS.	33	313·0	2	·5	
6	BAS.	875	1565·0	10	·5	XXIII
7	HAEM.	15	78·3	1/2	·6	
			3133·9	20	·7	SEE D
8	BUFF LIM.	14	19·6	1/8	·8	
9	BAS.	325	78·4	1/2	·8	
4010	BAS.	331	156·8	1	·8	
1	BAS.	314	156·8	1	·8	
2	BAS.	27	784·4	5	·9	
3	GY.QTZOSE	54	1568·6	10	·9	XXIII
4	BAS.	38	3138·8	20	·9	
5	BAS.	26	78·5	1/2	157·0	
6	BAS.	254	78·5	1/2	·0	
7	GY.MARB.	81	157·0	1	·0	
8	RED FELSP.	63	157·0	1	·0	XII
9	BAS.	384	785·1	5	·0	
			157000·	1000	·0	SEE D
4020	LIM.	32	785·8	5	·2	
			78602·	500	·2	SEE D
1	BAS.	33	1572·7	10	·3	
			31466·2	20	·3	SEE D
2	BAS.	331	315·2	2	·6	
3	BAS.	338	315·3	2	·6	
4	BAS.	338	3153·0	20	6	
5	QTZITE	313	7885·8	50	·7	
6	BAS.	256	78·9	1/2	·8	
7	BAS.	429	315·8	2	·9	
8	BAS.	15	789·3	5	·9	AMARNA
9	BAS.	27	789·8	5	158·0	
4030	BAS.	338	1579·8	10	·0	
1	BAS.	331	1580·3	10	·0	
2	ALAB.	923	1580·	10	·0	QUFT,−24,XVIII
3	LIM.	452	31600·	200	·0	−60
4	GY.SERP.	235	158·1	1	·1	
5	ALAB.	886	1581·1	10	·1	
6	HAEM.	499	79·1	1/2	·2	SYRIA XVIII
			3164·8	20	·2	SEE D
7	BAS	33	158·4	1	·4	
8	LIM.	452	792·0	5	·4	
9	GY.SY.	338	792·1	5	·4	
9A	BK.QTZOSE	144	1584·6	10	·5	ABYDOS
4040	BAS.	DUCK	31700·	200	·5	−1400
1	BAS.	33	158·6	1	·6	
			3174·0	20	·7	SEE D
2	BAS.	334	794·1	5	·8	
			3178·6	20	·9	SEE D
			3178·8	20	·9	SEE D
			7945·	50	·9	SEE D
3	BAS.	392	1590·	10	159·0	

No.	MATERIAL	FORM	GRS.	X	UNIT	DETAIL
4044	BAS.	406	159·1	1	159·1	
5	ALAB.	922	398·1	5 1/2	·2	∴ AMARN, XVIII
6	BAS.	446	318·7	2	·3	
7	LIM.	305	1592·8	10	·3	
			3187·1	20	·3	SEE D
8	ALAB.	4954	79·7	1/2	·4	XVIII
9	BAS.	429	159·4	1	·4	
4050	ALAB.	9156	478·2	3	·4	TARKHAN 1
1	GY.SY.	23	797·2	5	·4	
2	BAS.	494	159·5	1	·5	XVIII
3	GY.VOLC.	922	159·5	1	·5	
4	CHLORITE	265	159·5	1	·5	
5	BR.BAS.	254	31900·	200	·5	−7
6	GY.SY.	185	79·8	1/2	·6	
			798·2	5	·6	SEE B
7	ALAB.	64	159·7	1	·7	KAHUN XII
8	BAS.	265	798·4	5	·7	
9	ALAB.	15	1597·2	10	·7	
4060	BK.QTZOSE	555	1597·4	10	·7	
			3196·8	20	·8	SEE D
			3198·4	20	·9	SEE D
1	ALAB.	14	20·0	1/8	160·0	
2	BAS.	27	80·0	1/2	·0	
3	HAEM.	499	160·0	1	·0	SYRIA, XVIII
4	BAS.	33	160·0	1	·0	
5	GY.SY.	392	1599·9	10	·0	
6	BAS.	705	15998·	100	·0	IV
7	HAEM.	49	80·1	1/2	·2	XVIII
8	BAS.	331	800·4	5	·1	
9	BK.JASP.	14	801·0	5	·2	
4070	BAS.	338	1602·9	10	·3	
1	GY.GRAN.	312	40100·	5	·4	⊓ −8
2	BAS.	27	321·3	2	6	
3	BAS.	268	80308·	50	·6	
4	QTZITE	313	8032·1	50	·6	
5	BK.QTZOSE	876	3215·0	20	·7	−2·2 XXIII
6	RED GLASS	47	40·2	1/4	·8	
7	HAEM.	491	160·8	1	·8	XVIII
			804·9	5	161·0	SEE B
8	GY.SY.	38	805·6	5	·1	
9	BK.W.PORPH.	31	1611·0	10	·1	
4080	RED HAEM.	406	40·3	1/4	·2	
			3224·8	20	·2	SEE D
			322·7	3	·3	SEE B
			3227·0	20	·3	SEE D
1	GY.QTZOSE	658	16129·	100	·4	IV
2	BK.STEAT.	32	80·7	1/2	·4	OVAL
3	BK.STEAT.	202	80·7	1/2	·4	QUFT
			3229·2	20	·4	SEE D
			8077·7	50	·5	SEE B
4	GN.STEAT.	365	80·8	1/2	·6	
5	BAS.	27	1616·7	10	·7	
6	BAS.	353	1617·2	10	·7	
7	BK.QTZOSE	9	3233·3	20	·7	
8	ALAB.	331	81·1	1/2	162·2	
9	BK.QTZOSE	149	8108·	50	·2	XXIII
4090	LIM.	435	324·6	2	·3	
1	BK.QTZOSE	55	811·6	5	·3	XXIII
			3245·8	20	·3	SEE D
2	BAS.	21	1625·7	10	·6	XXIII
			3253·1	20	·6	SEE D
3	BAS.	338	162·7	1	·7	

No.	MATERIAL	FORM	GRS.	X	UNIT	DETAIL
4094	RED GRAN	9	8136·5	50	162·7	
5	BAS.	338	3257	2	·8	V?
6	BAS.	197	1628·8	10	·9	
			3257·9	20	9	SEE D
7	BAS.	312	81·5	1/2	163·0	
8	ALAB.	625	326·0	2	·0	XII
			3260·0	20	·0	SEE D
9	BAS.	314	163·1	1	·1	
			3261·8	20	·1	SEE D
4100	GY.QTZOSE	11	8180·	50	·6	GIZEH V?
			8198·	50	·9	SEE B
1	RED MARB	15	164·0	1	164·0	XP mor og?
2	BAS.	369	8202·	5	·0	
			3282·8	20	·1	SEE D
3	DIORITE	658	3290·2	20	·5	IV
4	BAS.	33	1645·7	10	·6	
5	BAS.	331	82·4	1/2	·8	
6	ALAB.	80	329·8	2	·9	XVIII
7	ALAB.	165	329·8	2	·9	
8	QTZITE	368	3297·5	20	·9	
9	GY.QTZOSE	311	16501·	100	165·0	rough
4110	GY.STEAT.	625	165·2	1	·2	XII
			3306·1	20	·3	SEE D
			3308·1	20	·4	SEE D
1	BAS.	331	8268·	50	·4	
2	BK.SY.	3	16536·	100	·4	XXIII
3	BK.SY.	264	16538·	100	·4	
4	BK.QTZOSE	11	8279·	50	·6	
5	BAS.	235	331·5	2	·7	
			8291·	5	·8	SEE B
			830·0	5	166·0	SEE B
6	BAS.	314	166·2	1	·2	
7	GN.JASP.	5	332·6	2	·3	
8	QTZITE	38	3329·0	20	·4	
			8320·	50	·4	SEE B
9	ALAB.	483	832·4	5	·5	
4120	BAS.	33	1665·6	10	·6	
1	BK.QTZOSE	14	3334·5	20	·7	
2	HAEM.	922	166·8	1	·8	TARTUS XVIII
3	BAS.	37	834·0	5	·8	
4	BAS.	27	1668·2	10	·8	
5	LIM.	496	334·6	2	167·3	XVIII
6	BAS.	39	335·1	2	·5	
7	BK.QTZOSE	11	8380·	50	·6	
8	BR.SERP.	144	8387·	50	7	
9	ALAB.	483	335·7	1	·8	
			839·0	5	·8	SEE L
4130	GY.SY.	392	167·9	1	·9	
1	HAEM.	803	168·0	1	168·0	XVIII
2	BAS.	328	336·0	2	·0	
3	BK.QTZOSE	55	1680·	10	·0	−64 XXIII
			3359·5	20	·0	SEE S
4	BK.STEA.	64	505·	3	·3	−5 XII
5	BAS.	33	337·0	2	·5	
6	ALAB	352	3382·8	20	169·1	
7	BAS.	338	339·0	2	·5	
8	BAS.	496	339·3	2	·6	XVIII
9	GY.SERP.	496	339·5	2	·7	XVIII
			3396·0	20	·8	SEE S
4140	BAS.	40	3397·0	20	·8	
			8500·	50	170·0	SEE B

KHOIRINE 170-189 GRS.

No	MATERIAL	FORM	GRS.	X	UNIT	DETAIL
4141	AMAZONITE	20	327	1/5	163.5	THEBES
2	BL.GL.SCHST	499	33.1	1/5	165.5	XVIII
3	BL.GLASS	929	33.5	1/5	167.5	
4	BR.SERP.	25	33.9	1/5	169.5	
5	BAS.	356	3401.8	20	170.1	
5A	GLASS VAR?	218	170.5	1	.5	
6	LIM.	924	85.4	1/2	.8	
7	BAS.	801	341.8	2	.9	XVIII
8	HAEM.	49	342	1/5	171.0	XVIII
9	BR.LIM.	646	1710	10	.0	IIIII -8 VI
4150	LIM.	202	171200	1000	.2	QUFT -300
1	GY.SY.	11	8565	5	.3	
2	LIM.	914	1713.2	10	.3	rough
3	BR.SERP.	342	85.8	1/2	.6	
4	BAS.	332	85.9	1/2	.8	
5	BAS.	165	17186	10	.9	
6	ALAB.	238	172	1/10	172.0	
7	GY.SY.	54	3440.1	20	.0	XXIII
8	BAS.	27	861.4	.5	.3	
9	BK.QTZOSE	54	3445.4	20	.3	XXIII
4160	GY.SY.	235	3447.0	20	.3	
1	BAS.	202	172.4	1	.4	
2	LIM.	50	86.3	1/2	.6	MEM.
3	BAS.	37	1726.1	10	.6	
4	LIM.	805	1726.6	10	.7	XVIII
4A	ALAB.	804	346.6	2	173.3	
5	BAS.	27	347.2	2	.6	
			3471.7	2.0	.6	SEE Q
6	BK.QTZOSE	165	3474.8	20	.7	
7	" "	54	3478.2	20	.9	XXIII
8	BAS.	331	3480.9	20	174.0	
			6962.1	40	.0	SEE Q
9	GY.STEA.	838	1741	1	.1	ROMAN
4170	GY.SY.	148	3487.5	20	.4	
1	HAEM.	691	3491	2	.5	
2	GY.QTZOSE	55	1744.8	10	.5	XXIII
3	GY.SY.	54	3491.5	20	.6	XXIII
4	ALAB.	918	349.4	2	.7	
5	BK.BAS	406	349.8	2	.9	HIERAKON? V
6	BAS.	338	1757.3	10	175.7	
7	BAS.	332	87.9	1/2	.8	
8	HAEM.	452	175.8	1	.8	MARATHUS
9	BK.JASP.	20	17.6	1/10	176.0	OVAL
4180	HAEM.	FACE	352.0	2	.0	
1	ALAB.	865	352.1	2	.0	
2	BRECCIA	801	352.2	2	.1	XVIII
3	BK.QTZOSE	10	3522.8	20	.1	
4	BAS.	356	352.6	2	.3	
5	BAS.	333	882	5	.4	-7
6	LIM	795	353.0	2	.5	MEM.
7	BK.QTZOSE	44	17650	100	.5	KAHUN
8	HAEM.	43	353.2	2	.6	XVIII
			3532.9	20	.6	SEE Q
9	BAS.	333	35400	200	177.0	
			3545.8	2.0	.3	SEE Q

No.	MATERIAL	FORM	GRS.	X	UNIT	DETAIL
4190	BAS.	33	88.7	1/2	177.4	
1	ALAB.	625	177.4	1	.4	XII
2	GY.QTZOSE	142	354.8	2	.4	
3	BK. "	54	3549.0	20	.4	XXIII
4	GY.SY.	54	3549.0	20	.4	XXIII
5	HAEM.	DUCK	35.5	1/5	.5	
6	GY.SY.	COWRY	53.3	3/10	.7	
7	BAS.	165	17769.	100	.7	
8	BK.SERP.	498	355.6	2	.8	XVIII
9	BK.SY.	16	17783	100	.8	XXIII
4200	HAEM.	485	177.9	1	.9	XVIII
			3553.2	20	.9	SEE Q
1	CHLORITE	31	35.6	1/5	178.0	
			3563.0	20	.1	SEE Q
2	YEL. PASTE	927	89.1	1/2	.2	
3	BAS.	40	891.2	5	.2	
			3567.1	20	.3	SEE Q
4	FOS.WOOD	54	1784.7	10	.5	XXIII
			3570.7	20	.5	SEE Q
5	BR.QTZITE	27	89330.0	500	.6	-6
5A	BK.WT.SY.	COWRY	53.6	3/10	.7	
6	GY.SY.	58	1787.4	10	.7	XXIII
7	GY.MARB.	147	357.6	2	.8	
8	BAS.	235	3577.6	20	.9	
9	ALAB.	625	178.9	1	.9	XII
4210	BAS.	332	179.1	1	179.1	
1	HAEM.	175	358.6	2	.3	
2	QTZITE	646	3590.6	20	.5	XVIII
3	BK.QTZOSE	7	17955	100	.5	XXIII
4	GY.SY.	COWRY	89.8	1/2	.6	QUFT
			3593.0	20	.6	SEE Q
			3596.0	20	.8	SEE Q
5	ALAB.	937	1799.4	10	.9	
6	GLASS	21	18.0	1/10	180.0	
7	GY.SERP.	873	36.0	1/5	.0	
7A	BK.WT.SY.	798	45.0	1/4	.0	COWRY
8	BK.QTZOSE	59	4500.5	25	.0	XXIII
9	GY.GRAN.	311	90122.	500	.2	
4220	OBSID.	20	36.1	1/5	.5	
1	BAS.	792	90.3	1/2	.6	XVIII
2	GY.SERP.	497	90.3	1/2	.6	XVIII
3	BK.W.PORPH	35	180.6	1	.6	
4	BAS.	33	361.8	2	.9	-.3
5	LIM.	65	181.0	1	181.0	XII
6	RED MARB.	436	362.0	2	.0	
7	RED SY.	347	9050.0	50	.0	
8	HAEM.	882	362.2	2	.1	rough
9	BK.QTZOSE	54	3621.4	20	.1	XXIII
4230	HAEM.	62	362.7	2	.3	XII
0A	LIM	4951	907.2	5	.3	rough
1	AMAZONITE	497	36.3	1/5	.5	THEBES, XVIII
2	BAS.	33	1815.1	10	.5	
3	BRECCIA	43	90.8	1/2	.6	
4	BK.SY	54	3632.7	20	.6	XXIII
5	BK.MARB	790	90.9	1/2	.8	XVIII
			3638.3	20	.9	SEE Q
6	ALAB.	65	182.0	1	182.0	XII

No.	MATERIAL	FORM	GRS.	X	UNIT	DETAIL
4237	HAEM.	51	364.0	2	182.0	XVIII
8	GY.QTZOSE	54	3641.0	20	.0	XXIII
8A	ALAB.	806	913.0	5	.6	
9	BK.SY.	54	3658.0	20	.9	XXIII
4240	ALAB.	334	183.1	1	183.1	
1	HAEM.	491	183.1	1	.1	XVIII
2	BK.QTZOSE	55	1832.6	10	.3	XXIII
			3665.6	20	.3	SEE Q
3	" "	65	3668.5	20	.4	XXIII
4	ALAB.	62	367.0	2	.5	-.8 XII
5	BK.QTZOSE	64	3670.2	20	.5	XXIII
6	BAS.	327	367.3	2	.6	
6A	BK.LIM.	287	2755.2	15	.7	IE ROMAN
7	GY.SY.	328	36.8	1/5	184.0	
8	" "	COWRY	368.0	2	.0	ΦIX
4250	HAEM.	80	184.3	1	.3	XVIII
1	BK.SY.	54	3691.4	20	.6	XXIII
2	GY.SERP.	311	3694.5	20	.7	
3	BK.SY..	646	36976.	200	.8	"IRON 10" XII
4	RED JASP.	653	1850.	10	1850.	IIIIIII -100 IX RETABEH.
5	HAEM.	484	185.2	1	.2	XVIII
6A	ALAB.	493	92.8	1/2	.6	XVIII
7	GY.SERP.	902	928.0	5	.6	
8	BAS.	646	4640	25	.6	-25 VI
			2785.	15	.7	SEE Q
9	ALAB.	801	92.9	1/2	.8	XVIII
4260	GY.MARB.	429	371.6	2	.8	-.8
1	BK.QTZOSE	54	3719.4	20	186.0	XXIII
2	BK.SY.	33	3719.4	20	.0	MEM.
3	QTZITE.	5	93100.	500	.2	-300
4	BAS.	33	931.9	5	.4	
5	BK.QTZOSE	58	4660.	25	.4	-22
6	BK.SERP.	397	934.7	1/2	.8	
			1494.7	8	.8	IIIIII SEE Q
7	ALAB.	917	934.8	5	187.0	
8	BAS.	235	3740.0	20	.0	
9	BR.QTZITE	54	3740.0	20	.0	XXIII
4270	LIM.	795	374.5	2	.2	
1	BR.CHALC?	925	935.9	5	.2	XXVI?
2	LIM.	646	4685.8	25	.4	QUFT VI
3	BAS.	313	37.5	1/5	.5	
			3751.4	20	.6	SEE D
4	HAEM.	499	187.8	1	.8	XVIII
5	BAS.	33	23.5	1/8	188.0	
6	BR.LIM.	801	375.9	2	.0	XVIII
			3760.	20	.0	-54 SEE B
7	BAS.	63	37.7	1/5	.5	XII
8	GY.SY.	882	377.1	2	.5	
9	BR.SY.	439	1884.8	10	.5	
4280	CARNEL?	258	94.3	1/2	.6	PIERCED
1	BK.QTZOS.	10	3776.3	20	.8	XXIII
2	BAS.	256	377.8	2	.9	
3	BK.QTZOSE	54	3783.5	20	189.2	XXIII
4	LIM.	646	4732.	25	.3	QUFT VI
5	PINK LIM.	801	94.8	1/2	.6	XVIII
6	HAEM.	430	95.0	1/2	190.0	XVIII

BEQA 187-214 GRS.

No.	MATERIAL	FORM	GRS.	X	UNIT	DETAIL
4287	SANDSTN	646	18515·	100	185·2	SINAI
8	BK.STEAT.	59	468	1/4	187·2	QUFT
9	HAEM.	891	187·6	1	·6	
4290	BK.SY.	16	3756·7	20	·8	XXIII
1	LIM.	65	3760·	20	188·0	KAHUN −55 XII
2	BAS.	458	47·1	1/4	·4	
3	GY.SERP.	742	1885·	10	·5	−17
			3776·3	20	·8	SEE K
			377·8	2	·9	SEE K
			3783·5	20	189·2	SEE K
4	GY.QTZOSE	11	3783·5	20	·2	XXIII
5	GY.SY.	64	3784·6	20	·2	XXIII
6	LIM.	881	5676·	30	·2	NAQ.107 PRE
			3786·0	20	·3	SEE D
7	ALAB.	499	47·4	1/4	·6	
8	CALCITE	65	47·4	1/4	·6	XVIII
9	ALAB.	62	569·2	3	·7	II/ XII
			3796·2	20	·8	SEE D
			7592·2	40	·8	SEE D
4300	BAS	452	47·5	1/4	190·0	
1	BK.QTZOSE	55	1900·0	10	·0	XXIII
2	ALAB. KAH	648	3801·	20	·0	IIIIII,−2, XII
3	LIM.	333	190·2	10	·2	−15
			3806·9	20	·3	SEE D
4	ALAB.	26	23·8	1/8	·4	
5	BAS.	26	23·8	1/8	·4	
6	BAS.	21	47·6	1/4	·4	
7	HAEM.	893	952·0	5	·4	
8	"	4	190·6	1	·6	ANTIOCH
			3816·1	20	·8	SEE D
			7633·	40	·8	SEE N
9	RED PORPH	642	9539·	50	·8	SINAI
4310	GY.STEAT.	932	191·0	1	191·0	
1	BK.QTZOSE	54	3820·0	20	·0	
2	LIM.	66	38200·	200	·0	KAH,−3000,XII
3	BAS.	14	47·8	1/4	·2	
4	BK.QTZOSE	55	1913·0	10	·3	XXIII
5	ALAB.	63	3828·	20	·4	−6 XII
			766·0	4	·5	SEE N
6	BK.MARB.	836	191·7	1	·7	
			766·7	4	·7	SEE N
			767·0	4	·7	SEE N
			3836·5	20	·8	SEE D
			3839·0	20	·9	SEE D
7	DURITE	425	48·0	1/4	192·0	
8	BAS.	14	48·0	1/4	·0	
9	LIM.	691	19200·	100	·0	−120 XII
			768·3		·1	SEE N
			3842·1	20	·1	SEE D
			768·7	4	·2	SEE N
4320	GY.MARB	892	961·7	5	·3	
			3846·	20	·3	SEE D
1	LIM.	881	7694·	40	·3	NAQ. PRE
			769·8	4	·4	SEE N
2	BAS.	235 356 331	961·9 1925·2 770·4	5 10 4	·4 ·5 ·6	HIERAKON P. SEE N
3	GY.SY.	331	9635·	50	·7	rough
4	BKQTZOSE	11	3859·7	20	193·0	ΦXVI
5	MARBLE	BRS	38600·	200	·0	BYBLOS −400
6	BK.QTZOSE	62	966·3	5	·2	XXIII
7	" "	54	38650·	20	·2	XXIII
			773·2	4	·3	SEE N
			3876·1	20	·8	SEE D
8	GN.QTZOSE	165	7745·	40	·8	XXIII

No.	MATERIAL	FORM	GRS.	X	UNIT	DETAIL
4329	GY.SY.	12	9693·	50	193·8	
4330	BK.STEAT.	617	97·0	1/2	194·0	⊂ = 1/2 XII
1	HAEM.	COWROID	97·0	1/2	·0	
2	LIM.	456	1163·8	6	·0	PRE
3	LIM.	55	9700·	50	·0	KAH,−120,XII
			777·4	4	·3	SEE N
4	GY.QTZOSE	11	1942·7	10	·3	
4A	LIM.	657	19434·	100	·3	MEDUM III
			777·8	4	·4	SEE N
5	ALAB.	626	389·0	2	·5	XVIII
			778·3	4	·6	SEE N
			3892·	20	·6	SEE D
6	GY.STEAT.	626	194·7	1	·7	Q QUFT XII
			778·8	4	·7	SEE N
7	BAS.	12	7788·	40	·7	XXIII
			779·4	4	·8	SEE N
			779·5	4	·9	SEE N
8	SANDST.	406	1949·2	10	·9	
8A	LIM.	802	97·5	1/2	195·0	MEM.
			780·1	4	·0	SEE N
9	LIM.	429	975·	5	·0	−15
			780·6	4	·1	SEE N
			780·6	4	·1	SEE N
			3902·5	20	·1	SEE D
4340	Y.BK.SERP.	314	24·4	1/8	·2	
1	BK.QTZOSE	55	975·8	5	·2	XXIII
			3903·5	2	·2	SEE D
			7807·	20	·2	SEE N
			781·2	4	·3	SEE N
2	" "	55	1953·2	10	·3	XXIII
			781·6	4	·4	SEE N
3	QUARTZ	11	7821·	40	·5	XXIII
4	Y.LIM.	937	391·3	2	·6	echinus
5	BK.JASP.	907	391·5	2	·7	−2 XXIII
			39150·	200	·7	SEE D
6	Y.BK.SERP.	347	24·5	1/8	196·0	
7	" "	427	24·5	1/8	·0	
8	BAS.	328	24·5	1/8	·0	
9	GY.SY.	328	24·5	1/8	·0	
4350	ALAB.	40	49·0	1/4	·0	
1	BAS.	202	49·0	1/4	·0	
2	ALAB.	9156	980·1	5	·0	TARKHAN. 1
3	LIM.	56	9800·	50	·0	KAH,−200,XII
			7844·	4	·1	SEE N
4	BK.QTZOSE	643	1177·4	6	·2	IIIIII VI
5	GN.MARB.	694	19621·	100	·2	HERFU,XII
			7851·	4	·3	SEE N
6	BAS.	891	392·9	2	·4	XVIII
			785·8	4	·4	SEE N
			786·0	4	·4	SEE D
			3929·2	20	·5	SEE D
			39300·	200	·5	SEE D
7	LIM.	452	393000·	2000	·5	
8	LIM	646	589·7	3	·6	NAQ. PRE
			3932·9	20	·6	SEE D
9	BK.QTZOSE	10	19667·	10	·7	MERNPTH
			39342·	20	·7	SEE D
4360	HAEM.	894	24·6	1/8	·8	TYRE
1	BAS.	7	49·2	1/4	·8	
2	BAS.	331	984·0	5	·8	
3	ALAB.	9156	985·0	5	197·0	TARKHAN 1
			7886·	40	·1	SEE N
4	ALAB.	892	394·5	2	·2	XVIII
			789·3	4	·3	SEE N
			3945·5	20	·3	SEE D
			3945·9	20	·3	SEE D

No.	MATERIAL	FORM	GRS.	X	UNIT	DETAIL
4364A	LIM.	INGOT	19735·	100	197·3	MEDUM III
5	PINK QTZ.	742	789·8	4	·4	QUFT
			789·3	4	·4	SEE N
6	BR.CARN.	902	395·1	2	·5	
7	ALAB.	64	3950·	20	·5	−75 XII
			7906·	40	·6	
8	BAS.	14	49·7	1/4	·8	
9	BR.SY.	54	1978·3	10	·8	XXIII
			792·0	4	198·0	SEE N
			792·1	4	·0	SEE N
4370	LIM.	372	19800·	100	·0	−130
1	WT.LIM.	264	1980·8	10	·1	THEBES
			3961·1	20	·1	SEE D
2	LIM.	652	991·	5	·2	IIIII,−8, VI
			3967·0	20	·3	SEE D
3	HAEM.	6	12·4	1/16	·4	
4	"	241	24·8	1/8	·4	
5	BAS.	232	24·8	1/8	·4	
6	BAS.	144	99·2	1/2	·4	DEFENNEH
			794·1	4	·5	SEE N
			3971·2	20	·6	SEE D
6A	ALAB.	805	993·5	5	·7	BORED
7	BK.QTZOSE	54	3979·1	20	·9	XXIII
			398·0	2	199·0	
8	LIM.	238	19900·	100	·0	−75
9	HAEM.	38	49·8	1/4	·2	rough
4380	BAS.	206	49·8	1/4	·2	
1	BAS.	7	49·8	1/4	·2	
2	HAEM.	893	199·3	1	·3	TYRE
			398·7	2	·3	XII
			797·2	4	·3	SEE N
4	POTTERY	924	996·9	5	·4	
4A	SANDSTN.	875	4985·0	25	·4	ABYD,146 1
5	MARBLE	BRS	39890·	200	·4	BYBLOS
			399·1	2	·5	SEE S
6	BAS.	63	798·2	4	·5	VI
7	LIM.	497	49·9	1/4	·6	XVIII
8	HAEM.	894	49·9	1/4	·6	TYRE XVIII
			798·4	4	·6	SEE N
8A	HARD LIM.	596	399·5	2	·7	ZET,AB329,1
9	CHLORITE	817	1997·	10	·7	−1·6
4390	BK.QTZOSE	18	39932·	20	·7	XXIII
1	HAEM.	505	99·9	1/2	·8	XVIII
2	LIM.	456	39966·	20	·8	NAQ. PRE
3	BAS.	33	199·9	1	·9	
4	LIM.	646	11995·	60	·9	ΠΠΠ,KAH,XII
5	DURITE	322	12·5	1/16	200·0	
6	BAS.	33	25·0	1/8	·0	
7	BAS.	442	1000·0	5	·0	
8	BK.W.PORPH	835	1000·2	5	·0	
9	CHERT	653	14000·	100	·0	ΠΠΠΠ −1300 V
			800·4	4	·1	SEE N
			801·0	4	·3	SEE N
4400	BR.SY.	59	2002·9	10	·3	XXIII
1	HAEM.	51	50·1	1/4	·4	TARTUS XVIII
2	COPPER	980	50·1	1/4	·4	
3	BR.LIM.	302	50·1	1/4	·4	
4	W.QTZITE	237	40100·	200	·5	rough
			40100·	200	·5	SEE N
5	BAS.	27	40152·	200	·7	
6	LIM.	38	100·4	1/2	·8	
7	BK.QTZOSE	10	40155·0	20	·8	XXIII
			8031·	40	·8	SEE N
			8032·	40	·8	SEE N
8	Y.LIM.	368	4019·0	20	·9	MERNPTH
9	GY.GRAN	364	40190·	200	·9	

No.	MATERIAL	FORM	GRS.	X	UNIT	DETAIL
4410	GY.SY.	618	201.0	1	201.0	VI
1	LIM.	643	1005.	5	.0	
2	BAS.	17	2009.5	10	.0	
3	BK.QTZOSE	347	4020.2	20	.0	XXIII
4	RED GRAN.	11	20100.0	100	.0	-60
5	BAS.	62	804.9	4	2	II VI
6	BR.SERP.	692	2011.8	8/10	251.5/201.2	⋂ HU 458 XII
			805.6	4	.4	SEE N
7	ALAB.	63	3828	19	.5	⋂ -6
8	BK.W.PORPH	356	4030	20	.5	-36
9	BAS.	33	25.4	1/8	.6	
4420	ALAB.	64	201.7	1	.7	DEFNEH VI
1	BAS.	16	8077.7	400	.9	XXIII
2	LIM.	232	50.5	1/4	202.0	
3	GY.STEAT.	932	101.0	1/2	.0	QUFT
3A	LIM.	653	24244	120	.0	MEDUM III
4	GY.SY.	62	202.1	1	.1	XII
4A	SANDSTN	54	8086.	40	.2	ZER,AB 729, 1
5	BAS.	23	25.3	1/8	.4	
6	BK.SY.	325	50.6	1/4	.4	
7	ALAB.	25	1012.	5	.4	
8	BAS.	339	2025	10	.5	MERNPTH
8A	LIM.	9202	1013.4	5	.7	END GROOVE 24.5.21
9	BAS.	347	40540	20	.7	
			8108.0	40	.7	SEE N
			12160.	60	.7	SEE P
4430	VIOLET GLS.	38	50.7	1/4	.8	
1	BAS.	425	50.7	1/4	.8	
2	BK.QTZOSE	55	1014.2	5	.8	XXIII
3	" "	10	4056.1	20	.8	XXIII
4	" "	63	6088.2	30	.9	XXIII
4A	GLZ.SCHIST	691	400	2	203.0	oⵝ? -30 XIII
5	BAS.	14	5073.	25	.1	XXIII
6	BK.SY.	54	4064.0	20	.2	XXIII
7	BK.QTZOSE	63	4066.0	20	.3	XXIII
8	" "	9	5085.	25	.4	XXIII
			8136.	40	.4	SEE N
9	BR.QTZ.	742	1017.8	5	.5	
4440	BK.QTZOSE	54	4070.6	20	.5	MERNPTH
1	RED GRAN	422	10175.	50	.5	rough
2	BAS.	19	25.5	1/8	204.0	
3	GN.JASP.	20	25.5	1/8	.0	THEBES
4	BAS.	33	51.0	1/4	.0	
5	BAS.	33	51.0	1/4	.0	
6	BAS.	26	51.0	1/4	.0	
7	BK.QTZOSE	881	5101.	25	.0	XXIII
8	GY.SY.	265	102.1	1/2	.2	
9	WT.GLASS	38	51.1	1/4	.4	
4450	BAS.	20	51.1	1/4	.4	
1	ALAB.	626	408.8	2	.4	XII
2	BK.QTZOSE	12	4090.8	20	.5	XXIII
3	BAS.	352	5112	25	.5	
			8180.	40	.5	SEE N
4	ALAB.	65	102.3	1/2	.6	I XII
5	RED VEINED LIM.	649	10433.	51	.6	⋂⋂⋂ QUFT, IV
6	BKQTZOSE	822	1024.2	5	.8	-12 XII
7	LIM.	64	5120.	25	.8	HARAGEH

No.	MATERIAL	FORM	GRS.	X	UNIT	DETAIL
4458	GY.SY.	12	5121.	25	204.9	XXIII
9	BK.SY.	347	8198.	40	.9	
			820.2	4	205.0	SEE N
4460	BK.STEAT	725	1640.0	8	.0	H=8 ROMAN
1	BK.QTZOSE	65	6153.	30	.1	XXIII
2	BAS.	38	25.7	1/8	.6	
3	BAS.	314	25.7	1/8	.6	
4	BAS.	38	51.4	1/4	.6	
5	GY.SILIC.	15	102.8	1/2	.6	
6	RED JASP.	653	1850.	9	.6	⋂⋂⋂⋂ -100, IX RETABEN
7	BRECCIA	11	2055.6	10	.6	XVIII
8	BK.QTZOSE	8	2056.5	10	.6	XXIII
9	" "	611	2057.4	10	.7	XXIII
4470	BAS.	33	51.5	1/4	206.0	
1	ALAB.	165	5156.	25	.2	
2	ALAB.	347	4126.5	20	.3	
3	BL.GLASS	303	25.8	1/8	.4	
4	BAS.	33	51.6	1/4	.4	
5	BAS.	33	51.6	1/4	.4	
6	BAS.	33	103.2	1/2	.4	
7	GY.SY.	16	20640	10	.4	
8	VOLC.ASH	264	2064.	10	.4	-12
9	BKQTZOSE	2	10319.	50	.4	XXIII
4480	GN.SY.	9	10326.	50	.5	KAHUN XII
			8268.	40	.7	SEE N
1	BAS.	33	51.7	1/4	.8	
2	BK.STEAT.	871	51.7	1/4	.8	
3	BK.QTZOSE	54	4137.5	20	.9	MERNPTH
			8279.	40	207.0	SEE N
3A	LIM.	653	24861.	120	.1	MEDUM III
4	GY.GRAN.	26	41416.	200	.1	
5	GY.JASP.	33	25.9	1/8	.2	
6	ALAB.	4	829.1	4	.3	HIERAKON?
7	BK.QTZOSE	2	5186.	25	.4	
8	LIM.	36	830.0	4	.5	
9	BAS.	203	51.9	1/4	.6	
4490	OBSID.	803	207.9	1	.6	LU.PIN
1	GY.SY.	165	20758	100	.6	⋂⋂⋂⋂ n
2	GN.QTZOSE	11	4157.1	20	.8	XXIII
3	BAS.	254	5197.	25	.9	
4	BONE	74	52.0	1/4	208.0	
			2080.0	10	.0	SEE Q 138.6
5	BK.QTZOSE	10	4160.1	20	.0	MERNPTH
6	LIM.	56	8320.	40	.0	KAHUN, -15, XII
7	LIM.	692	31200	150	.0	SINAI, -500
			832.4	4	.1	SEE N
8	W.QTZITE	54	2081.4	10	.1	XXIII
9	GY.MARB.	126	208.3	1	.3	
4500	BK.QTZOSE	55	2083.5	10	.3	
1	" "	38	4165.2	20	.3	XXIII
2	RED.QTZ.	54	4166.8	20	.3	XXIII
3	HAEM.	485	52.1	1/4	.4	XVIII
4	RED GLSS	15	104.2	1/2	.4	
5	GY.QTZOSE	38	4168.6	20	.4	XXIII
6	GY.STEAT.	63	417.0	2	.5	II XII
			834.0	4	.5	SEE N
7	RED VEINED LIM.	649	10433.	50	.7	⋂⋂⋂ QUFT IV

No.	MATERIAL	FORM	GRS.	X	UNIT	DETAIL
4508	BAS.	142	26.1	1/8	2088	
9	LIM.	232	26.1	1/8	.8	
4510	Y.BK.SERP.	33	52.2	1/4	.8	
1	BK.JASP.	63	417.9	2	.9	II VI
2	GY.QTZOSE	PEB	2090.0	10	209.0	
3	LIM.	429	20900.0	100	.0	-100
4	GN.STEAT.	725	209.1	1	.1	BORED
5	SANDST.	625	5229.	25	.1	XII
6	GY.STEAT.	63	209.2	1	.2	I XII
7	Y.QUARTZ	742	418.7	2	.3	
8	LIM.	917	837.8	4	.4	KAHUN XII
			8380.	40	.5	SEE N
9	ALAB.	265	41900.0	200	.5	-50
4520	BAS.	33	131.1	1/16	.6	
1	BAS.	20	52.4	1/4	.6	
2	HAEM.	894	52.4	1/4	.6	SYRIA
3	BK.JASP.	748	209.6	1	.6	
4	BK.QTZOSE	2	4192.1	20	.6	XXIII
5	" "	446	4192.1	20	.6	XXIII
6	" "	54	4192.4	20	.6	XXIII
			839.0	4	.7	SEE L
7	LIM.	816	4193.6	20	.7	
			8387.	40	.7	SEE N
8	BK.QTZOSE	11	4196.5	20	.8	XXIII
9	Y.LIM.	646	839.5	4	.9	II XII
4530	BR.QTZITE	11	41990.	200	.9	-4
0A	LIM.	653	42004.	200	210.0	MEDUM III
1	GN.QTZOSE	11	5256.	25	.1	MERNPTH
2	GY. "	7	10506	50	.1	XXIII
3	BK.BAS.	33	42022.	200	.1	
4	BK.W.SY	311	263.	1/8	.4	
5	QTZITE	64	6313.	30	.4	-.7 VI
6	DIORITE	652	10526.	5	.5	IIIII IV
7	LIM.	934	842.5	4	.6	
8	ALAB.	626	210.9	1	.9	XVIII
9	BK.QTZOSE	10	10543.	50	.9	XXIII
4540	BAS.	15	10546.	50	.9	⋂⋂ HIERAKNP.
	GY.GRAN.	231	21096.00	100	.9	
			5277.	25	211.1	SEE L
1	GLASS	395	264.	1/8	.2	DEFENNEH
2	ALAB, KA"	648	3801.	18	.2	IIIIIIII, -2, XII
3	HAEM.	883/4351	4224.6/1113.6	20/10	.2	NAR. PRE
4	PINK.QTZ.	742	1270.4	6	.7	QUFT
			5293.	25	.7	SEE L
5	GY.SY.	2.6	265.	1/8	2120	
			4241.	20	.0	SEE L.
6	LIM.	625	8500.	40	.5	KAH"-200, XII
7	BR.SERP.	691	1276.2	6	.7	III QUFT XII
8	RED V". LIM	649	6405.	30	213.6	⋂⋂⋂ " IV
9	PINK.SY.	165	10686.	50	.7	
4550	LIM.	29,6	1070.	5	2140	-60
1	CHLORITE	618	6447.	30	.9	HIERAKON P. ⋂⋂⋂ XII
2	Y.STEAT.	64	3227.	3/2	2153	III XII
3	LIM.	458	2180.2	10		
3A	LIM.	653	43848.	200	219.2	MEDUM III
4	WT.QTZ.	742	8853.	4	221.3	
5	LIM.	458	118.0	1/2	2360	

✶ A D D E N D A   MARKED ✶

No.	MATERIAL	FORM	GRS.	X	UNIT	DETAIL
2139A	P.BR.LIM.	799	241.2	2	120.6	P
2142A	P.GY.LIM.	797	1208.2	10	8	P
2183A	P.PINKLIM	702	245.4	2	122.7	P
2237A	P.BR.LIM.	792	124.4	1	124.4	P
2261A	D.PURP."	797	1250.3	10	125.0	Q↯D
2407A	D.VAR.GLS	711	128.4	1	128.4	D
2540A	PINK LIM.	803	392.0	3	130.7	D.
2618A	ALAB.	49	1319.5	10	131.9	D. chicker
2705A	HAEM.	808 DOVE	1330.	10	133.0	S. -20 HUMAN HEAD
2786A	GY.LIM.	435	4025.	3	134.2	S. ⵠIX
3073A	BR.LIM.	436	1387.3	10	138.7	S.
3151A	BK.JASP.	817	694.3	5	138.9	PEBBLE Q
3157A	HAEM.	442	69.5	1/2	139.0	Q
3337B	HAEM.	446	142.0	1	142.0	Q
3403A	BAS.	331	143.1	1	143.1	Q
3630A	BAS. thin	22	49.0	1/3	147.0	Q
3991A	IVORY, lowct	926	78.	1/2	156.	N -2

SELA 209–227 GS

No.	MATERIAL	FORM	GRS.	X	UNIT	DETAIL
4555A	BR.SERP.	740	418·2	2	209·1	
			209·2	1	·2	SEE B
6	ALAB.	265	41900·	200	·5	-50
7	HAEM.	938	839·0	4	·7	
			839·5	4	·9	SEE B
8	BR.QTZITE	11	41990·	200	·9	-4
9	BAS.	392	52·5	1/2	210·0	
4560	BK.BAS.	33	42022·	200	·1	
			6313·	30	·4	SEE B
			1052·6	5	·5	"
			210·9	1	·9	"
			10543·	50	·9	"
			10546·	50	·9	"
1	BR.QTZITE	343	42180·	200	·9	rough
2	HAEM.	11	211·0	1	211·0	
3	BK.QTZOSE	11	5276·	25	·1	XXIII
			3801·	9	·2	SEE B
			4224·5	20	·2	SEE B
4	BK.QTZOSE	378	423·0	2	·5	
5	LIM.	711	21149·	100	·5	
6	BAS.	71	423·4	2	·7	
7	GY.QTZOSE	2	5293·	25	·7	XXIII
8	BK.SERP.	744	847·5	4	·8	ROMAN
9	LIM.	15	53·0	1/4	212·0	AMARNA
4570	HAEM.	505	53·0	1/4	·0	XVIII
1	HAEM.	498	4240·6	20	·0	XVIII
2	GY.QTZITE	256	42400·	200	·0	-3000
3	BAS.	33	42400·	200	·0	-220
4	RED GRAN	32	106086·	500	·2	
5	GY.SY.	33	53·1	1/4	·4	
6	BK.CLAY	88	53·1	1/4	·4	
7	FELSPAR	824	425·1	2	·5	MEM.
8	LIM.	267	42500·	200	·5	-170
			1277·0	6	·8	SEE D
9	LIM.	RAM	21277·	100	·8	MEM.
4580	BK.SY.	14	5325·	25	·9	XXIII
1	BR.SY.	338	8521·	40	213·0	
2	BAS.	392	53·3	1/4	·2	
3	HAEM.	898	426·6	2	·2	XVIII
4	BK.QTZOSE	32	1280000·	2 TAL	·3	
5	BAS.	11	8535·	40	·4	
			6405·	30	·5	SEE B
6	BAS.	327	8547·	40	·7	
			10686·	50	·7	SEE B
7	BK.QTZOSE	7	4276·5	20	·8	
7A	BAS.	314	5348·	25	·9	GHUROB
8	HAEM.	494	107·0	1/2	214·0	XVIII
8A	HAEM.	495	2141·	10	·1	END GROOVE 24.V.21
9	BAS.	256	2142·	1	·2	rough
4590	LIM.KAH	64	8570·	40	·2	nn -34 XII
1	SY.		13·4	1/16	·4	
2	GY.GRAN	331	42900·	200	·5	-130
3	BR.LIM.	64	429·4	2	·7	II VI
4	GY.QTZOSE	10	5373·	25	·9	XXIII
			6447·	30	·9	SEE B
5	HAEM.	482	430·1	2	215·0	MERNPTH
5A	BR.LIM.	495	4300·	20	·0	G -270
6	BK.BAS.	364	43000·	200	·0	-50
7	BK.QTZOSE	3	4302·5	40	·1	XXIII
8	BRECCIA	498	26·9	1/8	·2	XVIII
9	HAEM.	897	107·6	1/2	·2	-·6 XVIII
4600	GN.SY.	2	8608·	40	·2	KAHUN XII
1	GN.JASP.	126	215·4	1	·4	
2	LIM.	702	21553·	100	·5	BENI HASAN XII
3	GY.GRAN	102	43112·	200	·6	
4	BAS.	143	2157·2	10	·7	
5	BK.QTZOSE	5	5393·	25	·7	XXIII
6	LIM.	701	21572·	100	·7	
7	GY.SY.	16	5397·	25	·9	XXIII

No.	MATERIAL	FORM	GRS.	X	UNIT	DETAIL
4608	CHLORITE	33	27·0	1/8	216·0	
9	WT.MARB.	14	432·0	2	·0	CARTHAGE, R0
4610	LIM.	33	2160·2	10	·0	
1	BK.BAS.		216100·	1000	·1	-400
2	ALAB.	64	432·4	2	·2	II ABYD.VI
3	BAS.	656 ROUGH	864·9	4	·2	IV
4	GY.GRAN.	465	43270·	200	·3	rough
5	BK.JASP.	875	865·8	4	·4	XXIII
6	BK.QTZOSE	55	1083·3	5	·6	XXIII
7	" "	4	4331·9	20	·6	XXIII
8	LIM.	12	1084·	1/2	·8	
9	BK.W.PORPH	10	4336·6	20	·8	QUFT XXIII
4620	LIM.	313	4336·8	20	·8	rough
1	BK.JASP.	14	216·9	1	·9	ROMAN
2	GY.SYEN	54	4338·6	20	·9	XXIII
3	RED GRAN	354	43380·	200	·9	rough
4	BAS.	422	5428·	25	217·1	XXIII
5	BAS.	313	54·3	1/4	·2	
6	BAS. WOLF	HEAD	1303·6	6	·4	√=3 ΦJX
7	GY.QTZOSE	5	43480·	200	·4	irregular
8	BAS.	422	5442·	25	·7	XXIII
9	GN.SERP.	887	54·5	1/4	218·0	
4630	BAS.	64	436·0	2	·0	I XII
1	ALAB.	406	1090·9	5	·2	
2	BK.QTZOSE	54	4367·3	20	·3	
3	HAEM.	899	218·4	1	·4	SMYRNA,XVIII
4	ALAB.	722	1092·0	5	·4	QUFT
5	BAS.	422	5459·	25	·7	XXIII
6	W.QTZITE	11	43700·	200	·5	
7	MARBLE	15	874·5	4	·6	IIII R0.
8	LIM.	406	437·8	2	·9	
9	ALAB.	368	1094·8	5	219·0	
4640	BR.SY.	2	43820·	20	·0	rough XXIII
1	BR.SY.	2	4380·3	20	·0	" "
2	RED GRAN	352	21900·	100	·0	-60
3	GY.GRAN	12	43800·	200	·0	
4	QTZITE	338	219000·	1000	·0	
5	GY.BAS.	892	876·5	4	·1	
6	ALAB.	26	54·8	1/4	·2	
7	HAEM.	494	109·6	1/2	·2	XVIII
8	BAS.	428	2192·4	10	·2	
9	BAS.	65	438·9	2	·4	ABYD.MENA.
4650	BAS.	165	4391·0	20	·5	XXIII
1	BK.SY.	5	4394·9	20	·7	rough XXIII
2	HAEM.	429	109·9	1/2	·8	+ ANTIOCH XVIII
3	BAS.	254	879·6	4	·9	
4	BAS.	149	4397·2	20	·9	XXIII
5	BAS.	33	27·5	1/8	220·0	
6	BAS.	33	55·0	1/4	·0	
7	ALAB.	795	110·0	1/2	·0	-1·4
8	BK.QTZOSE	54	22025·	10	·2	XXIII
9	W.QTZITE	27	220310·	1000	·3	
9A	Y.GLASS	926	110·2	1/2	·4	BEHNESA,R0
4660	BK.QTZOSE	55	881·8	4	·4	XXIII
1	LIM.	917	441·0	2	·5	
2	BK.QTZOSE	2	5512·	25	·5	XXIII
3	" "	12	5513·	25	·5	XXIII
4	HAEM.	232	110·3	1/2	·6	XVIII
5	BR.SERP.	13	882·4	4	·6	Δ=4 ROM.
6	GY.SY.	38	4411·2	20	·6	
7	BAS.	314	883000·	4000	·7	
8	BAS.	33	55·2	1/4	·8	
9	LIM.	5	3534·4	16	·9	H=8 ROM.
9A	CLEAR GLS.	215	110·5	1/2	221·0	
4670	HAEM.	232	110·5	1/2	·0	
1	NUM.LIM.	64	2210·2	10	·0	IIIII VI
2	GY.GRAN	326	44195·	200	·0	
3	W.QTZITE	27	44195·	200	·0	MEM.
4	QTZITE	54	4422·5	20	·1	XXIII
5	BK.QTZOSE	12	22130·	100	·3	-15
6	GY.GRAN	33	44256·	200	·3	

No.	MATERIAL	FORM	GRS.	X	UNIT	DETAIL
4677	BAS.	331	44300·	200	221·5	-1100
8	GY.QTZOSE	54	4432·5	20	·6	XXIII
9	BK. "		2217·3	10	·7	irregular
4680	" "	10	5543·	25	·7	XXIII
1	RED LIM.	325	221·8	1	·8	
2	LIM.	645	1109·2	5	·8	AMARN, XVIII
3	GY.SY.	348	5544·	25	·8	
4	BK.QTZOSE	55	2221·2	10	222·1	XXIII
5	GY. "	54	4443·9	20	·2	XXIII
6	HAEM.	49	444·7	2	·3	TARTUS XVIII
7	SARD	505	55·6	1/4	·4	XVIII
8	LIM. KAHN	64	8900·	40	·5	nn -200 XII
9	BAS.	11	2229·	10	·6	
4690	BK.SY.	10	5566·	25	·6	XXIII
1	DURITE	31	27·6	1/8	·8	QUFT
2	BAS.	63	2228·	10	·8	-8 XII
3	BAS.	14	8917·	40	·9	
4	GY.SY.	345	11144·	50	·9	
5	W.QTZITE	18	44574·	200	·9	
6	BAS.	26	5575·	25	223·0	-26
7	MARB.MAN	64	44600·	200	·0	LEBANON-170 ΦXVI
8	DIORITE	37	27·9	1/8	·2	
9	BAS.	33	55·8	1/4	·2	
4700	BK.QTZOSE	38	4465·2	20	·2	XXIII
1	BR.QTZITE	27	89330·	400	·3	-6
2	ORANG.GLS.	43	1117·7	1/2	·4	
3	Y.LIM.	429	1117·	5	·4	-4
4	BK.QTZOSE	8	5584·	25	·4	XXIII
			2011·8	9	·5	HIIIIII SEE B
5	" "	54	4471·0	20	·5	XXIII
6	" "	10	5588·	25	·5	XXIII
7	BAS.	2	2236·	10	·6	-7
8	BK.BAS. COWR0		111·9	1/2	·8	XVIII
9	HAEM.	499	111·9	1/2	·8	XVIII
4710	BK.JASP.	64	447·8	2	·9	VI
1	LIM.	526	448·5	2	224·2	
2	BK.QTZOSE	4	4483·3	20	·2	XXIII
3	GY.SY.	54	5609·	25	·3	XXIII
4	LIM.	701	11215·	50	·3	"HORA
5	BK.QTZOSE	4	4489·0	20	·4	KAHUN XXIII
6	GN.JADE	874	449·0	2	·5	"PTAH" XII?
7	GY.QTZOSE	54	6985·	40	·6	XXIII
8	BAS.	26	562·1	1/4	·8	
9	SLATE DUCK HEAD		562·1	1/4	·8	Φ IX
4720	LIM. rough	916	899·4	4	·8	KAHUN XII
1	BK.QTZOSE	11	5622·	25	·9	XXIII
2	BAS.	313	450000·	2000	225·0	
3	GY.QTZOSE	38	2253·5	10	·3	
4	GY.GRAN	351	90122·	400	·3	
5	HAEM.	893	112·7	1/2	·4	TYRE
6	HAEM.	2	1127·0	5	·4	HELIOPOLIS
7	Y.SERP.	13	225·5	1	·5	Λ R0.
8	BK.SY.	14	4509·5	20	·5	XXIII
9	BK.STEAT.	323	564·	1/4	·6	
4730	HAEM.		225·6	1	·6	irregular
1	GY.QTZOSE	3	4513·	20	·6	XXIII
2	BK. "	54	4514·8	20	·7	XXIII
3	BAS.	237	11289·	50	·8	
4	W.MARB.	14	4519·3	20	226·0	ROM.
5	BK.QTZOSE	54	4520·8	20	·0	XXIII
6	" "	10	5655·	25	·2	XXIII
7	" "	10	45272·	20	·3	XXIII
8	GY. "	54	2267·2	10	·7	XXIII
9	CHALCEDNY	925	226·9	1	·9	XXVI?
4740	BAS. FIG.656	656	454·0	2	227·0	QUFT IV NEFERMAOT
1	BK.QTZOSE	313	227·1	1	·1	
2	" "	10	4549·1	20	·4	XXIII
3	HAEM.	12	227·5	1	·5	
4	GY.STEAT.	64	227·6	1	·6	QUFT XII
5	ALAB.	914	457·0	2	228·5	

METAL WEIGHTS.

AS ALL OF THESE HAVE ALTERED BY
CORROSION THEY ARE LISTED SEPARATELY.

BRONZE PEYEM. L = LEAD.

No.	FORM	NOW	CH	ORIGIN	X	UNIT	DETAIL
4746	252	115·5	1·7	114	1	114·0	
7	605	4576·3	32	4570	40	·2	ANCHOR L
8	254	115·8	1	115	1	115·0	DEFNEH
9	CALF	59·0	1	58	½	116·0	ALEX. ΦIX
9A	505	228·4	4	232	2	·0	BEYRUT
4750	60	1169·8	36	1166	10	·6	L
0A	895	232·5	2	233	2	·5	
1	605	3533·0	30	3503	30	·8	ANCHOR
2	206	118·8	1·4	117	1	117·0	DEFNEH
3	338	236·0	1·8	234·2	2	·0	AMARNA
4	742	469·4	0	469·4	4	·4	B BK·MARBᴸ
5	628	2363·4	67	2356	20	·8	
6	256	60·7	1·3	59	½	118·0	
7	575	247·3	10	237	2	·5	
8	265	596·8	3·2	594	5	·8	
9	12	127·1	8	119	1	119·0	
4760	9196	240·0	1·7	238	2	·0	
1	623	251·0	13	238	2	·0	ALEX. L
2	334	28·7	5	24	1/5	120·0	
3	252	119·6	28	120	1	·0	
4	353	1209·2	5	1208·	10	·8	
5	605	1764·0	65	1816·	15	121·1	ANCHOR ΠΑΠΙΟΥ
6	26	246·6	3	243	2	·5	
7	263	1221·9	8	1218	10	·8	
8	345	60·7	·7	61	½	122·0	
9	26	123·5	2	122	1	·0	
4770	38	251·2	7	244	2	·0	
1	267	659·4	45	610	5	·0	
2	264	1235·6	13	1223	10	·3	
2A	49	121·8	2	123·5	1	123·5	
3	DISC	497·5	5·5	495	4	·7	TARTUS ΥΥ
4	338	62·1	1·4	62	½	124·0	
5	FROG	123·9	1·1	124	1		ΦIX
6	373	126·8	2·5	124	1		
7	369	125·4	1·5	124	1		
8	152	250·3	2	248	2		SMYRNA
9	331	251·6	2·5	249	2	124·5	
4780	338	246·8	35	250	2	125	
1	252	252·2	2·	250	2		

BRONZE DARIC   L = LEAD

No.	FORM	NOW	CH	ORIGIN	X	UNIT	DETAIL
2	60	975·2	7	968	8	121·0	MAGNESIA SIP.
3	17	998·9	22	977	8	122·1	EPHESOS, SEVERUS ΦIX
4	245	371·4	22	369	3	123·0	DEFENEH
5	155	1981·9	7	1975	16	123·4	L
6	364	248·4	1·4	247	2	·5	DEFENEH
7	724	989·8	·5	990	8	·7	ALAB.
8	LION	63·0	·7	62	½	124	TYRE ΦIX
9		994·6	1·3	993	8	·1	LPMᴀᵀOYP JAFFA ΦIX
4790	60	1991·1	10·	1987	16	124·2	L
1	60	998·6	0	999	8	·9	
2	60	1889·1	53	1882	15	125·5	L
3	382	635·3	66	629	5	·8	MEM.
4	51	21·0	·2	21	1/6	126·	
5	28	43·2	1·5	42	1/3		QUS
6	364	62·9	1·2	63	½		DEFENEH
7	264	63·5	1·6	63	½		
7A	507	123·9	2·	126	1		AMARNA

No.	FORM	NOW	CH	ORIGIN	X	UNIT	DETAIL
4798	26	127·2	1·5	126	1	126	DEFNEH
9	605	1895·9	6	1890	15		LACHISH PHILIP II L
4800	PL·XII	3232·2	72	3160	25	126·4	EPHESOS TRIPOD L
1	RAM	1289·0	21	1268	10	·8	ΦIX
2	499	126·9	3	127	1	127·	
3	343	129·2	45	127	1		
4	DUMP	127·4	·3	127	1		
5	334	256·4	22	254	2		
6	60	1014·4	8·	1016	8		E.M.L = 8
7	254	386·8	5	382	3	127·3	
8	262	393·0	10	383	3	·7	
9	26	16·1	·4	16	1/8	128·	
4810	26	32·7	·6	32	¼		
1	312	64·7	1·8	64	½		
2	321	127·1	2·5	128	1		
3	321	130·1	17	128	1		
4	DUCK HEAD	129·5	1·5	128	1		ΦIX
5	DUCK	260·1	4·	256	2		ΦIX
6	BULL HEAD	2509·8	113	2560	20		ΦIX
7	60	521·0	14	573	4	128·2	L
8	33	388·5	36	385	3	·3	
9	265	643·8	15	642	5	·4	
4820	95	3260·7	50	3210	25	·4	EPHESOS L
1	725	642·9	·1	643	5	·6	Π=5 BR·LIMSᵀ
2	353	44·0	1·	43	1/3	129·0	
3	321	127·4	25	129	1		
4	378	127·0	3·	129	1		
5	255	clean	0	388	3	·3	
6	60	535·3	17	518	4	·5	L
7	329	262·7	37	259	2		
8	333	66·8	3·	65	½	130·0	
9	63	65·1	1·5	65	½		
4830	328	126·5	5·	130	1		
1	3255	128·2	3·	130	1		
2	364	127·4	3·	130	1		
3	353	261·0	4·	260	2		
4	422	389·0	6·	390	3		
5	19	658·7	8	651	5	130·2	
6	60	1049·8	4·	1042	8		L
7	285	388·3	2·5	391	3	·3	
8	338	394·5	3·	391	3		
9	254	1304·8	6	1303	10		
4840	364	656·0	35	652	5	·4	
1	LION	2613·5	3	2610	20	·5	ASSYRIAN ΦIX
2	60	658·0	5	653	5	·6	
3	33	130·2	·9	131	1	131·0	
4	LION	131·2	·6	131	1		
5	364	659·4	3	655	5		
6	53	785·5	8	786	6		
7	605	3298·4	23	3275	25		ΦIX L
8	LION	2648·4	13	2635	20	131·7	ASSYRIAN THUNDER BOLT BULL
9	PL·XIII	527·7	·6	527	4	·7	
4850	33	448·	1·	44	1/3	132·0	
1	337	667·	1	66	½		
2	26	67·4	1·4	66	½		DEFENEH
3	23	132·9	35	132	1		
4	321	132·6	17	132	1		
5	328	137·0	5·	132	1		
6	724	527·9	·1	528	4		B BR·LIMSᵀ
7	26	658·1	8	660	5		
8	381	665·8	6	660	5		
9	66	265·1	3·	265	2	·5	

LEAD STATER B = BRONZE

No	FORM	NOW	CH	ORIGIN	X	UNIT	DETAIL
4860	621	19·7	·7	19·0	1/6	114·	· · = 2 OBOLI
1	60	21·5	21	19·4	1/6	116·4	· ·
2	60	183·4	7·	176	3/2	117·3	ALEX.
3	621	178·1	1·6	176·5	3/2	·6	Γ=3 DR. SMYRN.
4	621	61·1	1·8	59	½	118·	
d	60	60·1	·8	59·3	½	·6	
5	60	487·0	10·	478	4	119·4	H=8 DR
6	58	245·5	5·	240	2	120·	
7	623	484·8	9	480	4	120·	H
8	58	30·0	·6	30·2	¼	·8	· · · 3 OBOLI
d	60	246·9	3·5	243	2	121·5	
9	58	67·4	6·7	61	½	122·	B
4870	623	243·1	7·	245	2	·5	
1	58	125·5	2·3	123	1	123·	
2	623	121·7	1·9	123	1		
3	60	298·5	21	246	2		
4	60	277·1	30	247	2		ALEX
5	58	64·4	2·	62	½	124·	
6	605	62·8	·9	62	1		A=1 SMYRNA
7	605	124·7	7	124	1		HIERAPOLIS
d		248·4	4·	248	2		
8	71	248·0	0	248·0	2	·0	8 QUFT BK·MARB
9	60	256·7	8·	250	2	125·	
4880	60	252·2	1·8	250	2		Δ=4 DR. ALE)
1	60	252·4	2·7	250	2		ALEX.
2	60	633·0	4·	629	5	·8	I=10 DR.
3	60	21·5	·6	21	1/6	126·	ALEX.
4	623	68·2	5·	63	½		
5	623	63·0	1·2	63	½		
6	58	64·0	1·0	63	½		
7	58	133·4	7·5	126	1		
8	58	131·5	4·5	127	1	127·	ALEX.
9	605	316·5	2·7	319	5/2	·6	Є=5 MACNESIA SIPYL.
4890	44	63·8	1·1	64	½	128·	#
1	623	63·9	1·2	64	½		
2	58	128·3	1·7	128	1		ALEX.
3	615	520·8	7·	514	4	128·5	MAGNESIA SIP.
4	58	32·2	·5	32·3	¼	129·2	
5	623	32·3	1·	32·5	¼	130·	W
6	60	65·3	7	65·	½		ALEX.
7	60	65·5	·5	65·	½		Λ=1 DR.
8	622	130·2	·3	130·	1		
9	23	280·2	26	260	2		
d	333	394·2	2·	392·	3	130·7	
4900	58	130·3	1·9	131·	1	131·	ALEX.
1	621	16·0	4	16·4	1/8	·2	ALEX.
2	621	32·8	3·	32·8	¼	·2	
3	60	33·3	7·	33	¼	132·	
4	58	34·2	1·1	33	¼		ALEX.
5	60	67·2	·9	66	½		ALEX.
6	623	71·1	5·	66	½		
7	623	530·6	3·8	528	4		H=8 DR
7A	623	128·3	4·	132·5	1	132·5	B=2
8	336	268·7	4	265	2		
9	623	275·7	11	265	2		
4910		17·1	1·1	16·6	1/8	1	·8
1	623	671·7	8·	664	5		
2	333	1341	1·3	133	1	133·0	
A3	58 FROG	132·3	1·4	133	1		· · · B=2 ALEX.
4	304	1324·9	16	1332	10	·2	ΦIX.

d = duplicate rejected

No.	FORM	NOW	CH.	ORIGIN⁴	X	UNIT	DETAIL
4915	333	258.5	14	2.67	2	133.5	
6	336	270.0	2.8	267	2		
7	60	70.5	3.5	67	1/2	134.	SLATE
8	60	67.3	7	67	1/2		ALEX.
9	60	133.6	.9	134	1		
4920	SNAKE HEAD	134.6	1	134	1		ΦIX
1	256	134.9	2.9	134	1		
2	58	133.0	2.5	134	1		
3	333	132.9	3.5	134	1		
4	301	136.5	2.5	134	1		
5	BULL HEAD	134.6	.3	134.3	1		ΦIX
6	MAN HEAD	270.8	2.3	268.5	2		ΦIX
7	53	271.0	2.8	268	2		RIQQEH
8	58	540.2	12	536	4		SMYRNA
9	26	674.8	4.6	670	5		B
4930	265	668.0	2.	670	5		MEM.
1	74	268.5	0	268.5	2	134.2	Δ=4 QUFT GY. STEAT.
2	52	415.0	12	403	3	.3	III
3	314	263.4	11.5	269	2	.5	
4	58	277.1	8.	269	2	.5	ALEX
5	327	271.6	1.9	269	2		
6	60	543.7	6.	538	4		
7	338	669.7	5.6	673.5	5	.7	
8	WOLF HEAD	1345.8	2.	1348	10	.8	HAEM T. ΦIX
9	BULL HEAD	1354.1	6	1348	10	.8	AMARNA B ΦIX
4940	321	44.5	1.2	45	1/3	135.	
1	326	45.1	1.3	45	1/3		
2	623	135.3	.7	135	1		
3	927	270.4	4.5	270	2		
4	3255	679.3	9.5	675	5		GHUROB
5	265	667.8	2.7	675	5		
6	605	677.1	1.	677	5	135.4	ASKLEPIOS B ΦIX
d	915b	270.4	2.4	271	2	.5	
7	64	17.0	0	17.0	1/8	136	
8	575	24.3	1.6	22.7	1/6		ALEX.
9	60	34.0	.1	34	1/4		
4950	60	35.1	.7	34	1/4		
1	63	68.5	1.2	68	1/2		
2	622	68.3	.4	68	1/2		
3	622	135.6	3.0	136	1		
4	262	134.8	1.5	136	1		ALEX.
5	58	137.0	.7	136	1		
6	58	274.3	2.	272	2		
7	58	540.8	3.1	544	4		SMYRNA
8	60	2041.0	17	2040	15		
9	623	2771	4.5	272.5	2		
4960	621	33.3	1.1	34.2	1/4	136.8	
1	57	136.5	2.5	137	1	137	QUS
2	623	548.8	10	539	8	137.2	III H ALEX.
3	623	23.5	.5	23.	1/6	138.	
4	254	45.6	1.2	46.	1/3		
5	58	67.4	3.3	69	1/2		ALEX.
6	SEED	69.5	.1	69	1/2		SICILY B
7	60	140.0	2.3	138	1		
8	58	138.3	.3	138	1		ALEX.
9	622	71.1	.5	71	1/2	142	A=1
4970	58	144.7	3.	142	1		
1	14	11.9	0	11.9	1/12	142.8	SMYRNA
2	58	72.4	.7	72	1/2	144.	ALEX.
3	60	289.0	4.5	289	2	144.5	
d	625	74.7	3.2	71.5	1/2	143	ALEX
4	62	24.0	9	24.1	1/6	144.6	
5	60	145.0	3.7	145	1	145.	
6	58	145.7	2.3	147	1	147.	
7	60	12.2	.3	12.3	1/12	147.6	

BRONZE QEDET

No.	FORM	NOW	CH.	ORIGIN⁴	X	UNIT	DETAIL
4978	324	141.5	4.8	137	1	137.	
d	337	690.3	10	686	5	.2	
9	26	69.6	7	69.	1/2	138.	
d	344	141.1	3.	138.	1		
4980	335	684.2	10.	690	5		
1	33	66.6	4.3	69.	1/2		O mark
2	326	696.8	9.7	6943.	5D	.9	LEAD FILLING
d	32	148.5	9.	139.	1	139.	
3	494	140.0	1.	139.	1		
4	235	136.0	2.8	139.	1		
5	262	272.7	7.5	278	2		"T" TREASURY
6	FROG	277.2	2.3	278	2		
7	338	699.5	3.	696	5	.2	
d	265	692.4	8.	696	5	.2	
8	262	47.1	7	465?	1/3	.5	
9	26	281.5	12	279	2		
4990	338	280.8	2.	279	2		
1	LION	27866.	30	27900	200		LIM.
2	339	140.4	2.6	140	1	140.0	
3	334	140.5	2.6	140	1		
d	338	150.7	11.	140	1		
d	338	281.7	5.	280	2		
d	33	299.7	20.	280	2		
4	265	672.8	30.	700	5		
d	324	692.4	12	700	5		
5	334	702.8	3.	700	5		DEFENEH
d	324	708.0	18.	702	5	140.4	
6	333	281.7	5.	281	2	.5	
7	331	468	1.2	47	1/3	141.	
8	623	47.1	.5	47	1/3		LEAD
9	428	140.5	2.1	141	1		
d	324	143.5	3.6	141	1		
d	23	146.1	5.2	141	1		
d	338	138.0	15.	141	1		
d	33	149.6	8.7	141	1		MEM.
5000	23	280.2	2.	282	2		
1	366	282.0	6.	282	2		
2	884	711.4	5.	706	5	141.2	LEAD
3	262	713.9	15.	707	5	.4	LEAD FILLING
4	643	284.5	1.2	283	2	.5	
d	356	704.5	9.	708	5	.6	
5	33	73.0	3.	71	1/2	142.	X
d	338	73.7	3.	71	1/2		
6	337	142.5	2.5	142	1		
7	337	142.5	2.6	142	1		
d	338	143.5	1.2	142	1		
8	364	283.6	4.	284	2		
9	324	287.6	3.	284	2		
d	366	288.0	10.	284	2		
5010		692.4	17.	710	5		
1	324	699.7	10.	710	5		
d	338	1430.1	9.	1421	10	.1	
2	327	718.0	7.	711	5	.2	
d	337	720.3	8.	712	5	.4	
d	324	729.0	17.	712	5	.4	
d	334	283.0	9.	285	2	.5	
d	366	288.0	6.	285	2	.5	
3	333	710.2	6.	714	5	.8	
d	33	72.7	1.2	71.5	1/2	143.0	
d	338	145.6	2.2	143	1		
4		144.5	3.7	143	1		LEAD
5	74	142.9	.1	143	1		BK. STEA.
6	366	285.4	3.	286	2		

No.	FORM	NOW	CH.	ORIGIN⁴	X	UNIT	DETAIL
5017	262	293.3	7.	286	2	143.	
8	33	145.5	2.4	143	1		
9	344	713.6	4.	716	5	.2	
d	364	283.5	3.5	287	2	.5	
5020	312	287.0	6.	287	2		
1	338	287.7	2.	287	2		1
d	344	287.8	5.	287	2		
d	335	721.2	3.	718	5	.6	
2	23	72.2	.2	72	1/2	144.	
3	336	72.9	1.	72	1/2		
4	338	138.5	8.	144	1		
d	''	145.0	3.6	144	1		
d	''	146.7	46	144	1		
d	33	150.8	7.	144	1		
d	338	287.4	5.	288	2		
d	338	723.0	1.	722	5	.4	
5	344	283.2	6.	289	2	.5	
d	338	288.0	5.	289	2		
d	338	300.0	19.	289	2		
d	265	293.8	9.	289	2		
d	262	742.1	18.	724	5	.8	
6	57	144.5	.5	145	1	145.	LEAD, ALEX
d	338	150.7	5.6	145	1		
7	63	144.3	1.9	145	1		
d	312	290.2	4.	290	2		
d	324	715.6	9.	725	5		
8	366	293.5	10.7	2907	2	.3	MEM. SET OF 4
d	324	730.6	3.	727	5	.4	
d	333	292.5	2.	291	2	.5	
9	337	293.7	3.	291	2		MERENPTH
5030	BULL HEAD	302.7	11.	291	2		GHUROB
d	338	725.4	45	728	5	.6	
1	265	731.6	3.	729	5	.8	
d	335	73.1	3.	73	1/2	146.	
d	338	145.6	2.	146	1		
2	353	147.1	3.	146	1		
3	36	292.5	14.	292	2		
d	364	298.8	7.	292	2		
4	306	1474.6	14.	1460	10		ΦIX
5	338	725.4	5.5	730	5		
6	337	729.6	4.	730	5		
7	324	710.8	20.	730	5		
8	337	1475.8	12.	1464	10	.4	
9	33	292.6	2.	293	2		
d	366	297.3	12.	293	2		
5040	339	304.3	23.	293	2		
d	338	735.5	8.	733	5	.6	
1	338	734.2	5.	733	5		
2	333	734.4	5.	733	5		
d	33	147.4	.6	147	1	147.0	
3	36	295.6	2.	294	2		QUS
4	304	693.5	46	735	5		Λ' ABYD, DEN
d	324	742.0	9.	735	5		
5	338	1471.2	6.	1470	10		
6	45	150.5	11.	1474	1	.4	MEM. SET OF 4
d	333	293.5	14.	295	2	.5	
7	354	590.4	0	590	4		
8	494	739.2	11.	738	5	.6	SYRIA
9	237	1495.2	24.	1476	10		MEM. SET OF 4
5050	DOVE	74.3	.6	74	1/2	148.0	ΦIX
1	623	74.7	3.7	74	1/2		LEAD
2	623	146.8	3.5	148	1		LEAD
d	335	149.3	3.	148	1		
d	335	150.5	2.	148	1		

No.	FORM	NOW	CH.	ORIGIN?	X	UNIT	DETAIL
5053	66	297.8	5.4	296	2	148.0	DEFENEH
d	33	299.0	3.	296	2		
d	333	297.8	3.7	296	2		
. 4	873	301	7.	296	2		LEAD PLUMMET
5	346	592.6	3.3	592	4		DEFENEH
6	262	712.9	30	740	5		
d	338	300.0	3.	297	2	.5	
d	337	744.8	1.7	743	5	.6	
d	337	742.2	4.	744	5	.8	
7	337	146.5	2.5	149	1	149.	ALEX. LEAD
8	425	148.4	7	149	1		
9	353	149.9	1.5	149	1		
5060	335	150.6	1.2	149	1		
d	335	151.6	2.	149	1		
d	353	294.5	7.	298	2		
d	33	295.1	17.5	298	2		
1	32	296.3	4.5	298	2		
2	338	297.8	2.	298	2		
3	267	731.9	22	745	5		
4	333	744.6	0	745	5		
5	206	601.1	17.	596	4		
6	36	300.0	2.	298.5	2	.2	
d	335	749.3	3.	746	5	.2	
7	337	1497.8	5.	1493	10	.3	
8	900	744.6	5.5	747	5	.4	
9	267	753.5	6.	747	5		
5070	623	39.6	1.8	37.5	1/4	150.0	
1	364	50.6	.4	50	1/3		
2	311	50.7	2.8	50	1/3		
3	BULL HEAD	75.3	.6	75	1/2		ΦIX
d	338	72.8	2.	75	1/2		
.d	335	74.6	1.1	75	1/2		
4	324	75.5	1.5	75	1/2		
5	FACE	149.5	17	150	1		
6	324	149.7	2.	150	1		
d	339	737.6	11.8	750	5		
d	338	769.5	20.	750	5		
d	334	744.4	8.	752	5	.4	
d	337	758.3	6.	752	5		
7	353	602.1	.5	602	4	.5	
8	33	749.8	3.	753	5	.6	
9	337	757.3	4.	753	5		
5080	306	1547.5	41	1506	10		
1	337	758	15	75.5	1/2	151.0	
2	SCARAB	152.9	1.7	151	1		SCARAB
3	FROG	150.3	1.	151	1		ΦIX
4	144	294.6	10.	302	2		
d	324	758.5	6.8	755	5		
5	335	748.2	7.	755	5		
d	338	763.6	9.	755	5		
6	304	746.8	9.	756	5	.2	
7	323	306.0	3.	303	2	.5	
8	33	745.9	12.	758	5	.6	
9	333	309.0	4.7	304	2	152.	
5090	337	296.8	7.	304	2		
1	338	310.6	11.	304	2		
2	327	761.0	1.	760	5		
3	264	470.0	4.6	51	1/3	153	
4	33	29710.	1300	31000.	200	155.	HANDLE LOST
5	33	315.2	4.4	313.7	2	156.8	MEM.SET of 4

BRONZE NECEF L=LEAD

No.	FORM	NOW	CH.	ORIGIN?	X	UNIT	DETAIL
5096	934	152.5	2.	150	1	150	
7	621	38.5	.2	38.3	1/4	153.2	TINNED
8	803	724.2	42	766	5		
9	264	77.8	2.5	77	1/2	154.0	
5100	691	155.4	1.4	154	1		
1	337	821.5	50?	770	5		
2	275	312.6	9.	309	2	.5	
3	LION	313.8	5.	309	2		LION ΦIX
4	324	788.7	9.	774	5	.8	X
5	328	157.8	3.	155	1	155.	
6	3255	312.9	9.	310	2		
7	327	781.1	57	778	5	.6	
8	33	784.0	5.	779	5	.8	
9	DOG	38.3	.5	39	1/4	156.0	DOG ΦIX
5110	58	39.6	.9	39	1/4		L
1	324	155.1	2.4	157	1	157.0	
2	LION	159.5	2.	157	1		LION
3	934	781.9	11	788	5	.6	GHUROB
4	306	7932.	38	7894.	50	.9	
5	506	79.2	2.	79.	1/2	158.0	DEFENEH
6	202			79.4	1/2	1 .8	IRON
7	26	349.8	47.	397.	2 1/4	.8	
8	327	774.5	26	794.	5	.8	SCORPION ΦIX
9		167.1	8.	159	1	159.	
5120		40.0	.3	40	1/4	160.	BIRD ΦIX
1		47.9	.6	48	3/10		IBEX ΦIX
2	265	80.8	2.	80	1/2		DEFENEH
3	623	158.1	3.6	160	1		X L
4	329	812.4	6.	806	5	161.2	
5	3255	803.0	19.	810	5	162.0	
6	337	819.7	2.5	817	5	163.4	
7		326.4	7.	327	2	.5	LION HEAD ΦIX
8	426	165.1	18	164	1	164.	X
9	325	1653.5	9.	1644	10	.4	IBEX CLEANED 309.5 ΦIX
5130		344.4	35	329	2	.5	
1	356	352.0	15	337	2	168.5	

BRONZE KHOIRINE L=LEAD

No.	FORM	NOW	CH.	ORIGIN?	X	UNIT	DETAIL
5133	61	17.0	.4	17	1/10	170.0	ROMAN
4	623	83.7	2.4	85	1/2		L
5	50	178.5	7.	171	1	171.0	L
6	LION	345.5	1.5	344	2	172.0	LION ΦIX
7	58	346.9	1.7	345	2	.5	.. BEYRUT
8	LION	348.1	0	348	2	174.	LION ΦIX
9	745	553.0	2.5	351	2	175.5	EPHESOS
5140	245	363.9	12.	352	2	176.	ΦIX
1	HEAD	352.0	0.	352	2		QUFT, HAEM. ΦIX
L 2	60	351.6	3.6	353	2	176.5	Δ. MAGN. SIP L
3	33	357.1	3.	354	2	177.	
4	HOOF	356.7	.5	355	2	178.	HOOF? ΦIX
5		179.9	0	180	1	180.	BEETLE ΦIX
6	FROG	183.2	3.4	180	1		FROG ΦIX
7	9212	378.6	22	361	2	.5	
8	304	183.3	2.5	181	1	181.	
9	HEAD	186.2	8?	181	1	181.	HEAD ΦIX
5150	623	18.2	.4	18.4	1/10	184.	/
1	338	371.4	14.	369	2	184.5	DEFENEH
2	71	374.4	6.	378	2	189.	

BRONZE BEQA (AEGINETAN) L=LEAD

No.	FORM	NOW	CH.	ORIGIN?	X	UNIT	DETAIL
5153	60	43.7	6.	44	1/4	176	
4		88.9	.9	88	1/2	176	TORTOISE ΦIX
5	602 SHELL	177.0	1.	176.	1		II=2 DR. ΦIX L
A		177.9.5	5.	178.0	10	178.0	
6	741	179.8	0.	180.	1	1800	BK.STEA.
7		89.0	1.5	90.5	1/2	181.	B=2 L
8	605	45.7	.3	45.4	1/4	.6	L
	Licinius COLonia			GNA eus BER yt us			
9		90.8	.2	90.8	1/2	.6	JERUSALEM
5160	622	24.3	1.3	23.	1/8	184.	I L
1	60	374.6	7	368.	2	184.	
2	614	155.6	1.3	154.	5/6	.4	
3	LAMB HEAD	279.6	1.5	278.	1 1/2	185.4	EPHESOS ΦIX
4	625	46.5	0	46.5	1/4	186.0	ALAB
5	612	89.8	3.	93.	1/2	.0	B. ANTIOCH, L
6	144	475.5	9.	466.	5/2	.4	E=5D.SMYRN,L
7	6242	93.3	1.9	94.	1/2	188.	P ALEX. L
8	624	380.7	15.	376.	2	.0	
9	RAM HEAD	475.0	7.	470	5/2		ΦIX
5170	602	474.8	5.	470	5/2		I MAGN.SIP. L
1	SHELL	944		944	1/2	.8	HAEM. ΦIX
2	60	385.2	7.	378	2	189.8	B L
3	623	470	2.5	47.5	1/4	190.0	
4	623	95.1	0	95	1/2		GALENA
5	58	279.5	66	285	3/2		
6	57	388.8	8.	381	2	.5	ALEX. L
7	614	480.0	2.8	477	5/2	.8	
8	HEART	190.9	2.2	191	1	191.	HEART ΦIX
9	26	23.9	.6	24	1/8	192.	
5180	14	24.0	0	240	1/2		EPHESOS, CALCITE
1	57	47.1	2.2	48.3	1/4		ALEX. L
2	60	95.1	1.	96.	1/2		ALEX. GALENA
3	622	96.6	2.	96.	1/2		
4	60	484.8	5.	480	5/2		L
5	614	1455.0	96.	1445.0	75	192.7	ΦIX TORTOISE
6		485.0	2.5	482.	5/2	.8	
7	58	99.6	2.9	96.7	1/2	193.4	
8	14	24.2	0	24.2	1/8	.8	EPHESOS,CALCITE
9	494	195.3	4.5	194	1	194.	
5190	622	196.7	24	194	1		L
1	621	52.1	3.	49	1/4	196.	L
2	621	16.5	.3	16.6	1/2	199.2	
3	15	37.4		37.4	3/16	199.4	EPHESOS,CALCITE
4	622	99.6	3.	100	1/2	200.	
5	RAM HEAD	158	5.6	152	3/4	202.7	ΦIX
6	268	92.9	21	102	1/2	204.	
7	57	414.4	3.5	411	2	205.5	
8	321	101.2	6.	103	1/2	206.	QUS
9	58	1038.4	6.	1036.	5	207.2	
5200	33	51.1	1.	52.	1/4	208.	
1	254	51.9	.2	52.	1/4		
2	36	52.2	0	52.2	1/4	8	
3	333	104.8	2.	105.	1/2	210.	
4	324	52.2	.5	53.	1/4	212.	

BRONZE SELA L=LEAD

No	FORM	NOW	CH.	ORIGINAL	X	UNIT	DETAIL
5205	612	194·6	2·4	197·	1	197·0	Δ BEYRUT L
6	612	50·8	·7	50·	1/4	200·0	A " L
7	612	397·0	6·	400·	2	0	H, MARATHUS L
8	612	202·8	1·3	201·	1	201·0	Δ BEYRUT L
9	57	12·9	·3	12·6	1/16	·6	L
5210	623	53·0	1·7	51·	1/4	204·	L
1	58	58·7	8·	51·	1/4		L
2	58	52·9	1·	52·	1/4	208·	L
3	9233	106·1	2·	104	1/2		
4	PAN	12810·	252	12560	60	209·3	
5	LION	20968·	2	20970	100	·7	
6	657	105·3	·3	105	1/2	210·	
7	60	113·7	9·	105	1/2		
8	721	12568	80	12650	60	210·8	L III = 3 librae BK. STEAT.
9	60	213·2	1·8	211	1	211·	ALEX. L
5220	625	2189·5	80	2110	10		L
1	623	28·8	3·	26·5	1/8	212·	
2	165	56·0	3·	53·	1/4		
3	254	54·3	1·3	53·	1/4		MEM.
4	25	52·5	·7	53·	1/4		
5	57	105·7	3·	106	1/2		
6	333	216·5	4·	212	1		
7	14	997·2	66	1060	5		TREVES, MARB
8	612	427·8	3·	425	2	212·5	H BEYRUT L
9	575	225·8	13·	213	1	213·	⊙ L
5230	RAM	21277	80	21360	100	·6	LIM.
1	9233	107·9	·6	107	1/2	214·	
2	261	111·0	4·	107	1/2		
3	IBIS?	209·7	5·	214	1		ΦIX
4	573	210·4	4·	214	1		O L
5	66	214	3·4	215	1	215·	≶ = SELA
6	60	4290·5	40	4310	20	215·5	L
7	612	108·2	1·2	108	1/2	216·	B BEYRUT L
8	338	109·4	1·5	108	1/2		+
9	623	214·1	2·1	216	1		L
5240	368	434·6	3·	432	2		
1	LION	867·7	7·3	864	4		ΦIX
2	60	877·7	12·	866	4	216·5	
3	621	44·0	·6	43·4	1/5	217·	∴
4	602	437·0	3·	434·	2		MAGN. SIP. L
5	TOAD	655·0	9·	654·	3	218·	ΦIX
6	602	14640	13·	1461·	20/3	219·1	MNΓL
7	52	435·6	9·	439·	2	·5	
8	313	55·4	·3	55	1/4	220·	
9	623	56·4	1·2	55	1/4	L	
5250	338	111·4	1	110	1/2		DEFENEH
1	58	442·4	2	440	2		CYPRUS JEWELER MOULD
2	57	447·1	5·	442	2	221·	MAGNES. SIP. L
3	CALF	2756·5	18·	2765	50/4	221·2	ΦIX
4	SHELL	1779·9	9·5	1774	8	·7	
5	26	112·2	·9	111	1/2	222·	+ DEFENEH
6	66	1381·0	16·	1397	25/4	223·5	} CYPRUS L
7	66	664·8	8·	673	3	224·3	} ALIKE
8	ΦIX	56·3	·5	56	1/4	224·	TORTOISE
9		113·5	1·2	112	1/2		HEDGEHOG ΦIX
5260	LION	225·4	1·	224	1		ΦIX
1	572	453·8	6·	450	2	225·	
2	58	112·5	·2	112·6	1/2	·2	L
3	723	4494·	16	4510	20	·5	
4	TOAD	909·5	3·7	906	4	226·5	ΦIX
5	58	227·8	1·2	227·	1	227·	L
6	252	57·4	·6	56·8	1/4	·2	
7	SER.	5276 to 81		113·7	1/2	227·4	AMARNA L
8	25	57·4	·5	57	1/4	228·	
9	60	114·3	·4	114	1/2		
5270	144	226·6	2·4	228	1		L
1	40	229·0	1·	228	1		
2	58	28·7	·6	28·9	1/8	231·2	L
3	612	233·9	1·3	232·	1	232·	Δ BEYRUT L
4	58	117·4	1·	116·	1/2		L
5	612	238·7	1·5	239·	1	239·	Δ BEYRUT L

SET FROM AMARNA, MEAN 113·7, ROMAN. L

No.	FORM	NOW	CH.	ORIGINAL	X	UNIT	DETAIL
5276	57	189·8	·7	189·1	5/3	113·5	MARK I/\
7	57	223·0	1·0	222·0	2	111·0	II
8	57	345·8	7·0	339·0	3	113·0	···
9	57	563·5	1·5	562·0	5	112·4	II III
5280	65	692·6	1·8	690·8	6	115·1	⁝⁝⁝
1	314	1373·5	4·1	1369·4	12	114·1	IIIIII IIIIII

BRONZE UNGIA MARK Γo OR Γ

No.	FORM	NOW	CH.	ORIGINAL	X	UNIT	DETAIL
5282	621	52·6	5·8	50·4	1/6	302·	N = NOMISMA
3	595	52·6	3·0	52·0	1/6	312·	N } DEFENEH
4	621	54·1	1·5	54·5	1/6	327·	N }
5	61	59·3	·5	59·6	1/6	357·	N SMYRNA
6	61	59·8	·2	59·6	1/6		N "
7	61	60·0	·1	59·9	1/6	359·	N
8	61	60·6	·4	60·2	1/6	361·	N
9	623	374·6	7·	368·	1	368·	I L
5290	602	313·8	2·	312·	5/6	374·	NE = 5 NOM
1	15	188·2	o	188·	1/2	376·	NΓ = 3
2	61	62·2	·8	63·	1/6	378·	N
3	58	126·8	·8	126·	1/3		SMYRNA
4	615	379·8	2·	378	1		A = 1
5	61	379·8	x	?	1		NS = 6 N cleaned
6	BUSTS 15	63·3	1·	64	1/6	384·	KHT CONSTANTIV HERAC, TIB.
7	BUST	56·4	?	?	DN	HONO	RIVS EXAGIVM SOLIDI
8	58	388·8	o	389	1	389	ΓA JERUSALEM
9	152	389·6	·7	389	1		N2 MAG. SIP. L
5300	61	64·9	o	64·9	1/6	·4	SET IN BOX
1	PAN	4697·0	20	4680·	12	390·	LIBRA BEYRUT
2	602	389·7	7·	391	1	391·	ALEX L
3	61	197·5	1·8	196	1/2	392·	H
4	61	32·6	·1	32·7	1/12	·4	IB = 12 SILIQUAE
5	60	4714·9	5·	4710·	12	392·5	ΛΑ LIB SMYRNA
6	60	2333·2	24·	2358·	6	·7	ΓS = 6 UN.
7	745	393·7	1·4	393·	1	393·	Γ+A ALEX.
8	59	780·6	7·5	787·	2	·5	SMYRNA
9	60	395·4	1·4	394	1	394·	Γ+A ALEX.
5310	745	1182·0	o	1182·	3		Γ+Γ
1	72	1184·6	o	1185·	3	395·	BK. STEAT.
2	61	22·7	·7	22·	1/18	396·	H = 8 SILIQUAE
3	15	198·5	o	198·5	1/2	397·	NΓ
4	61	66·6	·2	66·4	1/6	398	N SMYRNA
5	60	265·6	o	265·6	4/6		NΔ
6	602	398·5	x	?	1		ΓA cleaned
7	723	2414·5	6·	2420·	6	403·3	IB, T ΠΑΛΥΛΟ ΑΛΑΒ.
8	605	1612·4	28·	1614	4	·5	Δ ANTIOCH, L
9	746	807·3	x	?	2		ΓB cleaned
5320	61	67·3	o	67·3	1/6	·8	ΔIKEON †N†
1	723	804·4	5·	809·	2	404·5	BR. MARB.
2	60	404·1	x	?	1		ΓA cleaned
3	607	405·0	o	405	1	405·	N+S
4	602	405·8	·6	405·	1		N+S III
5	60	202·5	·4	203·	1/2	406·	N+Γ
6	716	201·5	1·5	203·	1/2		I+B = 12 SCRUP.
7	602	810·9	2·5	813·	2	·5	ΓB SMYRNA
8	711	406·8	o	407·	1	407·	BK. MARB.
9	HEAD	1640·1	11·5	1628·	4		ΦIX
5330	711	1221·4	1·	1222·	3	·3	BK. STEAT.
1	61	68·0	o	68·0	1/6	408·	N
2	622	68·3	·4	68·	1/6		L
2A	61	69·4	1·4	68	1/6		AS 5341
3	60	202·0	2·	204·	1/2		N+Γ CYPRUS
4	61	827·5	12·	816	2		Γ+B QUFT
5	606	820·8	5·	816	2		
6	60	822·7	3·7	819	2	409·5	SMYRNA
7	15	200·7	5·	205	1/2	410·	NΓ "
8	60	1231·0	o	1231·	6	410·3	Γ+Γ
9	60	821·7	o	822·	2	411·	Γ+B SOL XII SMYRNA
5340	57	414·4	3·	411	1		
1	61	68·6	o	68·6	1/6	411·6	2 HEADS STAMPED
2	152	550·8	5·5	549·	8/6	·8	NH = 8 NOM.
3	60	415·4	3·	412·	1	412·	ΓB
4	60	413·3	1·7	412·	1		Γ+A
5	602	410·8	1·2	412·	1		2 SAINTS ΓA
6	625	206·0	1·4	206·	1/2		IB ΦIX

No.	FORM	NOW	CH.	ORIGINAL	X	UNIT	DETAIL
5347		829·0	4·	825·	2	412·5	MAGN. SIP. L
8	602	1247·3	9·5	1238·	3	·7	NIH = 18 NOM.
9	15	34·6	·2	34·4	1/12	·8	IB = 12 SILIQ.
5350	716	825·9	o	826·	2	413·	NIB = 12 NOM. CYPRUS
1	60	827·1	1·	826·	2		Γ+B QUFT
2	602	207·5	·7	207·	1/2	414·	NΓ
3	152	414·4	·5	414·	1		SMYRNA
4	61	69·3	·2	69·1	1/6	·6	N ALEX
5	60	414·3	x	?			CYPRUS, cleaned
6	60	419·6	4·5	415·	1	415·	SMYRNA L
7	60	1240·4	5·5	1246·	3	·3	MNΓ inlaid
8	HEAD	835·5	5	831·	2	·5	ΦIX L
9	60	208·5	·6	208·	1/2	416·	N+Γ GIZEH
5360	14	208·0	o	208·	1/2		N+Γ
1	602	414·9	1·9	416·	1		Γ+A MARATHUS
2	61	835·3	3·5	832·	2		ΓB
3	63	2523·2	22·	2500·	6	·7	GHUROB L.
4	745	139·4	·4	139·	1/3	417·0	NB
5	605	1245·2	7·	1252·	3	·3	Γ+Γ
6	60	835·9	o	836·	2	418·0	Γ+B
7	740	418·2	o	418·2	1	·2	A. BR. SERP.
8	745	2494·0	26·	2510	6	·3	Γ+S
9	61	69·8	o	69·8	1/6	·8	N. SET IN BOX
5370	60	2478·8	37·	2513·	3		ΓS+
1	61	70·0	o	70·	1/6	420·	N SET IN BOX
2	57	105·7	·8	105	1/4		
3	15	209·6	·5	210	1/2		N+Γ SMYRNA
4	71	854·7	14·	840	2		
5	605	5037·1	38·	5047	12	·6	L
6	746	1275·2	12·	1263·	3	421·	ΓΓ
7		71·5	1·2	70·3	1/6	422·	N DEFENEH
8	616	1261·4	4·5	1266·	3		Γ+Γ
9	61	70·5	·1	70·4	1/6	·4	N
5380	60	845·3	o	845·	2	·5	Γ+B
1	15	138·8	2·?	141·	1/3	423·	NB cleaned
2	602	1274·6	2	1276·	3	425·3	Γ+Γ
3	60	212·0	·7	213·	1/2	426·	N+Γ
4	58	211·0	1·9	213·	1/2	426·	Δ
5	71	2555·0	11·	2544·	6	424·	
6	621	46·9	·5	47·4	1/9	427·	3 BUSTS
7		71·5	·2	71·3	1/6	428·	N DEFENEH
8	71	2568·0	13·	2573·	6	·8	ϚC = 6 UN. M. HABU
9	711	107·9	o	107·9	1/4	431·6	RED PORPH.
5390	71	874·0	18·	864·	2	432·	
1	61	144·6	·4	144·	1/3		IB ALEX.
2	602	144·4	·7	144·	1/3		NB SMYRNA
3	71	216·5	o	217·	1/2	434·	BI = 12 SCRUPUL.
4		80·5	11·	73·	1/6	438·	N DEFENEH
5	PLUG RING	5288·	?	?	12	440·	LEAD PLUG, IRON RING
6	60	2676·2	13·	2663·	6	443·8	ΓS
7	623	81·6	1·4	82·			DEFENEH
8	608	992·9	1·	992·	2	496·	Γ*B

SET IN SCALE BOX, 350 A.D. MEAN 427·2 M.E. 2·4

No.	DESIGN	GRS.	MEAN SCALE	ERROR +	ERROR −	ΦXVI
5399	WREATH Γo S	2568·4	2563·2	5·2		SET IN
5400	" Γo Γ	1279·0	1281·6		2·6	LOWER
1	Γo B	855·9	854·4	1·5		BOX.
2	Γo A	424·8	427·2		2·4	PERFECT
3		141·2	142·4		1·2	STATE.
			MEAN	2·4		
4	·I·	30·1				LOOSE
5		427·0	427·2		·2	SET
6		205·7	213·6		7·9	IN
7	CONSTANTIUS II	28·0	26·7	1·3		UPPER
8	CONSTANS I	25·6	26·7		1·1	TRAY
9	GLASS	7·7	6·7	1·0		
5410	GLASS	6·0	6·7		·7	
			MEAN	2·0		

SET IN SMALLER SCALE BOX.

No.	DESIGN	GRS.	MEAN SCALE	ERROR +	ERROR −
1	N	72·6	72·6	·0	
2	GLASS	35·7	36·3		·6
3	"	24·6	24·2	·4	
4	" SILIQUA	3·19	3·02	·17	

MEAN UNGIA 435·6 ·3 MEAN ERROR

PEYEM

No.	X	UNIT
392	4	114.2
393	2	.2
396	50	.4
400	1	115.6
816	10	.7
401	8	.8
817	10	.8
819	1	116.2
404	2	.4
405	40	.9
409	5	117.1
777	6	.4
768	20	.9
779	10	.9
821	1/2	118.0
163	1/2	.4
627	1/2	.4
*645	20	.6
770	20	.6
1148	1/2	.6
*655	3	.7
772	20	.8
430	200	.8
773	20	119.2
774	20	.4
432	200	.4
822	10	.5
166	5	.6
1150	1/2	.6
167	5	.8
631	6	120.0
886	4	.0
1275	20	.0
168	1	121.4
171	20	.5
174	20	.8
175	5	.9
180	2	122.6
643	1	.6
181	5	.7
644	1/2	.8
648	20	123.0
649	10	.1
183	1/2	.2
650	1	.2
185	30	.4
186	30	.5
187	1/2	.6
782	400	.7
189	2	124.0
652	10	.0
655	30	.3
K499	100	.4
*444	5	.4
195	5	.6
656	30	.7
*439	1	.8
657	15	.9

DARIC

No.	X	UNIT
200	12	125.6
201	30	.8
661	30	.8
*454	2	.9
203	20	126.0
204	6	.0
K419	1	.0
1165	1	.0
664	30	.1

No.	X	UNIT
1246	1000	126.1
207	10	.1
208	2	.2
209	1/2	.2
665	4	.2
666	10	.3
667	20	.4
668	6	.4
888	10	.4
1167	1/2	.4
210	2	.5
1169	6	.5
*458	1/2	.5
212	12	.6
214	2	.7
1170	120	.7
216	1	.8
217	1	.8
*482	5	.8
*329	5	.8
671	30	.9
672	12	.9
673	6	.9
1171	30	.9
218	6	127.0
220	15	.1
676	5	.1
677	5	.2
678	1	.2
*397	50	.2
224	60	.3
225	2	.3
679	30	.3
680	10	.4
226	2	.5
1176	60	.5
1177	10	.6
227	2	.7
228	5	.8
229	5	.8
273	5	.8
681	5	.8
1179	24	.8
682	10	.9
683	6	.9
231	1	128.0
684	12	.0
685	1	.0
686	20	.1
*460	1/2	.1
*445	1	.1
234	10	.3
235	5	.3
236	12	.4
238	10	.5
688	15	.5
689	10	.5
*327	5	.6
691	10	.6
1183	5	.6
1277	40	.6
240	5	.7
242	2	.7
243	1	.7
692	20	.7
1185	10	.7
*424	1/2	.7
*386	10	.7
693	15	.8

No.	X	UNIT
246	10	128.9
247	1	.9
1187	6	129.0
249	20	.1
698	24	.1
250	240	.3
251	5	.3
1189	20	.3
696	30	.4
252	1	.5
697	5	.5
253	10	.6
255	120	.8
256	10	.8
698	20	.8
699	1	.8
257	1	.9
279	1/2	130.0
704	60	.0
280	50	.0
706	2	.2
707	10	.3
715	25	.4
281	50	.4
261	2	.4
282	20	.4
708	20	.5
716	10	.5
283	50	.6
*283	2	.6
710	2	.7
717	100	.8
718	1000	.9
287	50	.9
712	6	131.0
1196	120	.0
1202	1	.0
720	10	.1
266	60	.2
289	2	.2
749	1	.2
1206	1/2	.4
290	20	.4
291	50	.6
722	2	.7
267	5	.7
723	1	.7
292	50	.7
293	5	.8
*496	500	.8
294	5	.8
295	20	.8
724	10	.9
301	1	132.0
725	100	.0
726	25	.0
1210	1	.0
1211	20	.0
*406	2	.0
728	25	.0
304	40	.1
729	25	.1
305	50	.2
306	1500	.2
731	10	.2
732	25	.3
733	10	.3
*438	1	.4

No.	X	UNIT
1212	1/2	132.4
1213	2	.4
307	50	.5
*393	20	.6
*388	10	.7
*502	20	.7
310	10	.7

STATER

No.	X	UNIT
*278	5	132.9
312	20	133.0
*352	6	.0
313	5	.0
*626	1	.0
314	1	.0
1215	2	.1
1217	1/2	.2
1218	1	.2
739	10	.2
315	5	.3
740	5	.4
741	5	.4
743	5	.5
317	5	.6
744	50	.6
745	2	.6
*271	1	.6
318	20	.6
319	10	.7
889	200	.7
748	1	.8
320	50	.9
321	50	134.0
322	10	.0
1221	2	.0
1222	5	.0
324	20	.1
*349	10	.1
*613	600	.1
325	1	.2
326	1	.2
749	1	.2
1224	2	.2
1223	1/2	.2
*667	1	.3
750	25	.3
327	50	.4
*322	25	.4
751	20	.4
752	1	.4
753	1/2	.4
*333	12	.4
754	10	.5
1226	1	.6
755	100	.7
331	1	.7
328	50	.7
330	10	.7
1227	1	.8
*384	5	.9
756	10	.9
333	1500	.9
334	25	.9
*404	2	135.0
*311	5	.1
335	50	.1
*668	1	.2
336	25	.2
1231	5	.2
1232	10	.2

No.	X	UNIT
337	20	135.4
338	5	.4
890	50	.4
*281	2	.5
*661	2	.5
*657	2	.5
757	2	.5
1233	2	.5
*334	20	.6
*381	5	.8
*449	2	.8
1235	5	.8
343	50	.9
344	5	136.0
758	20	.0
346	1	.1
347	10	.2
348	20	.3
349	5	.3
350	5	.4
760	20	.4
761	1	.4
1237	5	.4
1238	2	.4
*350	10	.4
352	5	.5
762	10	.5
1239	1	.6
*456	1/2	.7
353	2	.7

QEDET

No.	X	UNIT
909	2	137.5
3	20	.6
766	2	.6
*636	50	.6
4	10	.7
*400	2	.7
912	10	.8
5	2	138.0
578	1/2	.0
915	1	.0
916	1	.0
7	20	.1
519	5	.1
8	2	.2
9	10	.3
*326	10	.3
*459	1/2	.3
10	2	.4
521	10	.4
522	20	.4
919	1/2	.4
920	10	.4
11	1	.5
12	5	.7
523	200	.7
891	20	.9
355	50	137.0
2	5	.2
1241	10	.2
1242	50	.2
763	1	.3
*357	60	.3
*500	200	.3
764	10	.4
1243	1/2	.4
765	50	.4

No.	X	UNIT
*302	10	138.7
*603	10	.7
13	2	.8
924	1/2	.8
925	1	.8
926	1	.8
14	1	.9
15	1	.9
16	1/2	.9
*358	10	.9
526	10	.9
927	10	.9
528	1	139.0
18	50	.1
19	1/2	.2
20	50	.4
21	40	.4
22	1/2	.4
529	1/2	.4
530	20	.4
*344	20	.4
*314	20	.4
23	200	.5
876	2	.6
523	1	.6
25	20	.7
*448	1	.7
*437	1	.7
*343	20	.7
*368	2	.7
*501	200	.7
936	1/2	.8
26	20	.9
27	20	.9
28	5	.9
29	10	140.0
33	1	.0
533	25	.0
938	1/2	.0
939	1/2	.0
943	10	.0
944	10	.0
*427	1/2	.1
*665	1	.1
*443	10	.1
*304	10	.1
36	2	.2
534	50	.2
535	50	.2
536	5	.2
948	5	.2
37	10	.3
537	20	.3
538	10	.3
*421	100	.3
539	2	.4
950	1	.4
38	2	.5
540	5	.5
951	1	.5
39	5	.6
*429	1/2	.6
*344	50	.6
521	20	.7
*453	2	.7
*403	2	.7
542	20	.8
952	50	.8
42	500	.9

No.	X	UNIT
953	5	140.9
543	5	141.0
954	1/2	.0
45	2	.1
544	1	.2
545	50	.2
*375	5	.2
*447	1	.2
546	20	.3
957	1	.3
46	10	.4
*426	1/2	.4
48	2	.5
547	10	.5
49	20	.6
548	10	.6
50	2	.7
959	2	.7
549	2	.8
960	1/2	.8
*307	5	.8
550	2	.9
51	200	142.0
52	20	.0
53	2	.0
963	10	.0
*428	1/2	.0
55	2	.1
56	10	.2
57	5	.2
551	1/2	.2
968	1	.2
969	1	.2
970	5	.2
58	5	.3
59	50	.3
971	10	.3
*356	50	.4
553	10	.6
975	1/2	.6
61	4	.7
554	50	.7
976	10	.7
62	10	.8
63	5	.8
535	100	.8
978	1/2	.8
979	1	.8
980	1	.8
64	10	.9
65	2	.9
557	10	.9
558	2	.9
*318	5	.9
67	1	143.0
982	1/2	.0
983	1/2	.0
68	10	.1
69	5	.1
580	20	.1
985	10	.1
986	1	.2
987	1	.2
988	5	.2
*432	1/2	.2
*365	2	.2
70	2	.3
561	2	.3
989	1	.3

QEDET cont±			No.	x	UNIT	No.	x	UNIT	No.	x	UNIT	NECEF No	x	UNIT	No.	x	UNIT	BEQA No.	x	UNIT
No.	x	UNIT																		
			577	10	145.3	117	20	147.2	141	20	149.1				835	20	160.5	425	1	188.5
			578	2	.3	118	2	.2	607	20	.1				478	1/2	.6	426	1/2	189.4
991	1	143.3	1027	1	.3	*385	10	.2	1100	5	.1	*412	1	152.3	*332	20	.7	433	3	191.2
995	1	.4	97	20	.4	1058	1	.4	*433	1/2	.1	*376	5	.6	480	1	.9	435	4	194.2
71	5	.5	98	5	.4	1059	2	.5	*308	1	.1	1129	10	.7	1283	5	160.8	441	25	195.4
562	200	.5	99	5	.4	1060	5	.5	*273	1	.1	1130	20	.7	836	20	161.0	442	4	.4
563	2	.5	100	5	.4	1061	5	.5	142	5	.2	*410	1	153.1	837	2	.4	443	25	.6
72	20	.6	*654	20	.4	120	2	.6	*275	1	.2	*450	2	.1	482	5	.6	459	10	.6
996	1	.6	*323	20	.4	121	1	.6	*359	10	.2	620	20	.2	483	50	8	825	20	.6
73	1	.8	101	5	.5	592	5	.6	143	50	.4	*360	5	.2	1285	20	162.0	444	4	.8
997	2	.8	579	5	.5	1064	1	.6	1102	1/2	.4	*417	1/2	.4	277	10	.3	445	20	.8
*457	1/2	.8	1030	20	.5	1065	2	.6	*347	10	.4	*436	1/2	.4	1286	50	.4	448	20	196.2
877	20	.9	*446	1	.5	1066	50	.6	*493	1000	.4	*363	2	.5	1287	5	4	778	1/2	.2
74	2	.9	102	20	.6	593	5	.7	*348	10	.4	1134	2	.6	838	5	.7	449	4	.8
75	1	.9	580	20	.6	1067	2	.7	608	10	.5	621	2	.7	895	1/2	.8	450	4	197.4
76	5	144.0	581	20	.6	1068	500	.7	1103	500	.5	*325	10	.8	839	20	.9	830	10	198.0
77	1	.0	1031	1	.6	1069	500	.7	1104	5	.5	452	40	154.0	840	10	163.0	451	4	199.4
565	20	.0	1032	2	.6	*364	2	.7	*352	5	.5	*394	20	.3	*420	1/2	.0	*306	2	.5
566	500	.0	1033	50	.6	122	50	.8	1105	20	.7	1138	1/2	.4	1288	20	.2	481	20	201.2
1003	10	.0	103	20	.7	123	10	.8	*312	10	.7	1139	1/2	.6	285	10	.4	484	20	202.6
79	10	.1	582	10	.7	124	5	.8	*382	5	.7	622	1/2	.8	842	1	.5	848	5	203.2
567	10	.1	583	2	.7	125	2	.8	*340	10	.7	885	1	.8	843	20	.5	*320	40	.2
80	50	.2	584	1	.7	594	10	.8	144	50	.8	453	20	155.0	1289	5	.6	485	10	.8
81	2	.2	1034	5	.7	1070	5	.8	145	20	.8	*396	30	.0	*414	1/2	.6	490	50	.9
1006	10	.3	104	20	.8	*418	1	.8	146	2	.8	454	1/2	.2	*653	10	.9	841	2	204.0
1007	100	.3	105	1	.8	596	10	.9	147	1	.8	455	1	.2	1291	2	164.2	844	20	.7
*656	2	.3	1038	1/2	.8	127	1/2	148.0	1106	1	.8	*285	5	.4	1290	20	.3	492	25	206.2
*423	1	.3	1039	1	.8	597	10	.0	1107	2	.9	*324	20	.4	845	5	.4	873	20	207.2
568	10	.4	585	2	.9	1071	1/2	.0	149	5	150.0	*328	20	.6	846	2	.5	*652	2000	.4
569	1/2	.4	106	20	146.0	1073	1	.0	1109	1/2	.0	824	20	.6	299	2	.9	874	50	209.1
570	2	.4	1040	50	.0	1074	1	.0	*339	10	.0	*310	1	.6	*398	50	165.0	783	5	209.5
878	5	.4	*434	1/2	.0	128	10	.1	*331	20	.0	*277	5	.6	*369	2	.2	363	20	.5
1008	1	.4	*669	1	.0	599	2	.1	610	2	.1	1142	10	.7	*602	1/2	.4	**SELA**		
82	20	.5	*387	10	.0	1076	1	.1	1113	5	.1	456	40	.8	311	10	166.0	366	1/2	211.2
83	1	.5	*371	5	.0	*366	2	.1	150	1/2	.1	1279	1	156.0	1292	5	.1	787	5	212.2
1011	50	.5	1041	10	.1	*287	5	.1	1114	1/2	.1	*474	1/5	.0	329	10	.4	*336	8	.7
*425	1/2	.5	*422	1	.1	*321	200	.1	1115	1/2	.1	*430	1/2	.0	*390	20	.4	491	10	.7
*659	2	.5	*405	2	.1	129	50	.2	611	20	.2	458	20	.2	847	10	.8	368	240	.9
*338	10	.5	*357	10	.1	130	10	.2	*411	1	.5	*409	1	169.2	**KHOIRINE**			788	1/4	213.2
*317	10	.5	108	2	.2	600	40	.2	*337	10	.5	460	40	156.6	849	20	171.2	*284	10	.4
*354	20	.5	586	1	.2	601	1/2	.2	152	500	.6	461	20	.8	*498	1/2	172.8	789	25	214.2
879	1/2	.6	1042	1/2	.2	1079	2	.2	153	2	.6	462	20	.8	850	20	173.2	*601	1/3	.7
1016	1/2	.6	1043	1	.2	1081	10	.3	612	5	.6	*372	5	.9	851	10	7	371	4	215.0
1017	100	.6	109	5	.3	*383	4	.3	1117	1	.6	826	40	157.4	1278	1	174.0	1252	40	.1
*413	1	.6	110	2	.3	131	50	.4	*435	1/2	.6	827	200	.4	868	2	175.1	493	10	216.2
*370	1	.6	1044	5	.3	132	5	.4	613	10	.7	*291	1/2	.4	*494	500	177.5	386	250	.5
84	20	.7	587	10	.4	602	10	.4	614	2	.7	1280	2	.5	799	10	7	792	10	217.2
1018	1	.7	111	10	.5	603	2	.4	154	20	.8	465	2	.8	870	20	178.0	887	200	.6
*362	2	.8	112	5	.5	1083	20	.5	155	1/2	.8	893	1	.8	867	1/2	2	375	2	.6
*345	10	.8	*379	5	.5	133	1/2	.6	615	1/2	.8	467	40	158.2	*408	1	3	1254	20	218.2
86	10	.9	*367	2	.5	*378	5	.6	881	20	.9	829	20	.2	*655	2	3	794	4	219.4
87	2	.9	588	20	.6	134	5	.6	*660	2	.9	*361	2	.2	869	10	179.6	1156	200	.7
88	2	.9	1045	2	.6	135	1/2	.8	1119	20	151.0	831	40	.6	871	20	7	361	8	220.8
573	2	.9	1046	2	.6	604	2	.8	*330	20	.1	832	10	.7	*452	2	8	380	2	221.3
574	1	.9	*377	5	.6	605	20	.8	*395	24	.2	469	20	.8	419	1/4	180.4	*407	1	.6
1019	2	.9	*380	5	.6	606	10	.8	156	2	.3	833	40	.8	872	20	182.7	797	20	.9
*341	10	.9	113	20	.7	1090	1/2	.8	616	1	.3	1281	1/2	.8	*309	1	183.6	798	25	222.4
*313	10	.9	589	2	.7	1091	10	.8	1122	1	.4	471	1/2	159.0	*415	1/2	185.8	1159	200	.5
90	50	145.0	*658	2	.8	1092	100	.8	*389	10	.4	1282	50	.2				399	40	.8
93	20	.0	*373	5	.8	*335	10	.8	*495	200	.8	472	10	.5				1260	1	223.0
1021	1	.0	114	5	.9	1093	10	.9	618	2	.9	*503	200	.7				422	5	.2
95	1	.1	1047	2	.9	*663	2	.9	1126	50	.9	894	1	.8				801	25	.3
575	2	.1	1048	5	.9	*288	5	.9	1127	1/2	152.0	475	10	160.0				385	20	.4
1023	1	.1	*401	2	.9	880	10	149.0	*412	1	.3	834	20	.0				1158	200	.5
*416	1/2	.1	*604	20	.9	1095	1/2	.0				*455	1/2	.2				804	10	225.0
*272	1/2	.1	1052	1/2	147.0	1096	1/2	.0				*632	2	.4				*316	5	.8
*442	1	.1	1056	5	.0	1097	1	.0				477	20	.4				1261	40	226.0
*402	2	.1	116	1	.1	139	20	.1										387	25	.3
1026	2	.2	1057	10	.1	140	20	.1										1262	4	.8
*342	20	.2																		

WEIGHTS FROM GEZER

PEYEM

P	GRNS	X	UNIT
4	112.2	1	112.2
2	456.0	4	114.0
3	114.2	1	114.2
2	460.8	4	115.2
1	468.6	4	117.1
4	468.9	4	.2
4	117.6	1	.6
4	1176.8	10	.7
4	118.1	1	118.1
3	473.0	4	.2
4	2397.0	20	119.8
3	601.0	5	120.2
2	120.4	1	.4
1	966.1	8	.8
4	241.9	2	.9
3	121.9	1	121.9
3	975.6	8	122.0
4	494.7	4	123.7
4	622.7	5	124.5
3	998.7	8	.8
3	624.9	5	125.0

DARIC

P	GRNS	X	UNIT
1	252.7	2	126.3
3	6327.	50	.5
4	2537.0	20	.8
2	847	2/3	127.0
1	852.1	2/3	.8
3	256.5	2	128.2
3	642.0	5	.4
4	128.7	1	.7
1	644.1	5	.8
1	2580.2	20	129.0
1	86.1	2/3	.2
4	258.8	2	.4
4	86.4	2/3	.6
3	2622.5	20	131.1
4	393.5	3	.2
1	656.3	5	.2
1	2627.7	20	.4
3	65.9	1/2	.8
3	264.9	2	132.4

STATER

P	GRNS	X	UNIT
3	1328.8	10	132.9
2	535.6	4	133.9
2	134.0	1	134.0
4	535.9	4	.0
1	536.4	4	.1
1	674.0	5	.8
2	675.1	5	135.8
3	1352.3	10	.2
4	1358.4	10	.8
4	136.0	1	136.0
3	680.5	5	1· ·1
2	1362.5	10	.2
4	137.0	1	137.0

QEDET

P	GRNS	X	UNIT
4	137.6	1	137.6
4	1376.5	10	.6
4	138.1	1	138.1
1	138.1	10	.1
4	3453.4	25	.1
4	138.5	1	.5
4	692.6	5	.5
2	692.8	5	.6
2	693.1	5	.6
3	138.7	1	.7
3	1386.8	10	.7
3	139.0	1	139.0
4	139.0	1	.0
4	139.0	1	.0
4	694.9	5	.0
3	2779.4	20	.0
4	2779.4	20	.0
1	696.0	5	.2
1	1397.7	10	.8
2	6994.	50	.9
3	28062	20	140.3
4	140.6	1	.6
4	1406.2	10	.6
1	1409.0	10	.9
4	141.0	1	141.0
4	705.0	5	.0
1	1409.6	10	.0
2	1410.3	10	.0
2	2820.2	20	.0
4	141.1	1	.1
4	1410.9	10	.1
3	1410.9	10	.1
4	706.0	5	.2
4	141.2	1	.2
4	7087.	50	.7
4	141.8	1	.8
3	1418.0	10	.8
4	1418.0	10	.8
3	142.0	1	142.0
4	142.5	1	.5
4	285.0	2	.5
3	1426.0	10	.6
2	1429.8	10	143.0
4	143.2	1	.2
1	716.5	5	.3
4	143.8	1	.8
2	1442.3	10	144.2
2	144.4	1	.4
2	1446.0	10	.6
1	2895.2	20	.8
4	1459.9	10	146.0
4	146.0	1	.0
4	146.3	1	.3
4	731.5	5	.3
1	734.0	5	.8
2	1469.3	10	.9
2	1470.1	10	147.0
2	295.6	2	.8
1	7042.	50	148.4
2	1495.8	10	149.6
2	149.7	1	.7

QEDET cont'd

P	GRNS	X	UNIT
2	299.4	2	149.7
3	150.0	1	150.0
1	150.1	1	.1
1	150.5	1	.5
2	76.1	1/2	152.2
3	152.3	1	.3
3	1523.1	10	.3

NECEF

P	GRNS	X	UNIT
1	1535.4	10	153.5
1	309.1	2	154.5
1	155.4	1	155.4
1	156.3	1	156.3
3	782.0	5	.4
1	1566.1	10	.6
2	157.1	1	157.1
3	157.3	1	.3
1	157.5	1	.5
1	157.5	1	.5
4	3152.0	20	.6
3	790.9	5	158.2
1	80.2	1/2	160.4
2	40.4	1/4	161.6
2	81.0	1/2	162.0
4	162.0	1	.0
4	162.0	1	.0
3	1631.2	10	163.1
2	331.6	2	165.8
4	1660.8	10	166.1
3	83.5	1/2	167.0
3	335.0	5	.5
3	167.7	1	.7
2	1686.9	10	168.7

KHOIRINE

P	GRNS	X	UNIT
3	85.6	1/2	171.2
4	343.7	2	.8
1	1718.2	10	.8
1	860.3	5	172.0
4	345.7	2	.8
2	345.6	2	.8
3	345.9	2	.9
4	173.6	1	173.6
4	347.2	2	.6
3	347.3	2	.6
3	173.9	1	.9
4	174.2	1	174.2
4	174.4	1	.4
3	174.7	1	.7
3	1754.7	10	175.5
4	175.6	1	.6
4	175.9	1	.9
4	351.9	2	.9
2	176.0	1	176.6
1	355.3	2	177.6
2	89.0	1/2	178.0
1	89.2	1/2	178.4
2	89.2	1/2	.4
3	178.6	1	.6
4	89.6	1/2	179.2
2	896.7	5	1· ·3
2	358.7	2	.3
2	359.4	2	.7

KHOIRINE cont'd

P	GRNS	X	UNIT
4	91.0	1/2	182.0
4	182.3	1	.3
4	1459.9	8	.5
3	1825.6	10	.6
3	365.6	2	.8
1	92.3	1/2	184.6
2	1847.2	10	.7
4	92.4	1/2	.8
3	370.5	2	185.2
4	92.6	1/2	.2
4	186.3	1	186.3
1	187.3	1	187.3
4	187.6	1	.6
4	94.1	1/2	188.2

BEQA

P	GRNS	X	UNIT
4	94.3	1/2	188.6
2	190.8	1	190.8
4	954.8	5	191.0
2	95.7	1/2	.4
3	95.7	1/2	.4
4	974.7	5	194.9
1	392.3	2	196.1
4	4923.	25	.9
2	1976.2	10	197.6
4	98.9	1/2	.8
2	198.0	1	198.0
2	99.2	1/2	.4
4	995.1	5	199.0
4	399.9	2	200.0
4	801.0	4	.2
1	1006.0	5	201.2
2	201.4	1	.4
3	101.6	1/2	203.2
4	4068.1	20	.4
4	1027.0	5	205.4
4	1029.7	5	206.0
1	1030.2	5	.0
4	2060.4	10	.0
3	103.5	1/2	207.0
2	207.2	1	.2

SELA

P	GRNS	X	UNIT
3	104.9	1/2	209.8
3	211.0	1	211.0
3	105.6	1/2	211.2
1	425.2	2	212.6
4	8537	40	214.4
3	108.6	1/2	217.2
4	108.6	1/2	.2
4	108.8	1/2	.6
2	1089.2	5	.8
2	2198.0	10	219.8
1	1100.3	5	220.0
3	221.1	1	221.1
4	8884	40	222.1
2	111.9	1/2	223.8
4	1123.0	5	224.6
4	1128.8	5	225.7
2	113.4	1/2	226.8
4	4552	20	227.6

FROM TROY

No.	D	SIZE M.M.	TYPE	GRAINS	X	UNIT
PEYEM						
2352	8	45×25	491	1141+	10	114.1+
2295	.	27 27	9?	581	5	116.2
2340	8	37 19	498	582	5	116.4
Sch⁴	8.5	40 20	14?	586	5	117.2
2322	.	30 25	805	591	5	118.2
DARIC						
Sch⁴	8.5	45×20	50	247	2	123.5
2345	.	28 15	495	250	2	125.
2349	8.5	60 25	491	1264	10	126.4
2348	10.	70 30	642?	2565	20	128.2
2291	.	22 22	9?	391	3	130.3
2358	8.5	31 13	496	262	2	131.
STATER						
2336	9.	54 22	496	1365	10	136.5
2347	7.	80 30	491	2738	20	.9
2221	.	26 26	9?	687	5	137.4
QEDET						
2330	9	55 14	50	280.	2	140
Sch⁴	8.5	50 10	14?	142	1	142
2343	.	31 16	149?	355	2½	142
2357	.	33 13	496	285	2	142.5
2359	8.	2 8	50	72	1/2	144
2328	.	27 8	899	72	1/2	144
2332	9.	62 32	810	2911	20	145.5
Sch⁴	8.5	50 20	50	293	2	146.5
2335	9.	60 22	810	1477	10	147.7
Sch⁴	8.5	36 15	50	301	2	150.5
KHOIRINE						
2360	.	26 9	899	86	1/2	172
Sch⁴	.			17450	100	174.5
BEQA						
2342	.	35 17	810	483	2½	193.2
2314	.	25 25	9?	497	2½	198.8
2350	8.5	50 25	691	1204	6	200.7
Sch⁴	.	90 50	17?	8010+	40	200.2+
2327	.	30 8	50	103	1/2	206
2354	.	47 16	505	208	1	208
Sch⁴	8.5	32 12	14?	208	1	208
SELA						
2315	.	28 25	805	532	2½	212.8
2331	9.	58 13	50	428	2	214.
2344	.	28 17	144	536	2½	214.4
2353	8.	45 20	491	868	4	217
2319	.	20 20	10?	332	1½	221.4
2337	8.	45 19	899	561	2½	224.4

Notes (column keys):
- Number in Berlin or Schliemann private
- Depth in metres
- Size in millimetres
- Types as these plates
- Grains reduced from grammes
- Multiple
- Unit in grains.

DARIC, BABYLONIAN, KYZIKENE, ANTIOCHIAN, OR ITALIC OF GALEN.

REGISTER	M	GRS.	CH	ORIGᵗ	X	UNIT	MINA	PL	DETAIL
67·8·14· 1	P	684·9	15·	692·	6	115·3	6920		TPIC. KYZI
68·1·10·123	B	574·4	30·	604·	5	120·8	7248	C	TUNNY?
68·1·10· 70	P	1801·4	22·	1813	15	120·9	7252	C	CLUB. TET. ΔΑ.
67·5·8·282	B	615·5	5·5	610·	5	122·	7320		
68·1·10· 79	P	620·5	3·5	617·	5	123·4	7404		CONVEX
66·5·4· 16	P	630·7	108	620·	5	124·	7440		E = 5 SHEKELS
68·1·10· 76	B	1863·0	6·	1866	15	124·4	7464	C	BULL'S HEAD
1872·P·511	P	1869·7	20·	1872	15	124·8	7488		½ TORTOISE
66·5·4· 3	P	3825·5	35·	3790	30	126·3	7580	C	
83·3·1· 1·	P	7201·	380·	7580	60	126·3	7580		TUNNY, KYZI, MNA
68·1·10· 96·	P	252·0	6·	256·	2	128·	7680	C	B = 2 SHEKELS
o	P	15396·	31·	15365	120	128·0	7682	LK	
85·10·13· 15	L	3846·	o	3846·	3	128·2	7692	Ky	ℐℐℐ
68·1·10·81	P	1936·9	13·	1924·	15	128·3	7696	C	
66·5·4· 26	B	3833·4	90	3850·	30	128·3	7700	C	ΣΩ monogᵗ
T·B·363	P	3866·8	12	3865·	30	128·8	7730	A	TORTOISE
63·8·9· 1	P	3925·0	40	3885·	30	129·5	7770	Cᵗ	AMPHORA BULL HEAD HMIMN

MARBLE BLOCKS, 2 BREASTS ON TOP (BR), SOME + HANDLE, (h). THE MINA IS 50 DARICS.

REGISTER	M	GRS.	CH	ORIGᵗ	X	UNIT	MINA	PL	DETAIL
59·12·26·457	M	563·0	50	610·	5	122·	6100	K	Br. h.
59·12·26·456	"	12290·	50	12340	2M	123·4	6170	K	Br. h.
74·2·5·105	"	25800	5200	31000	5M	124·0	6200	E	Br.
59·12·29·461	"	18544	80	18620	3M	124·1	6207	K	HEADS h.
87		37364	24	37340	6M	124·5	6223		Br.
59·12·26·459	"	6042	210	6250	M	125·0	6250	K	Br. h.
59·12? 56?	"	26508	5000	31500	5M	126·0	6300	K	Br.
59·12·26·448	"	32036	600	32000·	5M	128·0	6400	K	Br. h.
82·12·4· 1	"	52461	420	52880	8M	132·2	6610		Br. h.

MARBLE DISCS, ROUNDED EDGES PROBABLY ROMAN. CARTHAGE.

REGISTER	M	GRS.	CH	ORIGᵗ	X	UNIT	MINA	PL	DETAIL
60·10·2·72	M	1458·2	14·	1472·	12	122·8		C8	
60·10·2·75	"	491·9	4·	496·	4	124·0			
60·10·2·79	"	125·2	o	125·2	1	125·2			⁚⁚⁚
60·10·2·74	"	377·1	2·	379·	3	126·3			⋯
57·12·18·228	"	128·3	·5	128·8	1	128·8			
57·12·23·224	L	774·3	6·	774·3	6	129·0			

LITRA OF CONFUSED ORIGINS, PEYEM, DARIC AND STATER.

REGISTER	M	GRS.	CH	ORIGᵗ	X	UNIT	MINA	PL	DETAIL
65·5·8·337	S	40·4	o	40·4	25	121·2	5818		·· = 2
	S	242·6	o	242·6	U/2	121·3	5822		Σ = SEMIS
65·5·8·344	M	60·7	o	60·7	35	121·4	5827		∴ = 3
	S	1460·2	·5	1460·7	3U	121·7	5843		
66·5·4· 9	P	1330	240	14·66·	3U	122·2	5864		Γ = 3 UNCIAE
		41·3	·8	40·9	2S	122·7	5878		II = 2
67·5·8·250	P	2969·4	6·	2963	6U	123·5	5926		
67·5·8·338	S	41·2	o	41·2	25	123·6	5933		··
		247·3	·5	247·8	U/2	123·9	5947		Σ
67·5·8·313	S	1489·9	o	1489·9	3U	124·2	5960		·:·
68·8·10· 75	B	2994·1	12	2990	6U	124·6	5980		ARRP ARPINUM
82·12·4· 3	M	23995·	30	24025	4L	125·1	6006		Δ
68·1·10·102	P	6022·	24	6030	1	125·6	6030		ΛEItra
	M	3021·6		3021·6	6U	125·8	6043		S = 6 or SEMIS
	B	127·6	·8	127·4	6S	127·4	6103		⁝⁝⁝
67·5·8·307	S	510·6	·6	511·2	1U	127·8	6134		·
T·B·	S	2075·5	6·	2082	4U	130·1	6246		
68·1·10·155	L	3133·9	1	3134·	6U	130·6	6268		
S·169	B	1546·0	90	1570	3U	130·8	6280		X
82·12·4· 8	M	662	o	66·2·3	35	132·4	6355		
68·1·10·107	P	3186·7	100	3200	6U	133·3	6400		
67·5·8·324	S	6491	o	6491	1	135·2	6491		↑
67·5·8·343	L	68·6	o	68·6	35	137·2	6586		··
63·7·28·304	B	6600·5	6	6594	1	137·4	6594		
81·7·9· 7	P	6630·3	80	6605	1	137·6	6605		CAST OF BAG
60·10·2·77	S	275·2	o	275·2	U/2	137·6	6605		GN. PORPH.
80·9·11· 1	P	6742·	80	6660	1	138·7	6660		ΛƐITPA ΑΠΟΛΛΩΝΙΟΥ
	S	299·0	o	299·0	U/2	149·5	7176		S

The divisions may be noted between the PEYEM and DARIC at 125·8 and 127·4 and the DARIC and STATER at 130·8 and 132·4.

STATER, ATTIC.

REGISTER	M	GRS.	CH	ORIGᵗ	X	UNIT	MINA	PL	DETAIL
68·1·10· 98	P	229·2	3·5	230·1	2	115·0	5752	C	
67·5·8·257	P	228·3	4·9	231·6	2	115·8	5790		Δ. FEM. HEAD
67·5·8·252	P	175·9	5·0	176·2	3/2	117·5	5873		ℋ = 3 DR.
67·5·8·268	P	10·2	·4	9·8	1/12	117·6	5880		⊏I = OBOLI
67·5·8·254	P	234·3	·5	237·	2	118·5	5925		ℋℋ = 4 DR.
67·5·8·266	P	60·6	2·	60·0	1/2	120·0	6000		⊢
67·5·8·256	P	244·9	3·5	245·8	2	122·9	6145		HALF CRESCENT
67·5·8·274	B	62·7	·6	62·1	1/2	124·2	6210		SILBANI▽⊢
67·5·8·263	P	128·3	4·	124·3	1	124·3	6215		ℋ = 2 DR.
67·5·8·246	P	309·1	3·	311·	5/2	124·4	6220		E = 5 DR.
T.B.380	P	1044·3	4·	1040·	M/6	124·8	6240	A	ΔEWO CRESCᵗ
68·1·10· 91	P	781·3	7·	785·	M	125·6	6280	C	½ CRESCᵗ, STAR
66·5·4· 17	P	634·1	21·	629·	5	125·8	6290	C	PEGASUS, FORE
T.B.398	P	253·3	1·3	252·	2	126·0	6300	A	ℋℋℋ
	B	624·3	8·	632·	5	126·4	6320		I = 10 DR.
67·5·8·260	P	126·5	1·9	126·6	1	126·6	6330		⊢
T.B.	P	3216·3	55·	3180	M/2	127·2	6360	A	TETAPT. TORTOISE
	B	1591·5	3·	1590·5	25/2	127·2	6362		LEGLESS BULL
67·5·8·245	P	5044·	12·	509·	4	127·3	6367		ℋ = 8 DR.
68·1·10 84	P	1280·4	6·	1274·	10	127·4	6370		IIII
65·7·20·117	P	1273·2	21	1275·	10	127·5	6375		CRESCENT.
67·5·8·240	P	509·0	8·	511·	4	127·7	6387		∏ℋ =5+3 DR.
67·5·8·239	P	638·2	14·	639·	5	127·8	6390		
75·4·20· 8	P	1070·	11·	1066·	M/6	127·9	6396	A	LADLE LUMP
61·1·10·88	P	1053·3	16·	1070·	M/6	128·4	6410	C	ΔEWO CRESCᵗ
58·8·26·262	B	1279·9	7·	1287·	10	128·7	6435	KL	ΔH.K=20DR.
T.B.379	P	1079·3	2·9	1076·4	M/6	129·1	6456	A	½ TORTOISE
56·6·26·674	P	1295·6	4·	1292·	10	129·2	6460	KL	
67·5·8·236	P	1286·4	8·	1293·	10	129·3	6465		CRESCENT
54·5·19·154	P	322·5	4·	323·6	5/2	129·4	6472	R	
67·5·8·279	B	21·6	·2	21·6	1/6	129·6	6480		ℋℋ = 2 OBOLI
68·1·10· 95	P	665·4	15·	650·	5	130·0	6500	C	
68·1·10·112	P	647·1	6·	651·	5	130·2	6510	C	CYLINDER
T.B.394	P	524·8	3·6	521·	4	130·2	6512	A	∏ℋℋ 5+3
T.B.373	P	1643·1	22·	1635·	25/2	130·8	6540	A	H
66·5·4· 14	P	816·6	14·	818·	M/8	130·9	6543	C	½ CRESCENT
T.B.397	P	387·8	9·	393·	3	131·0	6550	A	
67·5·8·233	B	823·5	4·	819·	M/8	131·0	6552		OM3Δ
67·5·8·242	P	807·4	13·	820·	M/8	131·2	6560		½ CRESCENT
68·1·10· 99	P	2197·5	25·	2192·	M/3	131·5	6576	C	TORTOISE?
T.B.362	P	4418·5	28·	4390·	2M/3	131·7	6585	A	AMPHORA
T.B.369	P	2288·0	12·	2196·	M/3	131·8	6588	A	½ AMPHORA
66·5·4· 11	P	1103·6	12·	1101·	M/6	132·1	6606		CRESCENT
67·5·8·244	P	522·2	8·	529·	4	132·2	6612		Γ777 ?5+3
69·1·10· 1	P	6639·	9·	6630·	50	132·6	6630		MNA DOLPHIN
67·5·8·258	P	189·0	16·	199·	3/2	132·7	6632		
85·10·10· 1	P	6665·	50·	6640·	50	132·8	6640	N	H
67·5·8·265	P	68·5	2·	66·5	1/2	133·0	6650		
76·8·10· 5	P	831·0	9·	832·	M/8	133·1	6655·5	Ae	ΔH GOAT
67·5·8·221	P	4439·6	110	4445·	2M/3	133·3	6667·		AMPHORA
66·5·4· 10	P	1107·7	6·	1112·	M/6	133·4	6672·	C	CRESCᵗ. STAR
68·1·10· 77	P	2213·8	10·	2224·	M/3	133·4	6672·	C	OMHΔ ½ΖΑΜPH·
T.B.400	B	177·5	2·	178·	4/3	133·5	6675·	A	
35·7·656·1843	P	531·7	4·	534·	4	133·5	6675		
78·10·19·276	B	179·8	3·	179·5	4/3	133·9	6694		H
54·5·22·53	P	665·2	7·	671·	5	134·2	6710		
67·5·8·267	P	32·0	5·8	33·6	1/4	134·4	6720		III = 3 OBOLI
65·7·20·114	P	1699·0	18·	1681·	25/2	134·5	6724	A	ΔHMO ½TORTᵉ
67·5·8·238	P	1121·1	4·	1122·	M/6	134·6	6732	C	CRESCᵗ. STAR
68·1·10· 71	P	1709·2	23·	1686·	25/2	134·9	6744	C	DOLPHIN
67·5·8·259	P	137·7	5·5	135·	1	135·0	6750		ΠΤΙΕΠΑΝΕ ℋℋ = 2 DR.
67·5·8·289	B	187·2	12·	180·	4/3	135·0	6750		
66·5·4· 21	P	340·5	3·	337·5	5/2	135·0	6750	C	FEM. HEAD

REGISTER	M	GRS.	CH.	ORIGIN	X	UNIT	MINA	PL.	DETAIL
T.B.396	P	410.5	5.5	405.	3	135.0	6750	A	IIIIII =6 DR.
T.B.375	P	1347.5	9.	1350.	10	135.0	6750	A	B
T.B.391	P	842.1	7.	845.	M/8	135.2	6760	A	1/2 CRESCT
T.B.372	P	1696.9	7.	1690.	25/2	135.2	6760	A	CRESCENT
67.5.8.222	P	3399.6	60	3389.	25	135.6	6778	A	ΔΗΜΟ TORTOISE
67.5.8.223	P	16865	22.	1695.	25/2	135.6	6780		OMHΔ 1/2 ,,.
T.B.390	P	852.2	2.2	850.	M/8	136.0	6800	A	OMHΔ OWL
T.B.393	P	540.0	10.	545.	4	136.2	6812	A	
67.5.8.231		1675.9	47.	1705.	25/2	136.4	6820		1/2 AMPHORA
52.9.4.18		4576.8	19.	4558.	2M/3	136.7	6837		
NEIKOΛAOC MAPKOY AΓOPA NOMWN ΛΕ BAΛΕΥC									
67.5.8.227	P	1714.6	12.	1712.	25/2	137.0	6848		1/2 TORTOISE
	P	687.4	11.	685.	5	137.0	6850		EX
T.B.361	P	7044.	500	6860.	50	137.2	6860	A	MNA DOLPHIN
68.1.10.85	P	2219.3	23.	2196.	16	137.2	6862		H
69.1.10.3	P	4590.5	40.	4587.	2M/3	137.6	6880		TPITH AMPHORA
67.5.8.234	P	1139.6	13.	1147.	M/3	137.6	6882		
53.6.16.1	B	41507.	425	41300.	6M	137.7	6883	H	
ΘΕΟΙΣ ΣΕΒΑΣΤΟΙΣ ΚΑΙ ΤΩ ΔΑΜΟ AΓO PA NOMOYN TΩΠ									
KAΩΔΙOY POYΦOY KAI TEPTIOY BE KI ΛIOY.									
65.7.20.111	P	4599.8	50	4590.	2M/3	137.7	6885	A	AMPHORA
T.B.365	P	3458.6	35.	3445.	25	137.8	6890	A	BUCKLER
W.T.1109	P	4596.5	12.	4595.	2M/3	137.9	6893		AMPHORA
68.1.10.87	P	1386.8	7.	1380.	10	138.0	6900	C	DOLPHIN
68.1.10.89	P	557.6	13.	552.	4	138.0	6900	C	
T.B.364	P	3478.3	20.	3450.	25	138.0	6900	A	OMΘΔ TORTOISE
65.7.20.112	P	3453.8	50	3460.	25	138.4	6920	A	MNIMN, DOLPH.
T.B.389	P	8655	6.	869.	M/8	139.0	6952	A	ROSETTE
76.5.10.4	P	1697.6	50	1740.	25/2	139.2	6960	SY	ANTIOXEION TETAPT. ANCHOR
67.5.8.219	P	6958.	75	6990.	50	139.8	6990		DOLPHIN
	P	3545.7	46.	3500.	25	140.0	7000		WITH BRONZE RING
66.5.4.1	P	7010.	5.	7005.	50	140.1	7005	C	MNA DOLPHIN
66.5.4.12	P	897.9	22.	876.	M/8	140.2	7008		TT
67.5.8.253	P	282.0	6.	281.	2	140.5	7025		IIIΔAEGN, +4ATT.
T.B.371	P	1765.8	15.	1759.	25/2	140.7	7036	A	HMITETAP, 1/2TORT
68.1.10.93	P	422.0	2.7	422.	3	141.0	7050		DIOTA
T.B.388	P	881.3	4.	882.	M/8	141.1	7055	A	ΞΔΟΔΤΟ, 1/8AEm
83.10.1.1	B	707.1	1.	708.	5	141.6	7080	Co	ΔΩ LION, FAUN
66.5.4.4	P	3556.9	12.	3545.	25	141.8	7090	C	plugged.
T.B.387	P	880.0	7.	887.	M/8	141.9	7096	A	ΔOMO CORNUCOP.
T.B.	P	7161.	26.	7167.	50	143.3	7167		MNA DOLPHIN
67.5.8.225	P	1800.4	4.4	1796.	25/2	143.7	7184		HMITE 1/2TORT.
T.B.386	P	898.7	5.	898.	M/8	143.7	7184	A	1/4 AMPHORA
68.1.10.97	P	143.6	4.7	143.9	1	143.9	7195	C	
65.7.20.115	P	1807.5	15.	1808.	25/2	144.6	7232	A	HMIT 1/2TORT.
68.1.10.101	P	7234.	28.	7250.	50	145.0	7250	A	
T.B.385	P	908.0	7.	910.	M/8	145.6	7280	A	1/2 CRESCENT
T.B.384	P	914.1	33.	911.	,,	145.8	7288	A	
67.5.8.228	P	1835.4	10.	1836.	25/2	146.9	7344		HMIT 1/2TORT.
T.B.383	P	921.4	5.	921.	M/8	147.4	7368	A	1/2CRESCT, STAR
T.B.382	P	925.0	2.5	922.5	M/8	147.6	7380	A	OMΘΔ OWL
67.5.8.226	P	1868.6	30.	1848.	25	147.8	7392		
T.B.395	B	449.8	1.8	448.	3	149.3	7467		HHH

NECEF, MINA OF AELIAN, ISLAND MINA.

REGISTER	M	GRS.	CH.	ORIGIN	X	UNIT	MINA	PL.	DETAIL
67.5.8.251	P	228.5	7.	234.	3/2	156.0	7800		•1·1·
68.1.10.100	P	7853.	40.	7810.	50	156.2	7810	C	
68.1.10.104	P	7901.	50.	7915.	50	158.3	7915	C	FULL FACE. OWL
	P	3949.2	10.	3959.	25	158.4	7918		1/2 AMPHORA
66.5.4.6	P	3978.6	6.	3985.	25	159.4	7970	C	ΔHMO, AMPH.
	B	162.7	1.3	162.9	1	162.9	8145		
87	B	165.7	2.7	163.	1	163.0	8150		
78.10.19.293	P	2036.7	36.	2047.	25/2	163.8	8188		1/2 AMPHORA
	Sy	2048.5	.8	2049.3	25/2	164.0	8197		
82.12.4.7	M	166.2		166.2	1	166.2	8310		

KHOIRINE, CHIAN, PERSIAN.

REGISTER	M	GRS.	CH.	ORIGIN	X	UNIT	MINA	PL.	DETAIL
	S	29.2	0	29.2	15	168.2	8410		•
68.1.10.80	P	2127.2	22.	2105.	3U	168.4	8420	C	
67.5.8.336	S	29.3	0	29.3	15	168.6	8430		-
64.10.7.1997	M	8476.	0	8476.	M	169.5	8476	Km	DUCK
68.1.10.106	P	4243.2	50	4240.	6U	169.6	8480	C	
	S	89.2	0	89.2	35	171.3	8563		∴
68.1.10.134	B	175.7	3.5	172.2	2K	172.2	8610		i.e. M/50 }LIABLE
	S	358.8	0	358.8	U/2	172.2	8611	T	TO
	GP.	179.5	0	179.5	U/4	172.3	8616		i.e. M/48 }CONFUSION
	B.	86.9	1.4	86.3	K	172.6	8630		Δ = QUARTER
68.1.10.72	P.	2167.2	24.	2159.	3U	172.7	8636	C	ϟ = SEMIS
	S	360.1	0	360.1	U/2	172.8	8642		Σ = SICILICUS
67.5.8.347	S	181.1	0	181.1	U/4	173.8	8692		
	P	344.7	7	350.	4K	175.0	8750		
	S	8756.	0	8756.	M	175.1	8756		
67.5.8.319	S	2208.8	.3	2209.	3U	176.7	8836		∴
	S	2342.6	1.	2343.6	3U	187.5	9374		

TWO SYSTEMS ARE MIXED HERE.
THE MINA ÷100 = KHOIRINE, K.
   ,, ÷12 UNCIAE, U; AND 288 SCRIPULAE, S.

BEQA, AEGINETAN.

REGISTER	M	GRS.	CH.	ORIGIN	X	UNIT	MINA	PL.	DETAIL
	P	46.4	1.1	45.3	1/4	181.2	9060		∴ =3 OBOLI
	B	99.0	11.	92.	1/2	184.	9200		I = 1 DR.
	B	369.7	1.4	370.	2	185.	9250		
68.1.10.103	P	9218.	170	9300.	50	186.	9300		
67.5.8.232	P	1157.7	7.	1164.	M/8	186.2	9312		HMIS 1/4AMPH.
T.B.378,1809	P	1168.0	5.	1168.	M/8	186.9	9344	A	CRESCENT
T.B.377	P	1169.6	5.	1170.	M/8	187.2	9360	A	ΔHMO CRESCT
67.5.8.253	P	282.0	6.	281.	3/2	187.4	9367		IIIAEGN, +IIII ATT.
68.1.10.122	B	373.9	3.	375.	2	187.5	9375		
T.B.392	P	752.3	2.	750.	4	187.5	9375	A	Δ = 4 STATERS BOARS HEAD ΔHMOΣION OTAΘON
R.P.K.	B	1166.6	7.4	1174.	M/8	187.8	9392	{	
	3	47.3	.8	47.1	1/4	188.4	9420		Γ
66.5.4.19	P	477.8	3.	475.	5/2	190.0	9500	C	
68.7.20.118	P	955.5	5.	954.	5	190.8	9540	A	1/2 CRESCENT
67.5.8.249	B	2389.9	7.	2388.	25/2	191.0	9552		TOΔYA OWL
70.11.5.1	P	2402.4	25.	2390.	25/2	191.2	9580		ΔHMO 1/2AMPH.
68.1.10.94	P	482.7	9.	479.	5/2	191.6	9580		
67.5.8.241	P	957.3	19.	959.	5	191.8	9590		1/2 CRESCT, STAR
67.5.8.246	P	480.9	1.2	479.7	5/2	191.9	9594		A
	P	577.1	5.	578.	3	192.7	9633		
66.5.4.2	P	4823.3	7.	4823.	25	192.9	9646	C	MN RAM'S HEAD
65.7.20.116	P	1204.6	8.	1207.	M/8	193.1	9656	A	1/2 TORTOISE
67.5.8.262	P	82.7	5.7	80.6	05	193.4	9667		IIIII = 50BOLI
67.5.8.220	P	2404.9	30.	2420.	25/2	193.6	9680		
66.5.4.18	P	583.9	1.4	582.5	3	194.2	9708	C	FULL FACE TORTOISE
65.7.20.113	P	2434.1	5.	2429.	25/2	194.3	9716	A	
67.5.8.224	P	2458.5	22.	2436.	25/2	194.9	9744		3/4 AMPHORA
67.5.8.243	P	973.0	6.	975.	5	195.0	9750		1/2 CRESCT, STAR
68.1.10.90	P	489.1	1.4	487.7	5/2	195.1	9754	C	
T.B.399	B	294.2	1.2	293.0	3/2	195.3	9767	A	K
T.B.359	P	9782.8	60.	9793	50	195.9	9793	A	DOLPHIN
T.B.376	P	1229.6	12.	1227.	M/8	196.3	9816	A	ΔHMO 1/4AMPHR
68.1.10.82	P	594.1	4.	590.	3	196.7	9833	C	DIOTA
T.B.381	P	985.6	5.	985.	5	197.0	9850	A	OMΘΔ
	B	298.5	.25	298.	3/2	198.7	9933		H+ =3
T.B.358	P	9970.6	62.	9942.	50	198.8	9942		MNA AΓOP DOLPHIN
67.5.8.229	P	1248.1	14.	1244.	M/8	199.0	9952		CRESCT, STAR
T.B.570	P	301.8	4.	299.	3/2	199.3	9967		EUROPA ON BULL

BEQA AS UNCIA OF LIGHT LITRA OF HESYCHIOS AND POLLUX.

REGISTER	M	GRS.	CH.	ORIGIN	X	UNIT	MINA	PL.	DETAIL
	B	95.0	1.5	95.7	U/2	191.4	2297		S=SEMIS
67.5.8.348	B	194.4	0	194.4	U	194.4	2333		-S=SEMIS OF HEAVY UNC.
48.3.15.2	B	2314.	50	2350.		195.8	2350		ΠAVI PIG.
67.5.8.277	B	33.0	.2	33.0	S	198.0	2376		A=1 SEXTVLA
67.5.8.248	P	404.2	3.6	405.6	2U	202.8	2434		B=2 UNCIAE
	S	68.2	0	68.2	2S	204.6	2455		•• 2 SEXT.
67.5.8.327	S	206.9	0	206.9	U	206.9	2483		• 1 UNC.
67.5.8.305	S	593.3	50	640.	3U	213.3	2560		∴ 3UNC.

BEQA ½ ROMAN UNGIA. S, SCRIPULA. U, UNGIA. N, NOMISMA. L, LIBRA

REGISTER	M	GRS.	CH.	ORIGINL	X	UNIT	MINA	PL	DETAIL
	B	297·7	2·	298·	6N	298·	3576		SOL·VI = 6 SOLIDI
68·1·10·130	B	52·2	2·7	50·1	N	300·6	3607	C	Νομισμα
67·5·8·339	S	50·2	∘	50·2	N	301·2	3614		
68·1·10·131	B	52·0	2·1	53·3	N	319·8	3838		N
	B	352·7	1·0	352·8	U	352·8	4234		Γ+A = Ιουγγια
	B	60·3	·6	59·7	N	358·2	4298		N
67·5·8·340	S	46·0	∘	46·0	3S	368·0	4416		∴ 3 SCRIP.
	B	60·9	1·1	62·0	N	372·0	4464		
	B	124·4	1·7	124·1	2N	372·3	4468		SOL. II
78·10·19·290	B	126·7	1·9	124·8	2N	374·4	4492		
67·5·8·285	B	186·5	·7	187·2	3N	374·4	4492		X = 10 SCRIP.
	B	375·2	1·8	377·	U	377·	4524		NS = 6 NOM.
50·1·7·70	B	379·7	20·	379·	U	379·	4548		
68·1·10·82	P	379·2	4·	379·	U	379·	4548	C	A = 1 UNC.
67·8·10·12	B	127·2	·3	126·9	2N	380·7	4568		⊙ R ⊙
	S	1148·2	·2	1148·	3U	382·7	4592		
	S	1534·7	∘	1534·7	4U	383·7	4604		
	B	64·2	·4	64·2	N	385·2	4622		N
	S	2311·9	∘	2311·9	6U	385·3	4624		
50·1·7·71	B	379·7	20·	386·	U	386·	4632		
67·5·8·283	B	386·0	16·	387·	U	387·	4644		
68·1·10·127	B	393·0	6·	387·	U	387·	4644	C	
68·1·10·121	B	206·3	12·	194·	3N	388·	4656	C	TH
78·10·19·287	B	392·2	4·	388·	U	388·	4656		• = 1 UNC.
48·8·19·201	B	388·8	·7	389·5	U	389·5	4674		ȣA, ουγγια 1
67·5·8·273	B	391·6	1·0	391·5	U	391·5	4698		ΓA " "
67·5·8·297	B	4645·	55	4700·	L	391·7	4700		EYT ··· ΛA =LIB. 1
	B	66·0	1·0	65·4	N	392·4	4709		N
	M	1181·4	∘	1181·4	3U	393·8	4726		
	S	2362·9	1·5	2364·4	6U	394·1	4729		V
67·5·8·316	S	2353·	12·	2365·	6U	394·1	4730		VIR. CL. EX. A. IVNI. R. PR. VR.
67·5·8·290	B	98·1	1·7	98·6	U/4	394·4	4732		IN = 10 NOM.
67·5·8·321	S	4731·	3·	4734·	L	394·5	4734		I LIBRA
61·5·20·1		394·6	·5	395·	U	395·	4740		–I SOLG = 6
67·5·8·321	S	4746·	1·	4747·	L	395·6	4747		
68·1·10·128	B	92·4	6·6	99·	U/4	396·	4752	C	
68·1·10·151	P	802·2	9·	793·	2U	396·5	4758	C	BALL + LOOP
	B	66·7	·6	66·1	N	396·6	4759		N
	B	198·0	·8	198·4	3N	396·8	4761		N Γ = 3 NOM.
	S	1191·8	·2	1192·	3U	397·3	4768		∴
68·1·10·124	B	395·8	6·	397·4	U	397·4	4769	C	
67·5·8·270	B	794·1	1·	795·	2U	397·5	4770		–II, SOL XII
	S	4783·	6·	4789·	L	399·1	4789		
50·1·17·73	B	798·9	2·7	798·4	2U	399·2	4790		
67·5·8·318	S	2396·0	∘	2396·0	6U	399·3	4792		S = SEMIS
	B	66·8	·2	66·6	N	399·6	4795		S = SOLIDVS
	B	199·7	1·2	199·9	3N	399·8	4798		
	B	403·2	7·	400·	3N	400·	4800		
T.B.1093	S	4801·	∘	4801	L	400·1	4801	Ro	
	B	133·2	1·2	133·4	2N	400·2	4802		SOL II
78·10·19·271	B	1189·7	11·	1201	3U	400·3	4804		ȣΓ ουγγια 3
	B	800·5	·5	801	2U	400·5	4806		
	S	14434·	2·	14436	3L	401·0	4812		III = 3 LIB.
	B	664·1	5·	669·	10N	401·4	4816		N I = NOM. 10
50·1·17·69	B	803·0	∘	803·0	2U	401·5	4818	G	VSLDN, SOL XII
50·1·17·74	B	399·1	2·6	401·7	U	401·7	4820	G	··LSN··· •
82·12·4·5	S	4822·	∘	4822	L	401·9	4822		
68·1·10·137	B	398·8	3·	402	U	402·	4824	C	ȣA
	B	803·1	3·	804·5	2U	402·2	4827		ES·CA
	B	804·5	·5	805·	2U	402·5	4830		
66·5·4·13	B	806·1	·5	805·6	2U	402·8	4834	C	Γ+B
67·5·8·349	S	201·5	∘	201·5	3N	403·0	4836		S = SEMI-UNC.
	B	201·8	1·4	201·5	3N	403·0	4836		BI = 12 SCRIP.
	S	2419·6	∘	2419·6	6U	403·3	4839		S = SEMIS
82·12·4·4	S	23534·	670	24200	5L	403·3	4840		
78·10·19·274	B	801·5	5·5	807	2U	403·5	4842		ȣB
	S	9685	∘	9685	2L	403·5	4842		
	B	67·4	·7	67·3	N	403·8	4846		⁞⁞ = 4 SCRIP
	B	84·0	1·5	84·7	O 10	404·0	4848		X = 10 OBOLI
	S	202·2	∘	202·2	3N	404·4	4853		
	B	401·6	5·	404·4	U	404·4	4853		N + S
68·1·10·138	B·	203·0	2·7	202·5	3N	405·0	4860		1B = 12 SCRIP.

REGISTER	M	GRS.	CH.	ORIGINL	X	UNIT	MINA	PL.	DETAIL
	B	831·0	30·	810·	2U	405·0	4860		SOL XII
	S	810·2	·3	810·5	2U	405·2	4863		
	S	405·5	∘	405·5	U	405·5	4866		
68·1·10·149	B	201·6	2·0	202·8	3N	405·6	4867	C	BI = 12 SCRIP.
	S	22658·	1690	24350·	5L	405·8	4870		
121	B	206·2	3·	203·	3N	406·0	4872		
68·1·10·147	B	404·2	1·8	406·	U	406·0	4872		ȣA
68·1·10·148	B	404·0	2·	406·	U	406·0	4872		ȣA
	B	203·0	1·1	203·2	3N	406·4	4877		
	S	406·6	∘	406·6	U	406·6	4879		
73·7·9·1	S	9698·	60·	9760·	2L	406·7	4880		EX·AVC·Q·IVNI. RUSTICI·PRAEF.VRB.
	S	813·2	·3	813·5	2U	406·7	4881		X•• = 12 NOM
	B	4876·7	12·	4888·	L	407·3	4888		+ΛHΔI
68·1·10·86	P	1626·5	12·	1630·	4U	407·5	4890	C	Δ = 4 UNC.
	S	24464·	20·	24484·	5L	408·0	4897		
S.170	B	821·7	5·	817	2U	408·5	4902		•• = 2 UNC.
68·1·10·125	B	408·0	·7	408·7	U	408·7	4904	C	N+S
67·5·8·281	B	815·3	2·2	817·5	2U	408·7	4905		
	S	1228·4	∘	1228·4	3U	409·4	4914		Δ ¼ LIB.
	S	14743·	1·	14744	3L	409·6	4915		
	S	49027·	145	49170·	10L	409·7	4917		EX·AVC·Q·IVN· RVSTICI.PRAEF.VRB.
67·5·8·275	B	410·1	·3	409·8	U	409·8	4918		ΓA 2 BUSTS
	S	24589·	2·	24591·	5L	409·8	4918		V = 5 LIB.
67·5·8·323	S	4910·	10·	4920·	L	410·0	4920		
	B	136·4	2·3	136·7	2N	410·1	4921		NB
	S	410·8	∘	410·8	U	410·8	4930		• = UNC.
	S	410·8	∘	410·8	U	410·8	4930		•
67·5·8·230	P	810·0	26·	822	2U	411·0	4932		B = 2 UNC.
	S	2459·9	6·	2466	6U	411·0	4932		S = SEMIS
67·5·8·327	S	2469·5	∘	2469·5	6U	411·6	4939		X
	S	1231·6	3·4	1235·	3U	411·7	4940		∴ 3 UNC.
67·5·8·314	S	1646·6	∘	1646·6	4U	411·7	4940		⁞⁞ 4 UNC.
67·5·8·315	S	2471·3	·4	2471·7	6U	411·9	4943		S
	S	412·3	∘	412·3	U	412·3	4947		•
67·5·8·300	B	19657·	130·	19790·	4L	412·3	4947		EYTYXI B. LΔ =LIB.4
	S	1237·4	∘	1237·4	3U	412·4	4950		
67·5·8·353	S	14850·	∘	14850·	3L	412·4	4950		III
83·11·10·1	L	4948·7	2·	4951·	L	412·6	4951	Ro	XI
67·5·8·326	S	9903·	∘	9903·	2L	412·7	4951		
	B	34·0	·4	34·4	2S	412·8	4954		1B = 12 SILIQVAE
	B	1239·3	2·	1239·	3U	413·0	4956		ȣΓ
	S	1648·6	3·5	1650·	4U	412·5	4950		⁞⁞
	S	1240·0	∘	1240·0	3U	413·3	4960		∴ Γ
68·1·10·150	B	211·4	5·	207·	3N	414·0	4968	C	
67·5·8·320	S	2484·4	·3	2484·7	6U	414·1	4969		S II
67·5·8·354	S	49691·	2·	49693·	10L	414·2	4969		X 10 LIB
	S	14911·	∘	14911·	3L	414·2	4970		
82·12·4·2	S	49777	100	49710	10L	414·3	4971		X 10 LIB
67·5·8·310	S	1243·2	∘	1243·2	3U	414·4	4973		∴
	B	51·7	·8	51·8	U/8	414·4	4973		TIBERIANI.PROC. MENATIS.PREF.
	B	829·0	1·	829·	2U	414·5	4974		
W.T.1759	S	14924·	1·	14925·	3L	414·6	4975		III
							4977		LYONS SET. SEE END
67·5·8·276	B	138·4	·8	138·3	2N	414·9	4978		NB
	B	414·7	1·4	414·9	U	414·9	4979		
	S	24839·	56·	24895	5L	414·9	4979		V
S·19	B	5206·	270	4980	L	415·0	4980		ASTRAGALVS
67·5·8·299	B	14806·	134	14940	3L	415·0	4980		EYT ···· ΛΓ
67·5·8·357	S	19940·	∘	19940	4L	415·4	4985		
67·5·8·329	S	206·5	1·3	207·8	3N	415·6	4988		
67·5·8·312	S	1248·8	∘	1248·8	3U	416·3	4995		
	S	4639·	360	5000	L	416·7	5000		
67·5·8·355	S	25001	2·	25003	5L	416·7	5001		V
68·1·10·129	B	105·3	1·1	104·2	U/4	416·8	5002	C	
78·10·19·272	B	417·9	1·1	416·8	U	416·8	5002		YA
	L	19998	15·	20013·	4L	416·9	5003		IIII
67·5·8·291	B	830·2	7·	834·	2U	417·0	5004		EYT IB NOM =12
	S	208·7	∘	208·7	3N	417·4	5008		S = SEMI UNC.
	S	1251·8	·6	1252·	3U	417·3	5008		∴
	S	1665·5	5·5	1671·	4U	417·7	5013		
67·5·8·272	B	413·1	6·	418·	U	418·0	5016		
68·1·10·146	B	418·8	2·	418·5	U	418·5	5022		ȣA
79·10·19·288	3	418·3	1·5	418·5	U	418·5	5022		
	B	838·3	·8	837·5	2U	418·7	5025		

REGISTER	M	GRS.	CH.	ORIGINL	X	UNIT	MINA	PL.	DETAIL
67·5·8·306	S	839·1	6·	839·	2U	419·5	5035		
	S	1656·5	24	1680·	4U	420	5040		
	S	2522·6	·4	2523·	6U	4205	5046		S
67·5·8·294	B	1683·8	2·	1683·	4U	420·7	5049		∴
	B	2104·	1·	2105·	3N	421·0	5052		
67·5·8·230	S	210·9	○	210·9	3N	421·8	5062		Σ
67·5·8·303	S	421·8	○	421·8	U	421·8	5062		·
	S	843·7	○	843·7	2U	421·8	5062		
67·5·8·283	B	416·2	10·	422·	U	422·0	5064		Γ NOM =6
48·8·19·202	B	1258·7	7·	1266·	3U	422·0	5064		𐅵Γ
W.T.1760	S	1688·1	○	1688·	4U	422·0	5064		∷
50·1·17·75	B	193·9	176	211·5	3N	423·0	5076	G	S
	S	2536·6	1·4	2538·	6U	423·0	5076		XS
	B	846·3	·3	846·	2U	423·0	5076		··
68·1·10·83	P	850·0	4·	846·	2U	423·0	5076	C	‖
67·5·8·311	S	1273·7	○	1273·7	3U	424·5	5095		∴
67·5·8·325	S	10190·	3·	10193·	2L	424·7	5096		‖
67·5·8·280	S	8494·	1·5	850·	2U	425·0	5100		𐅵B
	B	1285·1	15·	1276·	3U	425·3	5104		
67·5·8·335	S	35·5	○	355·	2S	426·0	5112		··
67·5·8·308	S	425·5	·5	426·	U	426·	5112		
82·12·4·6	S	1704·1	1·5	1705·6	4U	426·4	5117		∷
78·10·19·277	B	5110·	10	5120·	L	426·7	5120		
	B	4·27·1	1·	427·	U	427·	5124		
67·5·8·334	S	17·8	○	17·8	S	427·2	5126		
	S	855·5	○	855·5	2U	427·7	5133		
	S	214·2	·2	214·4	3N	428·8	5145		
67·5·8·298	B	10076·	240	10320·	2L	430·0	5160		EYT···ΛB
67·5·8·301	B	25635·	250	25840·	5L	430·7	5168		EYTYXI.B.ΛE
	S	215·9	○	215·9	3N	431·8	5181		S
67·5·8·304	S	216·2	○	216·2	3N	432·4	5188		
68·1·10·120	B	109·2	·8	108·4	U/4	433·6	5202	C	CPAB·····M
	S	218·8	·2	219·	3N	438	5256		
67·5·8·271	B	430·0	12·	438·	U	438	5256		

SET OF LEAD SCRIPULA, LOYASSE, LYONS.

50·1·7·95		173·8	·1	173·9	10	⊢·			10 STROKES
96		155·2	○	155·3	9		·2	9	,,
97		135·4	○	135·4	8		2·8	8	,,
98		121·9	·1	122·0	7		1·0	7	,,
99		103·8	○	103·8	6		·1	6	,,
100		86·7	○	86·7	5		·3	5	,,
101		68·3	○	68·3	4		·8	4	,,
102		ABOUT		31	3			3	,,
103		35·6	·2	35·4	2		·8	2	,,
104		·17·9	○	17·9	1		·6	1	,,
		MEAN		17·283	±·01	LIBRA	4977	±3	

SELA, HEAVY PHOENICIAN MINA.

	B	1218·8	120	1340·	1/8	214·4	10720		HD. OF PALLAS
66·5·4·20	P	447·0	11·	446·	1/25	223·	11150	C	ΟΓΔΟ··KAICAPOC X
68·1·10·74	B	1404·1	2·	1402·	1/8	224·3	11216	C	EYΔH· H

SELA, LIGHT PHOENICIAN MINA. OR ITALIC

S.SCRIPUL N.NOMISMA D.DRACHM S.UNCIA M.MINA Sh.SHEKEL

	B	24·9	·1	24·9	D/2	199·2	4980		
67·5·8·278	B	25·6	·7	25·3	D/2	202·4	5060		
67·5·8·351	M	25·6	○	25·6	D/2	204·8	5120		
67·5·8·237	P	1023·0	7·	1026·	20D	205·2	5130		ΓΔ . K=20
	B	52·2	·4	51·8	D	207·2	5180		Θ
	M	5245·6	2·4	5248·	M	209·9	5248		{C=centum dr; M.P.=Mina pond.
78·10·19·275	B	218·8	1·1	219·9	U/2	439·8	5278		1-B
	P	103·9	2·3	105·6	2D	211·2	5280		1 & ⊢III
67·5·8·302	S	440·6	○	440·6	U	440·6	5287		·
67·5·8·328	G	220·9	○	220·9	U/2	441·8	5302		
T.B.374	P	1599·5	4·5	1595·	30D	212·7	5317		ΓΔ. Λ=30
68·1·10·105	P	5415·4	90·	5325·	M	213·0	5325	C	·
	S	15967·	13	15980·	3M	443·9	5327		
	S	55·6	○	55·6	3S	444·8	5338		∴ =3 SCRIPL
67·5·8·356	S	26694·	○	26694·	5M	444·9	5339		V
67·5·8·293	B	1331·8	4·	1335·	3U	444	5340		𐅵·Γ
67·5·8·346	S	148·7	○	148·7	2N	446·1	5353		
67·5·8·333	L	18·6	○	18·6	S	446·4	5357		
78·10·19·291	B	223·9	·4	223·5	U/2	447·0	5362		
67·5·8·296	B	2653·	31·	2684·	6U	447·3	5368		N VΛΛ····

REGISTER	M	GRS.	CH.	ORIGINL	X	UNIT	MINA	PL.	DETAIL
68·1·10·154	L	10718·	50·	10770·	2M	448·7	5385	C	‖
69·1·10·2	P	5327·4	112·	5395·	M	449·5	5395		M.AMPHORA
67·5·8·292	B	1331·2	19·	1350·	3U	450·	5400		EYΘΑ𐅵Γ
67·5·8·295	B	2655·4	45	2700·	6U	450·	5400		EYΘY𐅵9
	S	112·7	○	112·7	U/4	450·8	5410		
48·8·19·203	S	224·9	·6	225·5	U/2	451·0	5412		S
53·2·25·1	B	1341·6	12·	1354·	3U	451·3	5416		MAPAC𐅵Γ
68·1·10·145	B	113·7	·8	112·9	U/4	451·6	5419		
67·5·8·235	P	1074·6	48·	1087·	5Sh	217·4	5435		Π=5
67·5·8·345	S	113·3	○	113·3	65	453·2	5438		∷∷
	S	2263·0	3·	2266·	5U	453·2	5438		∵
67·5·8·309	S	909·2	·2	909·4	2U	454·7	5456		
	S	229·0	1·7	228·3	U/2	456·6	5479		ΠΥΟ
	S	457·4	·1	457·5	U	457·5	5490		
67·5·8·341	B	57·4	○	57·4	3S	459·2	5510		
68·1·10·78	P	1377·9	19·	1379·	3U	459·7	5516	C	
66·5·4·20	B	9·34	·14	9·2	P/6	220·8	5520	C	ΙΘΛ Odysseus hd.
	B	114·9	·7	115·6	U/4	462·4	5548		
	S	2779·5	○	2779·5	6U	463·2	5559		
67·5·8·288	B	232·1	1·7	231·8	U/2	463·6	5563		
	S	154·6	○	154·6	2N	463·8	5565		
	B	58·5	·5	58·0	3S	464·0	5568		∴
67·5·8·286	B	231·5	2·	233·5	U/2	467·0	5604		
67·5·8·261	P	112·6	1·6	112·4	D	224·8	5620		+
	P	1404·0	7·	1411·	3U	470·3	5644		
67·5·8·287	B	235·6	1·7	235·3	U/2	470·6	5647		
T.B.368	P	2859·7	20·	2850·	6U	475·	5700	A	ΟΜ3Δ TORTOISE
78·10·19·292	P	2851·9	23·	2865·	6U	477·5	5730		1/2 AMPHORA
67·5·8·284	B	231·6	1·1	231·7	Sh	231·7	5792		Ψ
68·1·10·126	B	101·9	14·	116·	2D	232·	5800		A & O

SELA. 2 BREASTS (BR) WITH BAR HANDLE (H).

59·12·26·455	M	2538·2	20·	2560·	1/2	204·8	5120	K	BR. H
77·8·8·1	M	1266·4	40·	1305·	1/4	208·8	5220	K?	,, ,,
59·12·26·447	M	40263·	240·	40260·	7 1/2	214·7	5368	K	,, ,,
68·4·5·1	M	22138·	4430·	27000·	5	216·0	5400	B	,, ,,
59·12·26·456	M	1341·1	13·	1354·	1/4	216·6	5416	K	,, H
353	M	36889·	5600·	42300·	7 1/2	218·4	5460	K?	,, ,,
68·7·5·164	M	42380·	220·	42600·	7 1/2	219·2	5480	KΓ	,,
	M	27447·	70·	27520·	5	220·2	5504		,, H
59·12·26	M	5459·	140·	5590·	1	223·6	5590	K	,, ,,
59·12·26·690	M	23647·	4730·	28000·	5	224·0	5600	K	,,
73·5·5·146	M	42778·	2700·	45500·	8	226·7	5667	E	DOLPHIN. H
59·12·26·454	M	5510·	160·	5670·	1	226·8	5670	K	BR. H
59·12·26·452	M	14250·	○	14250·	2 1/2	228·0	5700	K	,, ,,
	L	32925·	1530·	34450·	6	229·7	5742		,,
59·12·26·458	M	460·6	20·	480·	1/12	230·4	5760	K	,, H
	L	67384·	1800·	69200·	12	230·7	5767	LK	THUNDERBOLT. H
59·12·26·451	M	35133·	○	35133·	6	234·2	5855	K	BR. H.
59·12·26·460	M	14641·	1A·	14655·	2 1/2	234·5	5862	K	,,

SELA. DISC WEIGHTS, CARTHAGE.

57·12·8·223	L	632·1	158?	790?	4	1975?			ROGATVS, XT
67·5·8·350	M	103·2	○	103·2	1/2	2064			
57·12·18·226	M	206·8	○	206·8	1	206·8			
60·10·2·73	L	823·1	12·	835·	4	208·7			
60·10·2·78	M	209·6	D·	209·6	1	209·6			
57·12·8·225	M	341·9	○	341·9	1 1/2	227·9			
60·10·2·80	M	233·2	○	233·2	1	233·2			
57·12·18·229	M	231·3	2·2	234·	1	234·			

BRONZE ⧗ SERIES.

MARK	∷		59·6	·6	59·7	5	11·94	191·0
	⁚⁚⁚		123·0	8·6	120·4	10	12·04	192·6
	⁚⁚⁚		119·9	1·5	121·4	10	12·14	194·2
&	⁚⁚⁚=H		98·0	·4	97·9	8	12·2	195·2
	⁚⁚⁚		148·3	1·3	149·6	12	12·47	199·5
	⁚⁚⁚		125·9	○	125·9	10	12·59	201·5
	⁚⁚⁚		127·4	2·3	127·7	10	12·77	204·3
	⁚⁚⁚		128·0	3·	129·0	10	12·90	206·4
	⁚⁚⁚		129·6	·4	129·2	10	12·92	206·7
	⁚⁚⁚		91·0	1·2	90·8	7	12·97	207·5

FRONT VIEW

SIDE VIEW